EARLY WARMING

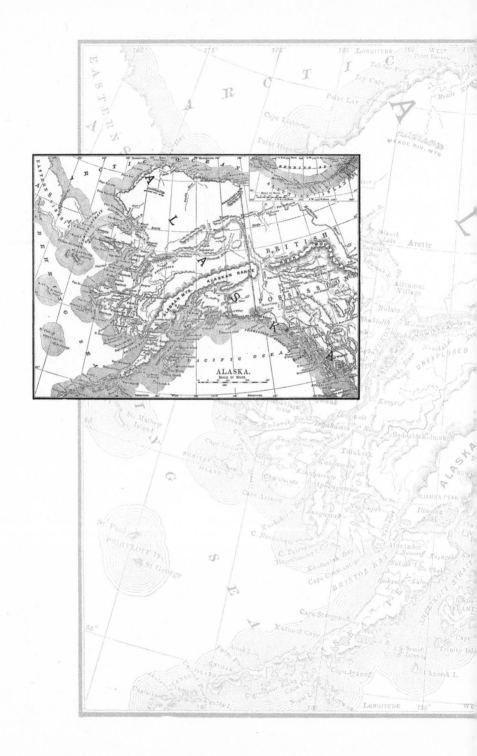

ALASKA.

SCALE OF MILES.

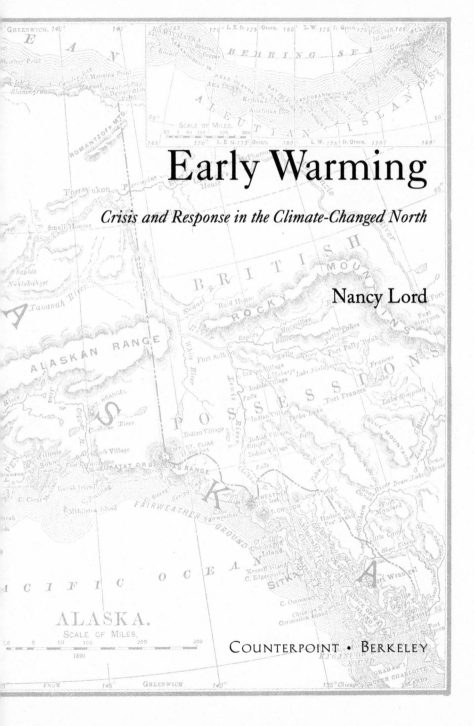

Early Warming

Crisis and Response in the Climate-Changed North

Nancy Lord

COUNTERPOINT • BERKELEY

To the memory of my parents,
who taught me to love nature and books.
Robert Nelson Lord 1916–2008
Mary Burpee Lord 1921–2008

Library of Congress Cataloging-in-Publication Data is available.

978-1-58243-802-3

Jacket design by Silverander Communications
Interior design by Gopa & Ted2, Inc.
Printed in the United States of America

COUNTERPOINT
2560 Ninth Street, Suite 318
Berkeley, CA 94710
www.counterpointpress.com

Distributed by Publishers Group West

10 9 8 7 6 5 4

Contents

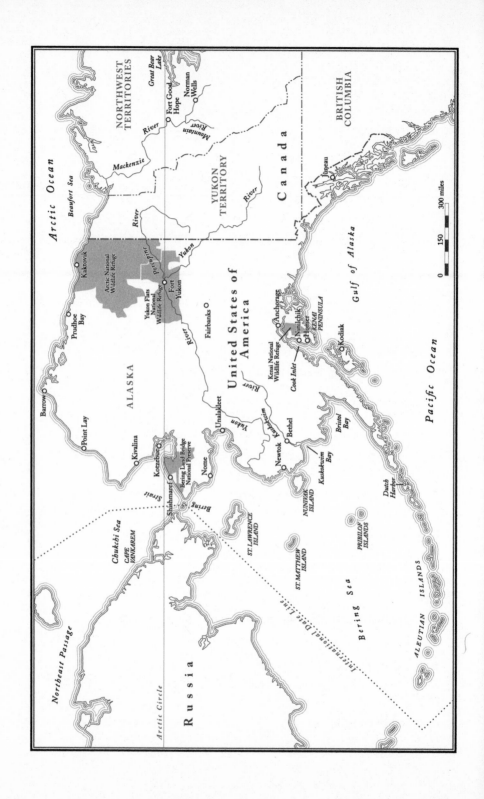

INTRODUCTION

Among the visuals that accompany reports and projections of global warming, there's typically a map of the world that uses color to indicate temperature change.[1] Blue stands for cooler than the mean for a given time period, yellow and orange for hotter. The reddest bands circle the high northern latitudes, and at least on the NASA map showing trends since 1955, the hottest spot of all lies like congealed blood over Alaska and the Canadian Northwest. This is where I live and where, like others from the north, I'm acutely aware of environmental change that has killed most of the spruce trees in my part of Alaska, eroded shorelines, and shifted our fisheries into different species and ranges. *Fish shifted to different ranges due to eroded shorelines and climate changes*

Globally, surface air temperatures have increased by a bit more than one degree Fahrenheit in the last hundred years. A measly one degree, and yet, already, the climate disruption that's resulted from that warming has been profound. Climate, it helps to remember, is the pattern of weather—encompassing averages, extremes, timing, and spatial distributions of temperatures, precipitation, and "events" like blizzards and tornadoes. Climate change refers to altered patterns. A small change in global average temperature (an index or indicator of the state of the global climate) can mean large changes in the patterns. *1 degree of change → can largely change climate patterns*

In Alaska and other parts of the north, average temperatures have

wt on pg 221
simile
def.

increased rapidly and dramatically. Just in the last fifty years, Alaska temperatures averaged across the state and through the year have risen by 3.4 degrees Fahrenheit. Winter temperatures have risen more sharply, by an average of 6.3 degrees. Temperature increases have varied by community.[2] My community—Homer, Alaska—has seen its year-round temperature increase by 3.1 degrees and its winter snows turn to rain. In February of 2010 even the slush melted away, moose knelt in our yards to eat green grass, and my neighbors and I went about without jackets or hats in sunny warmth as temperatures shot toward fifty. Then in March a blizzard dumped four feet of snow, temperatures dropped to zero, and schools were closed for the first time in decades.

Def.

"Polar amplification," the science phrase for the tendency of temperature change to increase with latitude, depends on a number of factors, some of which are not yet well understood.[3] The main process at work is the "ice-albedo positive feedback," which simply means that when ice and snow melt, the darker land and water surfaces absorb more solar heat, causing more ice and snow to melt. More open water allows for strong heat transfers from the ocean to the atmosphere.

The Intergovernmental Panel on Climate Change (IPCC) expects that climate change in the Arctic will be among the largest and most rapid on earth, with wide-ranging physical, ecological, sociological, and economic effects. Its fourth assessment, in 2007, noted that the polar regions are "extremely vulnerable to current and projected climate change," of considerable geopolitical and economic importance, and are "the regions with the greatest potential to affect global climate and thus human populations and biodiversity."

In other words, what happens in the Arctic doesn't stay in the Arctic. The polar regions function as the cooling system for our planet. As the climate and environment of the north change, so will the climate and ocean systems that regulate the entire world. The Kansas farmer and Florida vacationer don't need to care about desperately swimming polar bears or Inupiaq hunters falling through ice to be concerned about what's happening at the top of the world.

In the north, we live with disappearing sea ice, melting glaciers, thawing permafrost, drying wetlands, dying trees and changing landscapes, unusual animal sightings, and strange weather events. We live with such change, and we respond to it, through the myriad of daily choices we make about when and how to travel, what to plant in a garden or when to hunt or harvest, where to build, or how much to invest in a business like salmon fishing or snow-plowing. Communities pull together to work on erosion control, wildfire prevention, and water supplies; some, like my town, have adopted (if not fully embraced and implemented) climate action plans.[4] Our universities and other institutions support research and publish information they hope will be useful at all levels, including that of policy making. Governments respond—slowly, hampered by bureaucracy and the political strength of certain industries and skeptics.

Deborah Williams, a former Department of the Interior official and passionate conservationist, has been called "Alaska's Al Gore." One day in 2008 in the Anchorage office of the organization she founded, Alaska Conservation Solutions, she gave me what amounts to her "stump speech." Alaskans are seeing the effects of global warming sooner than the rest of the world and "as witnesses have a moral responsibility to talk about what we're seeing, the cause of what we're seeing, and the imperative need to act." Alaska, she said, should not just be the poster child for global warming but set an example by reducing its own carbon footprint. Alaskans can show what it takes to be both resilient and transformative. We're first, in consequences and opportunity.

Two years later, in early 2010, President Obama's secretary of interior Ken Salazar announced the selection of the University of Alaska as home to the first of eight planned regional climate science centers in the nation. He said this: "With rapidly melting Arctic sea ice and permafrost, and threats to the survival of Native Alaskan coastal communities, Alaska is ground zero for climate change. We must put science to work to help us adjust to the impacts of climate change on Alaska's resources and peoples."

Yes, there is a great variability, as the scientists say, to weather and climate, and the earth's interconnected systems are immensely complex. None of us can say that a particular event is solely attributable to global warming. The trends, however, are clear, and the changes occurring in the north have been well documented by the IPCC in its series of reports, the Arctic Climate Impact Assessment, ongoing scientific studies, and the popular press.

This book is not about the fact that climate change is occurring on regional and global scales (faster than the models predicted), that the emission of greenhouse gases from human activities (rising at an increasing rate) is driving it, or that we may be reaching "tipping points" after which the earth will likely be a very different and less hospitable place than that which has supported the human species since its members first learned to rub two sticks together.[5] Although many people have chosen to ignore and even deny the peril we've brought upon our world, the scientific community has been in agreement for many years about the basics and seriousness of global warming, and publications on the subject abound.[6] Some of them are listed in my bibliography.

This book, instead, takes a look at my reddish corner of the world and the ways that its people and communities are learning from, struggling and coping with, and adapting to the climate-related changes they encounter on a daily basis.

Of course, there's a lot of change going on in the north besides climate. There's environmental change brought on by resource development, land use, and the accumulation of toxins, and there's continuing socioeconomic change. Native peoples in particular have leaped, in just decades, from traditional to modern lives. Changes related to global warming aren't easily teased out of the entire fabric of change, and climate change isn't usually the first thing that northerners—who face so many other challenges, from cultural loss to high energy costs and competition over resources—worry about.

Still, northerners live in and depend on the environment in more intimate ways than most Americans and tend to be keen observers. The indigenous among us, with ancestors who survived and thrived in a harsh and unforgiving climate for thousands of years, hold a particularly close and generational knowledge of their home places. These Native people, whose values are grounded in respect for the land and in cooperation, have in the past demonstrated great resilience and innovation.

An ecologist who has worked among northern communities for many years said to me, "These people are really good at adapting—and proud of their abilities. They're not sitting ducks getting washed out to sea." Their adaptation to date has been assisted by such things as strong community networks, an acceptance of uncertainty, flexibility in resource use, and government support.

And yet, the ability of individuals and communities to adapt, today, is constrained by political decisions made (or neglected) at every level—regional, national, and international. It's also challenged by the unprecedented speed and degree of environmental change.

I have on my desk a brittle and yellowing scrap of newsprint I tore from somewhere a few years ago. The one paragraph reads, "'We basically have three choices: mitigation, adaptation, and suffering,' said John Holdren, the president of the American Association for the Advancement of Science and an energy and climate expert at Harvard. 'We're going to do some of each. The question is what the mix is going to be. The more mitigation we do, the less adaptation will be required and the less suffering there will be.'"

Holdren is now President Obama's science adviser. In testimony to Congress in July 2009, Holdren again pointed out the need to reduce carbon emissions and sequester as much carbon as possible and to make parallel efforts in adaptation. Adaptation strategies—such things as improving the efficiency of water use, managing coastal development with sea level rise in mind, and breeding drought-resistant crops—need, he said, to be employed at every level from the individual on up. This commitment, he said, would take leadership, coordination, and funding.

Until a few years ago, "adaptation" as related to climate change was rejected by many of us, from Al Gore on down, who were concerned it diverted attention from the critical need to reduce carbon emissions. "If temperatures increase, if sea ice decreases, we'll just adapt," was a toss-off response from those who wanted to continue business as usual. They posed adaptation as a simple solution, on the order of providing more air conditioners and, more positively in their view, taking advantage of ice-free Arctic waters for shipping and oil production.

Alaska's representative Don Young, who at every opportunity mentions "the myth of global warming," likes to talk about adaptation. He has opposed an endangered species listing for the polar bear and insisted that the bears can just switch from living on ice to living on land. He complained on a radio show, "We're the only ones that are not adapting to climate change. We're the only ones. All the other species will adapt. They'll all change, and they will survive."[7] Rep. Young is apparently unaware that the current rate of species extinction is one thousand to ten thousand times faster than at any time in the last sixty-five million years, or that there's a distinction between the common use of the word *adapt* (to adjust) and the biological one (in which species genetically evolve over time, through natural selection, to improve their conditions in relationship to their environments).[8] The IPCC has estimated that global temperature increases in the next hundred years may match those that occurred over five thousand years at the end of the last ice age—a rate far too rapid for evolutionary change by all but the fastest-breeding (think fruit flies) species.[9]

The mitigation part of Holdren's triad clearly isn't going too well, as global emissions continue to rise and the international community fails to brake a disastrous course. Adaptation—as in making human choices about how we'll live with the changes already set in motion by global warming—is now taking over much of the discussion, as it must. Even then, it's important to realize that adaptation as Holdren and others intend it involves proactive planning for the long-term—making changes to activities, rules, institutions, and so on in order to minimize risk. It is not the same as coping, which is a short-term response to protect, right now, resources or livelihoods. Coping mechanisms can get you through an event or year but can easily be overwhelmed.

Lara Hansen, an ecologist who started a nonprofit called Eco-Adapt, lamented to me as I began this book the lack of a "field" of adaptation.[10] (This has been described elsewhere as an "adaptation deficit"—the difference between what we know and what we need to know to help with adaptation. This gap exists both in scientific research and in policy making.) Resource managers, community planners, and others working in areas affected by climate change, Hansen told me, "know at some level they need to work on this, but they feel completely disempowered to do anything because they've never had any formal training on what adaptation is. Generally when I talk to people at state agencies, the response I get is, 'Yeah, we know we need to be doing something about this, but we don't know what it is, and we don't even know how to start approaching it.' There's very little in the world to help a person define a good adaptation versus a bad one, or to decide what is effective and fis-cally wise or not." Hansen founded EcoAdapt to train people in what she called "unfortunately a growth industry."

The north, Hansen said, is a very useful place from which to learn. "The changes are happening so fast that the people and eco-systems have already started to do things. It's not been formally called adaptation, but it's happening. We need to know what those things are and try to learn lessons from them. What's working? How did people come up with the ideas of what they thought would work? What kinds of decision-making processes generated success-ful responses? What kinds of partnerships helped? How can we facilitate the kinds of conversations that need to happen? And how can we use those experiences to empower vulnerable communities in other parts of the country or world as they deal with their unique responses to climate change? How do we build the network so that people in analogous situations talk to each other and share what they've learned—and do it in a manner that works for them?"

Hansen had found most of the guides dealing with climate change adaptation to be written in language that was incompre-hensible or alienating to ordinary people and "wildly inappropriate to deal with the problem at the level that it needs to be dealt with. It's not a problem that's going to be dealt with by individuals sitting in high government offices."

What will adaptation in the north look like? One thing we pretty well understand—it will be expensive. A study by the Institute for Social and Economic Research at the University of Alaska esti-mated that the changing climate will make it between 10 and 20 percent more expensive to build and maintain public infrastruc-ture in Alaska over the next couple of decades.[11] These additional costs (billions of dollars) are mostly associated with the effects on roads, runways, and water systems of thawing permafrost, erosion, and flooding. Analyses show generally, though, that the costs and difficulties of adapting will be much greater if action is delayed. Other adaptation strategies that have been discussed include things like more flexible and more conservative management of fish and wildlife resources, protection of key lands and waters, technological assistance, and training for new jobs. Adaptation, for some living in coastal areas, will also involve building seawalls and/or moving to higher ground.

In a perfect world, climate change adaptation in the north might be integrated into broader objectives to solve additional social, economic, and cultural problems while acting as a proving ground for particular strategies.

One way or another, the early-warming north *will* be a proving ground. The north is where we'll find out just how creative and responsible humans can be. Maybe, we'll show how to turn a crisis into stronger communities and a more sustainable future. Or maybe the lessons will be quite different; maybe what we'll learn is how hard it is to lose homes and livelihoods, the costs of ignoring risk and peril, what it means to suffer.

My homeplace, Alaska's Kenai Peninsula, depends for its life on salmon. Salmon have fed people here since the first Pacific Eskimos showed up, salmon kept the early homesteaders going, and salmon today support families engaged in commercial and sport fishing. For twenty-five years I fished commercially for salmon in Cook Inlet, and I love this place in all its weathers and sea conditions but especially in its bounty. The nutrients that spawning salmon deliver upstream feed bears, birds, other fish, plants, the entire ecosystem. To the degree that climate change alters rainfall, evaporation rates, plant cover, stream temperatures, and ocean conditions, salmon may find themselves living in an environment quite different than in the past. Or not living—not surviving, at least not as well or in the same places as they do now.

I set out, first, to learn in my own neighborhood about streams and salmon. I wanted to know what was happening relative to climate, and I wanted to understand how science—so much of it scaled globally and so bound in scientific conservatism and jargon—could be explained and made useful on a local level. I would start at home, and then I would head northward, to see how people elsewhere were responding to their own climate change challenges. My inquiry would be, by necessity, more opportunistic than comprehensive—based on visits to a scattering of communities, with their disturbing climate news and the occasional example of promising innovation. I wanted to see if people in the forefront of so much change were getting information and the assistance they needed, and how their expertise was informing others. Even as I knew that in North America—with our collective wealth and privilege—we have so many more options than most of the planet's people, I wanted to catch a glimpse of what the future might hold for us all, the world over.

Part One

My Salmon Home: Kenai Peninsula

On a mid-May Friday, the Ninilchik River on Alaska's Kenai Peninsula was running high, fast, and dark. Sue Mauger, stream ecologist for the nonprofit Cook Inletkeeper, and I stood on the muddy bank, among piles of moose turds, willow bushes close-cropped by those same moose and just beginning to tint into green, and a crushed pop can. A pair of harlequin ducks beat past us, low over the water and heading upriver, the male in its colorful clown plumage, the duller female sporting white cheek patches like silver dollars.

Somewhere in that muddy water whipping past us, the first king salmon of the year were likely forcing their way upstream. In another week, Memorial Day weekend would launch the sport fishery on the Ninilchik and neighboring rivers, and barbecue grills throughout the region would be put back to work. The economy of the Kenai Peninsula, in fact, largely runs on salmon—not just the sportfishing that occurs along the rivers and in the inlet, but also commercial fishing by seiners, drifters, and setnetters and the subsistence and personal use fishing that nets Alaskans food for their freezers. The early king salmon would be followed by the big push of red salmon in the rivers that lead to lakes, then late-run kings, pinks, and silver salmon later in the summer.

We had driven north from Homer for forty miles in an effort to collect a "TidbiT," a temperature data logger, left in the Ninilchik

River since the previous October, and replace it with a new one to begin to record the spring and summer water temperatures. Mauger pointed toward the middle of the river, where the logger, an item not much larger than a quarter, was housed in a piece of PVC pipe and anchored to the river bottom with rebar. The whole apparatus was well out of sight below the surface, in a low spot behind a rock, where fishermen should not have snagged it and, Mauger hoped, where ice and logjams should not have scraped against it. This was her first visit to the river since fall, and she was eager to get the logger back to the Homer lab to download its winter's worth of temperature data.

In chest waders and long plastic gloves, Mauger stepped off the bank and braced herself against the current. A slight and athletic woman who has run marathons and had just been telling me about a triathlon she was entering in Anchorage the next day, Mauger worked her way over the mud-and-gravel bottom, careful not to lose her footing in the swift current. The tannin-brown water reached her knees, then her waist, and she was nowhere near the logger's location. She turned and shuffled back to the bank. "This is what they call 'bankful,'" she said. Indeed, the river filled its banks from one side to the other, about forty-five feet away. On both sides the willows were hung with grasses and other debris, deposits from even higher water levels a few weeks earlier.

Spring that year—2008—had been late and cool, and a surprise snowstorm in April had left snowpack still melting in the hills. There were even late snow patches in the shadowy places along this lower stretch of the river, just a mile from where it emptied into Cook Inlet. The morning was overcast and cool—thirty-eight degrees Fahrenheit when we'd left Homer—and rain during the night had swelled the river.

The late spring and cooler temperatures had local people saying things like, "There goes the global warming theory." I was also used to seeing a popular bumper sticker that read ALASKANS FOR

GLOBAL WARMING and knew there were plenty of Alaskans who were suspicious of the underlying climate change science but also thought that warmer temperatures could be a *good* thing—more shorts-and-sandals weather, a longer gardening season, lower winter fuel bills. Certainly the difference between weather and climate had more than a few people confused, and erratic weather events—even sometimes involving colder temperatures and more snow—were hard for many to connect to a warming planet.

Besides the climate change effects of increased greenhouse gases in the atmosphere, we needed to contend with natural cycles, including what scientists call the "El Niño Southern Oscillation." The shifting in the equatorial Pacific from warmer masses of water to cooler ones, and back again, affects the wind patterns that carry warmer or cooler air to Alaska. We were just coming off of a strong La Niña, which, according to the models, should be followed by an El Niño and warmer than average winters.

If air and water temperatures were not alarming all Alaskans, there was one thing almost everyone cared about passionately—our wild salmon. Salmon evolved as cold-water animals, and Alaska today supports tremendous runs of five species. In some recent years the commercial fisheries have caught upward of two hundred million salmon valued at hundreds of millions of dollars at the dock. The sport fishing industry, which claims twelve thousand jobs, boasts hundreds of millions of dollars of additional value to the state's economy.

And salmon are anadromous, meaning they travel up rivers and streams, and sometimes into lakes, to spawn, and are thus sensitive to both marine and freshwater conditions.

Cook Inletkeeper was all about protecting the Cook Inlet watershed and the life forms that depend on it and since 1998 had been monitoring twelve sites on four Kenai Peninsula salmon streams for pollutants, along with water temperature, pH, dissolved oxygen, turbidity, and nutrients.

The biggest surprise was finding that in recent summers stream temperatures on the lower Kenai often exceeded state water-quality standards set to protect salmon spawning and the survival of eggs and fry. And water temperatures were trending upward, tracking air temperature increases.

Here at the Ninilchik River, the number of summer days that water temperatures had exceeded state standards for the upper limit of egg and fry incubation (55.5 degrees Fahrenheit) increased from fifty-six days in 2002 to seventy days in 2005. The number of days that the standards for the upper limit for fish migration and spawning (59 degrees) were also high—to more than fifty days. Other Kenai Peninsula streams showed similar temperatures and trends. In 2005 the Anchor River close to Homer topped the 55.5-degree limit on eighty-eight days and the "do not exceed" temperature of 68 degrees on six days.

Mauger is well aware that a few years of data mean, by themselves, very little. (In fact, in the couple of years after 2005, the stream temperatures were a little less alarming, before shooting back up in 2009.) She also knew that increased stream temperatures could be due to a number of factors. Like a detective, she'd set out to discover associations and meaning.

Stream temperatures can increase as a result of land development—the cutting of shade trees, paved surfaces where water warms before running off, water withdrawals. It was true that much of the spruce forest on the Kenai Peninsula had died from a beetle infestation, but an analysis of the subsequent logging that occurred on different watersheds, with changes in stream shade, could not account for the warming. Neither could the very small amount of development that dotted woods and fields with cabins and connected them by roads and trails.

What did correlate with the warming streams was warming air. At the Homer Airport, air temperature records go back to 1932—a long time for Alaska, where most baseline data is sorely lacking. Those records show that most of the warming has occurred since 1977, following worldwide trends, with summer air temperatures warmer by two degrees Fahrenheit and December and January temperatures by four degrees. Beginning in 2005, Cook Inletkeeper started hanging temperature data collectors in trees near the stream data loggers and found that the water temperatures generally tracked the air temperatures. That is, when we have a warm summer, the water temperatures are warmer, and when we have a cooler summer, the water temperatures are cooler. (The relationship also changes with water volume, which relates to the amount of rain and snowmelt.) With that relationship established, Mauger and others can "backcast" to estimate earlier stream temperatures as well as begin to predict future stream temperatures if air temperatures continue to rise.

We were not, Mauger emphasized to me, at temperatures where we were seeing any visible changes in survivorship. That is, fish were not dropping dead in the streams. The effects could be more subtle—stress that might affect growth or susceptibility to disease. It was time, she said, before we had catastrophic results, to "get people comfortable with using the data. The trajectory that we're on gets us there. What we don't know is the time scale."

Mauger had, in the last couple of years, begun making public presentations about her work to various audiences.[1] She'd presented at science conferences and to conservation groups, to chambers of commerce and fishing organizations. In 2007 she'd been an invited guest to speak to the Alaska Climate Impact Assessment Commission appointed by the state legislature. The commission, a "balanced" group of government employees, industry representatives, and citizens, included members who did not believe that human activities contributed to global warming, and Mauger described the group as "a little bit of a hostile audience." (One person in particular wanted to argue the science with her, and others accused her of having "no proof" that salmon were being affected.) As we turned back from the river, Mauger half grimaced, half chuckled. "I didn't feel like I had a very aggressive message, so I was kind of surprised by the feedback I got."

Her recommendations to the commission, about what should be done in Alaska, had been straightforward:

1. Collect stream temperature and flow data in key watersheds across the state.
2. Incorporate temperature data (both stream and marine) and climate information into salmon management models and plans.
3. Encourage actions to increase watershed resiliency to climate warming.

One of the points she tried to make in all her presentations was, she acknowledged, the need to control greenhouse gas emissions. But even if we stopped burning fossil fuels immediately, past actions had already committed us to a certain amount of environmental change, and she wanted people to think about what that meant. "We need to understand what that change is going to look like on small, regional scales," she explained. By starting to collect stream temperature data, "we're helping communities understand what role fishing will play in their future. This project is about getting people the information they need to make good economic decisions." It was up to those people, then, to decide what they wanted to do, both to ameliorate the negative effects of climate change and learn to live with them.

Mauger and I returned to Inletkeeper's Ford hybrid and drove the short road down into the village of Ninilchik. There, a huddle of homes crowded the lowest bend of the river and a small boat harbor accessible only at the highest tides.

Ninilchik has a unique history among Alaskan towns, having been settled as a retirement colony for Russians and their "creole" families (the results of Russian and Alaska Native unions) who chose to stay in the country when control passed from Russia to the United States in 1867. Many of the residents today are direct descendants of those settlers, and the onion-domed Russian Orthodox church on the hill is surrounded by a graveyard filled with more of those Russian names. From where we stopped by the river to check a stream gauge, I spotted the notched-log house once owned by a friend, who, when he stripped the inside for a bit of modernizing, found old Russian newspapers used as insulation. The Russian colonists, the Dena'ina Athabascan people who preceded them, and all comers since have relied on the river and its salmon for their lives and livelihoods. It was unthinkable that the people of Ninilchik should have to turn away from that history and dependence.

What does it mean when stream temperatures exceed state standards for salmon spawning and rearing? Nobody quite knows. Alaska's temperature standards are actually a modification of research-based recommendations from the Pacific Northwest, not based on any Alaska-specific data—and not adjusted regionally to match Alaska's huge geographical spread. A former governor, Frank Murkowski, had eliminated the Department of Fish and Game's Habitat Division, so there was no one home to figure out what effects, if any, warmer temperatures might actually be having on Alaska's wild salmon.

We do know, from testing and experience elsewhere, that higher temperatures can have profound effects on salmon and other cold-water fish. Higher temperatures can reduce growth rates (when fish have to put more energy into respiration and metabolism), reduce the survival of eggs and fry, affect the timing of out-migration (reducing marine survival), increase disease, and make fish more vulnerable to pollution (since some chemicals and metals increase in toxicity with higher temperatures). Warmer waters can also influence food supplies, vulnerability to predators, and competition with other species including exotics that move into waters made more hospitable to them. And we do know that when fish (and living organisms generally) are stressed by any one process, they're less able to deal with other stressors.

Along the West Coast of the United States, salmon runs have been in serious decline, with the collapse of California's Sacramento River Chinook runs resulting in a complete closure of sport and commercial salmon fishing off the coast of California and most of Oregon. The reason for the collapse was not clear. Some biologists pointed to unusual weather patterns that disrupted the upwelling of nutrient-rich water in coastal waters that normally supported the marine food web. Other people pointed to water quality issues related to damaged habitat, agricultural pollution, and altered flows and temperatures related to development and water diversions. Greenhouse gas–induced climate change might be just one factor among a series of environmental insults.

In the Sacramento River, engineering efforts had already been made to try to keep temperatures from becoming overly warm; in 1996 a temperature control system was added to the Shasta Dam to release deep, cold water from the lake bottom. As early as 1976 and 1977, thousands of Sacramento River salmon died when water temperatures rose to sixty-two degrees Fahrenheit. (Recall that Alaska's "do not exceed" temperature is sixty-eight degrees, and that in 2005 our Anchor River exceeded that on six days.)

Michael Healey, a professor emeritus at the University of British Columbia, is a nationally recognized expert in both the ecology of Pacific salmon and the design of resource management systems. He has noted that the effects of climate change on salmon are of major concern to resource managers and that the degree of warming expected in both freshwater and marine habitats over the next century "will have uncertain but potentially devastating effects on salmon and their ecosystems."[2] By focusing on the sockeye salmon of British Columbia's Fraser River (the most valuable—commercially and ecologically—salmon river in Canada), he has developed a model for examining the cumulative effects of climate change on the many stages in the salmon life cycle and across generations. What he lays out is not pretty.

First, he notes that in recent years large numbers of adult salmon that enter the Fraser River have failed to make it to the spawning grounds and many that did died without spawning, and that a late run has been entering the river weeks earlier than in the past. Extremely poor survival in the Fraser in 2004 was linked to exceptionally high temperatures. Sockeye returning to the Fraser have been both smaller than in the past and with lower energy reserves, suggesting that "energetic exhaustion" may be one cause of the observed mortality, perhaps along with temperature stress and disease.

For his analysis, Healey recognized eight stages in the life of the sockeye and detailed the effects of increasing temperature (drawn from previously published scientific studies) on each stage, then looked at how the effects on each stage affected performance at later stages. He has shown that global warming has negative effects on productivity at every stage and that the effects at one stage carry through to the next and then generationally. He further considered how the effects of high temperatures at each stage might be mitigated or adapted to—biologically and by management and policy decisions. For example, management options might include releasing cool water from reservoirs upstream of spawners, fertilizing lakes to make up for nutrient deficits related to the mismatch of plankton bloom times, and preventing overfishing. Policies might include reserving adequate stream flows in salmon rivers, managing predators, and establishing "salmon first" for the use of estuarine habitats.

Healey wrote to me, "I had been stuck a bit trying to find anything positive to say, but I think I have a found a thread (melting Arctic is opening new habitat for salmon)." Given time, he says, salmon will naturally colonize the Arctic, but he fears that their rate of moving into new habitats might be too slow to keep ahead of global warming. It was his opinion that managers and policy makers should be thinking now about assisting salmon to colonize the Arctic (by transplanting them or developing freshwater nurseries), not only to keep salmon in the world but also to retain the option of eventually restoring populations to the south, when the climate there is favorable again.

Alaska has its own example of temperature-stressed salmon not making it back to their spawning beds. A five-year study of Yukon River salmon infested with *Ichthyophonus* linked the microscopic parasite (commonly called "ick") to warmer stream temperatures.[3] Before the mid-1980s, *Ichthyophonus*, which causes "white spot disease" in fish, had never been reported from the Yukon River. Today, it infects more than 40 percent of the river's adult Chinook salmon.

This disease, which can be fatal to fish, doesn't harm people but makes the salmon meat mealy, with an odd smell and unpleasant texture, fit only for feeding to dogs. Richard Kocan, a fish disease expert from the University of Washington, has linked the emergence of the disease to increased river temperatures. Average Yukon River temperatures have been rising for three decades. Since 1975 June water temperatures at the village of Emmonak, on the river's delta, have increased from less than fifty-two degrees to fifty-nine degrees Fahrenheit with July temperatures even higher.

Kocan found that the number of infected fish, and severity of the disease, was highest in the study years with the highest temperatures and highest during the times of summer when the water was warmest. Laboratory studies have also shown that *Ichthyophonus* thrives as a host's temperature increases (as would be the case of cold-blooded salmon in warming water). Kocan's peer-reviewed study concluded, in the conservative manner of science, that water temperatures above fifty-nine degrees appeared to correlate with increases in *Ichthyophonus* infection, and that rising average water temperatures in the Yukon River in the last three decades may be an important cause of increased disease and mortality among Chinook salmon. He believed—but did not have good data to support—that as much as 20 percent of the Yukon's Chinook were dying from the disease en route to their spawning grounds. *Ichthyophonus* has also been detected, in limited surveys, in salmon in other rivers, and in other fish species. Kocan considers it to be a classic emerging disease—defined as a disease that has either newly appeared in a population or has been known for some time but is rapidly increasing in incidence or geographic range. In this case, the triggering factor for its emergence appears to be warming waters.

To put it simply, *Ichthyophonus* may have always been with us, but a warming climate may be redistributing it, allowing it to flourish in parts of the north where cold temperatures once acted as a barrier to its spread and where species, themselves stressed by warmer temperatures, lack individual or evolutionary resistance.

And more of the same may be on the way.

In a spitting rain, Mauger and I headed back south on the highway, past an eagle's nest in a bare cottonwood right next to the road, to our last stop, at Stariski Creek. Stariski is a smaller watercourse than Ninilchik but still an important salmon river, with spawning runs of king, silver, and pink salmon, along with steelhead and Dolly Varden trout. At Stariski, culverts running under the highway had been recently replaced with a bridge, and Inletkeeper was hired by the Alaska Department of Transportation to check turbidity around the project. The project included a fancy new boardwalk that led from the road to the river, so that even someone in a wheelchair could easily roll to streamside for fishing. The whole bridge project, including riverbank stabilization with rock and willow plantings, was necessitated by not one but two "hundred-year (that is, expected to occur only once in a century) floods" in 2002. Those major floods had dramatically reshaped channels, scoured beds, and undercut banks.

The landscape remodeling brought home to me those other likely effects of global warming—not just an increase in air and water temperatures, with their direct implications, but lower stream flows in summer (reducing habitat areas and increasing stream temperatures even more), stream-scouring floods in the fall (wiping out eggs and egg-laying habitat), changes in the timing of freeze and thaw cycles, and sedimentation.

Sedimentation could come from sources previously unthought of. Alarms had sounded recently about Skilak Lake, a critical rearing habitat for red salmon that ascend the nearby Kenai River.[4] There, the glacier that feeds the lake is melting more rapidly, depositing more ground-up rock "flour" into the water. The resulting turbidity means sunlight can't penetrate the lake water as far, which means less photosynthesis, less plankton production, less food for the young salmon.

Downstream of the Stariski bridge, Mauger took a water sample to check turbidity and filled out a data sheet to describe the current river conditions, high and fast. I watched a pair of mergansers, looking like passive wooden decoys, take a wild ride downstream. Then we crossed the highway and walked upstream, past riverbanks restored with fabric and willow plantings and a section where more recent erosion had undercut a bank. We walked through dead, flattened grasses and twisted alders and into the shade of cottonwoods, where snow patches still lingered. Mauger pointed away from the river. "It's interesting," she said. "This area's never been logged, but it's all open." Indeed, the "forest" was more grass than trees; most of the spruce trees were broken off, leaving splintery stumps at various heights, and the deadfall of their tops lay under and over the twining grasses.

This was a story that Mauger and I knew all too well. In the warmer temperatures of the last couple of decades, spruce bark beetles in the region had flourished. They not only survived the winters that had previously kept them in check with cold temperatures, but were able to complete their life cycle in a single year instead of two. They loved the hot summers that enticed them from their galleries beneath the bark and propelled them to new trees. The infestation, which eventually killed thirty million trees (decimating four million acres of spruce forest—that is, a land area larger than all of Connecticut)—was the largest insect infestation ever documented in North America. (It was recently overtaken by an even larger attack of pine beetles in British Columbia, also linked to climate warming.)

Spruce bark beetles (*Dendroctonus rufipennis*), like the *Ichthyophonus* salmon parasite, are a natural part of the ecosystem in our region—thought perhaps to be *the* instrument of forest succession, rather than fire—but their success in attacking and killing nearly every adult spruce tree across an entire landscape is unprecedented in either historic or prehistoric (judged by tree-ring evidence) times.[5] I well remember the summer "flights" in the 1990s, when a series of overly warm days would release swarms of beetles, like a biblical plague, that would, literally, drive people to the shelters of their closed homes. And I remember the march of death across the landscape—the forest turning red as needles died, then gray, then splintered as the dried-out trunks shattered in winter winds.

Parts of the peninsula were logged, the dead trees turned to chips and shipped to Asia, while others were left "natural" as habitat for insect-eating birds, for building new soil, for eventual regrowth. In both cases, our woods were being replaced with grasslands; it's thought that the tall native grasses may, for a long time, keep any trees from gaining a foothold.

The changed landscape can, of course, have profound effects on water resources and salmon. Trees provide shade, which can help cool rivers. Trees also provide woody debris, beneficial to salmon streams for breaking up the flow and providing resting and hiding spots for fish.

Mauger waded into the raging stream to take another water sample. She pointed out, against the far bank, a pole and instrument she uses, when she can reach it, to measure stream height. A dead tree had fallen against it, and next visit, when she hoped to be able to wade across, she'd bring a chainsaw to clear the area.

All around us, grasses and other debris were hung in the willows, showing how high the water had been earlier. Mauger surveyed the banks, alert to another climate change threat: invasive species. Two that had devastated habitats elsewhere on the peninsula were northern pike—a toothy, predatory fish that can take down ducks and muskrats while also gobbling up young salmon—and exotic grasses. Neither had moved in naturally, as some species did, mile by mile, as the climate changed. They had been introduced—pike by people who valued them as a sport fish, and exotic grasses by being mixed with grass seed, seed packets, or imported hay. Still, in a hospitable climate, they can flourish. Such "weedy" species can outcompete native ones.

Reed canary grass (*Phalaris arundinacea*)—"a huge deal," Mauger said—grows into mats that turn flowing streams into marshes. It's been used for revegetation of roadsides precisely because it spreads rapidly and builds sod that helps with erosion. All along the West Coast, from California to British Columbia, it's destroyed wetlands and salmon habitat. Plant specialists once thought that in Alaska's cold the grass wouldn't produce viable seed, but recent surveys had found infestations in at least 259 locations on the Kenai Peninsula, including along salmon streams.

"It's all additive," Mauger said, capping her water sample. Warmer temperatures, more flooding, greater drying, less shade and debris, human alterations to the river corridor and uplands, invasive species—"the system is getting hammered."

We made our way back along the river, past the fallen forest and the eroded muddy banks, to the highway. We drove back toward Homer through more dreary rain, and I asked Mauger whether, with all that she knew about consequences, she considered herself an optimist or pessimist about the future.

She hesitated a few seconds before drawing a breath. "I do have optimism that some of the repercussions of climate change can be minimized. We're going to do that with having better information. That's what this project is about—getting the information that we need so that we don't have a collapse in fisheries with no warning."

She paused again and then added that she was also hopeful that, after so much delay and denial from our political leaders, our national politics would change enough, soon enough. "To make the transitions that we need to make, I think it will be a painful ten years. But we have to start now."

That summer, the stream temperature work Mauger had pioneered on the four Kenai Peninsula rivers was being extended, with state funding, to the rest of the Cook Inlet watershed—forty-eight sites in all. Mauger had worked all winter on the protocols so that data would be collected in a consistent, reliable manner. "We want to try to identify what types of streams are likely to warm fastest, and what types of systems are likely to remain coolest, so we can make some decisions about where to study more about the habitats and the fish. This is really a first cut at looking at different stream sizes and types, the role of wetlands, the role of lakes." The plan was, after that, for the same monitoring system to be employed by partners and volunteers in the major salmon streams of Bristol Bay (the location of the most valuable salmon runs) and elsewhere in the state.

In this way climate data would be broken out of the broad models and brought down to a local, real-time, and real-place level, to empower communities with the tools and data they need to protect salmon habitat and watershed health. Biologists and land use planners, it's hoped, will use the data to identify streams most vulnerable to change, then apply it to decisions about further research, habitat protection, water use, and restoration activities. In that ideal world, fishery managers will incorporate temperature information into their modeling of run strengths and escapements (the numbers of fish allowed upstream to spawn). They will also use everything they know about stock structures and life histories to maintain genetic diversity within Alaska's salmon, knowing that such diversity is critical to the ability of salmon populations to respond to climate change; elsewhere in the world, where individual stocks have disappeared due to overfishing or habitat loss, there's been little left for filling voids. (This need for genetic diversity, of course, applies to all species.)

We drove along and then across the swollen Anchor River, and Mauger offered up an example of practical application, one way that stream temperature data had already been used in decision making. She'd worked with a university student to identify and map "temperature refugia" along the Anchor. Areas of cool water—shaded by banks with overhanging vegetation—would be most essential to maintaining the river for salmon, and the local land trust added that information to their conservation priorities for working with willing land owners on maintaining vegetative cover in those key areas.

I was listening and making notes, but I was thinking about that eagle in the nest we'd passed, in the cottonwood tree right beside the highway. We used to think that eagles were shy birds that needed plenty of undisturbed space around them; now we know they don't—or that some have adapted to our busy presence.

Eagles—like bears, belugas, other large and small birds, trout, microbes, even the trees enriched by the spawned-out salmon carcasses that are carried into the forest by the birds and the bears—depend on the salmon. So, of course, do we. I can hardly imagine my home place without them. How would we live?

Salmon are adaptive; we know this. The five Alaska species have managed to survive in this part of the world for six million years, through periods of warmth and cold. Over the course of time, individual stocks have been challenged by change—whether it came from glaciers and ice sheets that overran streams or tied up water in ice, from volcanoes that buried streams in ash or mud, from rock slides, floods, earthquakes that raised or lowered the land and its streambeds. Some stocks perished, while others survived, adapting to conditions and colonizing new habitat.

The challenge, this time, looks to come from climate change that modifies both freshwater and marine conditions on a large scale, and rapidly. Despite all of Alaska's bragging about our sustainable salmon management, we may find ourselves up the proverbial creek. This time, the degree and speed of change may be more than salmon, as species, can adapt to.

Freshwater—not just in streams but also in lakes, wetlands, and the water table, and in its various forms of precipitation and storage, including in glacial ice—is absolutely key to the Kenai Peninsula landscape and everything that landscape supports. Despite the high water I witnessed in May, I knew that the western peninsula was drying, and I wanted to understand both what that might mean and how the people who decide what it might mean do their work. On a coolish July morning, I joined my neighbor Ed Berg for a day trip into the heart of the Kenai National Wildlife Refuge, where he works as the refuge ecologist. We were joined by Dick Reger, a retired geologist who volunteers with Berg just for the fun of it, for a trip to the middle of the five Finger Lakes. Or Middle Finger Lake.

"We definitely got the idea why it's called that," Reger laughed as we readied gear at his cabin. A few days earlier, the two men, both in their late sixties, had canoed the length of that longest of the Finger Lakes against the wind.

Now, Berg, wearing an orange field vest with multiple bulging pockets and with his ever-ready hand lens on a cord around his neck, waited patiently while Reger showed me how to look at aerial maps with a stereoscope and pick out their three-dimensional features. Reger put on his own orange vest—with the six pens and pencils lined up in their pocket compartment—and tossed his lunch into a backpack. And then we were off, bumping down Swanson River Road into the refuge, nearly two million acres of federal land characterized by mostly scrubby forest, lots and lots of small lakes and two really big ones full of red salmon, plenty of wetlands, and on the southeast side, the Harding Icefield and its glaciers. This northern part of the refuge, near the town of Sterling, had been entirely burned in a 1969 forest fire and was now largely covered by skinny birch trees.

Berg and Reger explained as we drove that this lowland had once been lake bottom; during the last ice age, ice sheets had formed dams and impounded freshwater. The lakes that pock the refuge today, including the Finger Lakes, are known as "kettle lakes," created from the melt of giant ice blocks left by retreating glaciers and filled by precipitation and groundwater; streams do not flow in or out of them, thus making them very useful for studying effects of climate change. Over time, they've been good recorders of what Berg calls "available water"—that is, precipitation minus the water that's lost to evapotranspiration (the combination of water transferred to the atmosphere by evaporation and from the leaves of plants). The record is long; although glaciers remain in nearby mountains, the land here has been free of ice for about eighteen thousand years.

Our goal was to again canoe the length of the lake, for further investigation of a key geological feature called an ice-shoved rampart. The mystery of that berm of earth, and others within the refuge, might, the men thought, be unlocked into an understanding of past climate—and thus be useful for imagining a future.

As soon as we were out of the truck and lathering on mosquito repellent, Berg and Reger were examining and debating, with tangible excitement, oddities in the bark of some birch trees. This supreme inquisitiveness is what I love about Berg, whom I've known for years—since the time he was a carpenter—and from whom I've twice taken a geology class at our local college. Before the carpenter period of his life, Berg had been both a geophysicist and doctor of philosophy, and when he tired of hammering, he became a botanist. Berg is also particularly skilled at making science understandable to the public. His study of the spruce bark beetle and its warm-weather success at devastating Kenai Peninsula forests has been oft-reported in the popular press, in which he tends to be very quotable.[6] "Beetles take no prisoners," he once told reporters during a tour of the refuge. "It's a Mafia-style execution."

The woods, as we slipped through, were full of carefully observed insects, seedlings, bird calls, and a spruce tree clawed by a bear.

At the edge of the lake, we maneuvered into the water the canoe they'd previously left there. Reger, lingering in the shallows, examined acorn-sized freshwater snails; on the earlier trip he'd collected some for his home aquarium, and now he told me of the snail's Asian origins and its passage—likely by birds—across Bering Strait. Berg, examining a sedge, quizzed Reger about its species.

Reger said to me, "Ed and I appreciate the same sorts of things. We have different backgrounds. He shows me this, and I show him something else. Everyone else thinks I'm a crackpot."

The two men paddled, and I rode like an Egyptian princess in the middle of the canoe. A slight breeze rippled the water, but there was no real wind. The lake, long and narrow but indeed "kettlelike," lay within steep sides and a surround of higher, forested land.

We stopped on a small island, and the two men went into high gear, digging holes and mixing soil samples with spit in their hands, referring to a soil color chart. This was not the day's project but a side stop to explore how long the island had been an island as opposed to lake bottom, which would say something about water levels and climate. The men engaged in a vigorous discussion about soil "platyness" and how sand is winnowed from silt and the age of the vegetation on top. The island, they could tell, was wave-flattened, and the sandy soil on top had to have been deposited by waves that had washed over the island, perhaps not that long ago. There was essentially no soil on the island—just that sand over the silt that had been lake bottom. The trees—some birch, a few short spruces, alders—were sparse, and the ground beneath them was mostly mossy, with a few wintergreen plants and dwarf dogwood and, in a moist spot near the shore, reddish sundews with their tentacles and seductively dewy tips.

After the 1969 fire that destroyed so much forest in the refuge, Berg said, he would have expected the water level in the area to rise, not fall; trees would be drinking less, so more water would stay in the lakes. But, in general, the refuge's lakes and wetlands were drying in the warmer temperatures and greater evapotranspiration associated with human-induced climate change.

In the expected cycles of warming and cooling, this part of Alaska should have been cooling. "Glaciers should be advancing," Berg said, as he paused to wipe his brow with a bandana. "Climate change may be overriding the natural order of things."

Then it was back into the canoe and only a short paddle to the south end of the lake, where we clambered out and approached a small berm with a hole dug into it and a pile of sandy soil to one side. This was it—our ice-shoved rampart, among the carpet of dwarf dogwood flowers and the dead leaves of the last year.

The men went back to work with a shovel, enlarging the hole they'd begun two days before on the landward side of the berm and from which they'd taken away a bit of woody evidence. Berg dug, and Reger squeezed and tasted soil samples, and then Reger dug and Berg talked to me about what they were doing. He spoke in his slow and always precise manner, in sentences that unfolded complete and orderly thoughts.

"What we're doing here at Middle Finger Lake is excavating a berm that's about two feet high, parallel to the shore, and it's back thirty or forty feet from the shore. The base of the berm is about eight and a half feet above the present surface of the lake. These berms are formed by the ice bulldozing the lake sediments. This happens in the spring when the lake ice is breaking up and getting blown around by the wind. We find them on the south and southwest sides. The remarkable thing about these is that they're so far above the present lake level—on other lakes we've found them twenty or twenty-five feet above the modern shorelines. Sometime in the past, the lake levels were very high—much higher than in the historic period. So we're excavating this berm—or ice-shoved rampart—in hope of finding some pieces of wood we can date with radiocarbon. That will give us an idea about when these berms were formed."

That—knowing when the lake levels were so high, the ice thick, and the northeast winds strong—could be matched to other climate data from that time period to tie regional effects to global ones and suggest linkages among conditions. An ability to "backcast," as Sue Mauger was doing with stream temperatures on a shorter time scale, could help with forecasting a climate future.

On their previous outing, Berg and Reger had collected two small pieces of wood that, from their placement between bulldozed lake material and forest floor, appeared to have been at the bottom of two different rampart-building "shoving events." Today, the goal was to get to a layer of soil underlying the whole berm. If they could find something woody there, they might get a maximum date—an upper limit on how old the berm might be.

Slate-colored juncos rustled through the underbrush, sparrows chattered, Reger paused to pinch some soil and what might have been part of a disintegrating root. He and Berg debated the theory they were working with—that the ramparts were created during the Younger Dryas period, some twelve thousand years ago. Younger Dryas was considered to be "a cold snap" after a warming period following the last big ice age, but there was some evidence from lake sediments and peat cores that it had been a wet period here on the Kenai.

That was the theory, but the first three radiocarbon dates they'd gotten from ramparts had dated from just fifteen hundred to five thousand years ago.

The two men argued the theory back and forth—whether the samples were good or might have been from deep roots, what the soil profiles told them, what it might mean if the ramparts were younger than they thought. Reger was leaning now to a mid-Holocene age. "That tells us a story, too."

"A stranger story," Berg said.

"It's not that we're arguing," Reger said to me. "It's just on the table."

Reger was standing in a pretty big hole now. "Look what I see down here—a thin possible silt layer." He and Berg studied the dirt, talked excitedly in technical terms, showed me—I could *kind of* see it—where the rampart ended and layers of overridden forest floor began. In another minute Reger was scraping, like an archaeologist, around a chunk of wood, and then a second one. Berg drew in his field notebook—the hole, the dimensions, notes on soil colors. He drew pictures of the little chunks of wood and then carefully wrapped them in aluminum foil.

Months later, when the radiocarbon dating was completed on those chunks of wood and twelve others from the ramparts at six different refuge lakes, the "stranger story" would be told. All the samples dated within the last fifty-two hundred years, in that recent interglacial period we know as the Holocene, when climate was thought to be reasonably stable. Why would there have been such high water at that time? What might have been going on with the climate then, here in this part of Alaska and globally? Were there other data sets that could support such a finding? Lake sediment studies in the refuge have suggested that the land in question had generally cooled and become wetter over the last nine thousand years, but there was, until now, no record of such extreme wetness.

Berg's new theory posits that the ice-shoved ramparts associate with a large regional climate trend, perhaps involving "a series of stormy, high-precipitation anomalies that have occurred over the last 5,200 years, reflecting major changes in the North Pacific weather system."[7]

We ate our sandwiches, and I wandered through the woods for a while, on animal trails that followed two smaller (and presumably more recent) ramparts that lay between the one we'd dug into and the shoreline. Had I come across any of these berms in the woods on my own, I would have guessed them to be glacial moraines or eskers, features I was more familiar with. In among the birch and the sweet-smelling balsam poplar stood a few blackened tree stumps, from the fire forty years earlier. Open areas around them were filled with bursts of purple fireweed.

I took a turn filling in the hole and then swatted more mosquitoes and listened to the far-off wavering call of a loon while Reger filled his plastic sandwich bag with lake plants to take home to his snail aquarium.

We boated back along the east side of the lake, watching for the indentation where we would portage to the next lake and then find a trail to the road.

I thought about the process of science—its posing of questions, all the tedious data collecting, the accumulation over time of observation, test results, reviews of results. The scientific process was slow and incremental, and conservative; it didn't respond well to crises.

I tried to think as a geologist might, back through time and the processes that work on landscapes. Imagine a woody plant on a forest floor, twelve thousand years ago. Or five thousand years ago. What kind of a world did either date define? Twelve thousand years ago humans were just coming across, or along the coastline of, the Bering Land Bridge, land exposed because so much water was tied up in ice caps and glaciers. Five thousand years ago our ancestors were primarily hunters and gatherers, although, at least in Asia, farming was developing on a largish scale; some clever beings invented both the wheel and systems of writing. In both those time periods the amount of carbon dioxide in the atmosphere (measured from Antarctic ice cores) was around 250–280 parts per million. Today atmospheric CO_2 exceeds 392 parts per million and is continuing to rise; levels of it and other greenhouse gases are higher than they've been at any time in at least eight hundred thousand years, which is as far back as ice core records go. Never in those eight hundred thousand years years did CO_2 levels increase at a rate anywhere near what we're experiencing today. Eight hundred thousand years ago *Homo sapiens* was still five hundred thousand years years away from evolving; our species has never had to cope with what are, indeed, unprecedented conditions—that is, unprecedented in our human history.

From his position in the stern, Berg talked about the Aleutian Low—that low-pressure center south of the Aleutian Islands in winter, characterized by high winds—that plays a major role in atmospheric circulation. If he and others could learn when the Kenai was particularly wet, climate modelers might be able to link that to other conditions at the time—for example the intensity of that Aleutian Low. Or to the advancement or retreat of glaciers in our part of Alaska, or to periods of intense storm activity in the Arctic. "That's the practical way this information will be used," Berg said. "This will help the climate modelers calibrate the models. In order to predict the future, we need to know the past. We need to run the model backward."

More locally, knowing something about climates of the past and conditions associated with them should inform decisions about land and water use, species conservation, and fire protection. Would it be a good thing to encourage beavers to build dams and store more water in the future? Would it be smart to reserve water for salmon streams, as opposed to using it for industrial or agricultural use? Should forest fires be allowed to burn, or should they be controlled?

We cruised past a flock of golden-eye ducklings, all paddling furiously with no parent duck in sight. When we got over that excitement, Berg told me about other research related to "available water." Various studies in the refuge, including analyzing photos that go back to the 1950s, have shown that wetlands are shrinking at accelerating rates. Ponds have disappeared, shrubs are filling in, and black spruces are expanding into areas that had once been too wet for them.[8] (I see this myself. Flying over, as I do when traveling to Anchorage, I look down on the "bathtub rings" around drying ponds, as well as the new, dark growth of little spruces pushing into open areas.)

Local meteorological records have shown a 60 percent decline in available water in the Kenai lowlands between 1968 and 2009; one-third of that, Berg has calculated, is due to higher summer temperatures and increased evapotranspiration and two-thirds due to lower annual precipitation. "That's a big change," Berg said. "That's 60 percent less water to recharge groundwater, fill up lakes and rivers, and be used by plants and animals. That's pretty dramatic."

With less water, areas once dominated by herbaceous plants—that is, leafy plants lacking woody stems—have been converting to shrubland at increasing rates—more than 12 percent per decade—and previously unforested areas are becoming forested at similar rates. Peat cores taken from the drying wetlands found no history of woody plant cover; that is, the sedge and sphagnum moss fens have dominated for eighteen thousand years. Only since about 1850 have those lands been drying—a drying that has greatly accelerated since 1970.

Let me repeat that: The current invasion of Kenai wetlands with shrubs and trees is unique in the last eighteen thousand years, and it is accelerating.

On the local level, the drying meant we were likely to see

more—and more damaging—fires. Berg said, "What were fire breaks in the past are becoming fuel bridges." A warmer climate, generally, will result in more fire activity. If the wetland areas that have acted as natural firebreaks between grasslands and forest dry out, they will no longer help control fires but will connect and speed them through the refuge and the rest of the Kenai lowlands. So far, the refuge has been experiencing more early-season fires—as early as April—in the grasslands that have replaced beetle-killed forests, and more fires have been ignited by lightning strikes. Lightning used to be a rare phenomenon on the peninsula, but has been increasing with the warming that builds thunderhead clouds. In 2005, six hundred lighting strikes started twenty-two Kenai Peninsula fires.

The conversion of our wetlands to a landscape of shrubs and trees is also significant for the global climate because of the major role wetlands play in the cycling of both CO_2 and methane. In the cycle that takes place everywhere on earth, trees and plants take up great quantities of carbon dioxide, release the oxygen, and store the carbon in their cells. (Wood is one-half carbon.) That carbon stays stored not just in the living vegetation but in woody debris and soil, until it's released by decomposition or burning. Methane (CH_4) is another form of carbon, created in the absence of oxygen. (When it's released to the atmosphere, where it's a powerful greenhouse gas, it eventually converts to CO_2 and water.)

Northern peatlands hold a tremendous amount of CO_2 and CH_4, equivalent to somewhere between a third and a half of that in the atmosphere. In the anaerobic (lacking oxygen) situation of wet soils, the gases stay in place. As the soils dry, the microbes get to work, decomposing the organic matter and giving off CO_2. But at the same time, the plants and trees that fill in the wetlands perform more photosynthesis, which takes in CO_2. The net result of this carbon "flux" (the transfer or rate of exchange between carbon "pools," as between, in this case, organic matter and the atmosphere) is not yet well understood.

A couple of months later, I returned to the refuge with a grad student, Sue Ives, helping her place a clear plastic box over vegetation plots and measure carbon flux with a gas analyzer machine. It was another example of small science steps, the necessary accumulation of place-specific data. It took most of the day to set the box over twenty plots marked out along a gradient—five very wet and mossy ones near the edge of a lake, five slightly drier ones with sedges and bog rosemary among the mosses, five dominated by brushy dwarf birches, and finally the driest, where small black spruce trees had begun to sprout up among cranberry and cloudberry plants—and to take readings with different cloud cover–imitating screens wrapped around the box.

So far it was looking as though, at least in summer, the drier plots were both respiring and photosynthesizing more than the wetter plots—with photosynthesis significantly outpacing respiration. The drier plots were sequestering more carbon than the wet ones.

On the surface, that seemed like a good thing—a landscape change that allowed for holding on to more carbon, keeping it out of the atmosphere. But summer measurements were, of course, not the whole story. In winter there would be little photosynthesis, but the microbes in the soil under the insulating snow would still be working, still be respiring. And there were other considerations: More plant growth would create a darker surface in winter, decreasing the albedo (surface reflectivity) and increasing the absorption of solar heat. The implications of more heat are earlier snowmelt, more drying, more plant and microbe activity, and more respiration and release of CO_2.

And this was just one type of wetland, in one place and set of conditionos.

In the next chapter, we'll look more closely at the role of carbon in vegetation, soils, and permafrost—what makes a particular landscape a carbon "sink" or a carbon "source."

Late that day, dark rain clouds rolled in over the mountains, threatening the whole day's work. Suddenly, we heard bugling. From the north, long skeins of sandhill cranes were coming our way, high in the sky and stretching for miles. The enormous flock—hundreds of birds—passed to our east, their calls echoing across the landscape, and I remembered the first time I saw cranes, my first fall in Alaska. I had stood then in the yard of a homestead house in the hills outside Homer and watched them spiral up into a great cloud, and I had thought they were magnificent. They were no less magnificent thirty-odd years later, flying high in their multiple twisting V formations. The two of us standing on a boardwalk in a bog stopped working to watch them pass, and then we turned to more bugling and another tremendous flock, spread out like musical notes across shifting staffs. And then, a third time—but now the birds came directly over our heads, and lower, so that we could see their long necks extended and their legs trailing, broad wings slowly flapping, the feathers on the wing tips separate and pointing like fingers. There were thousands, and the noise was deafening.

The cranes were flying from their nesting grounds on the Yukon-Kuskokwim Delta and the tundra areas of northern Alaska and Siberia. They scatter in those places—wetland places, peat bogs and muskegs, wet tundra near water—into their nesting pairs and raise one, sometimes two, "colts" while they fatten on insects, seeds, frogs, even small rodents. They were going to wintering grounds, in the southwestern United States, Texas, Mexico, where they—birds with the longest fossil record of any bird still flying, going back perhaps ten million years—have adapted well, in recent time, to feeding on the waste grain in agricultural fields.

I wondered where they'd settle for the night, what field or wetland they'd find, and how different that field or wetland might be in another year, ten years, within the lifetime of a long-lived crane.

PART TWO

BOREAL FOREST: AT THE ARCTIC CIRCLE

The boreal forest is that swath of stunted forest that circles the Northern Hemisphere, south of the treeless tundra and north of the temperate forest and grasslands, named for Boreas, the Greek god of the north wind. It is the largest, most intact wilderness area left on earth. A third of all the boreal lies in Alaska and Canada, and Russia has most of the rest, where it's called taiga, the "land of little sticks."

The boreal is also a massive storehouse of carbon; its trees, plants, and soil hold more carbon, on an acre-to-acre comparison, than the famed tropical forests. As more carbon dioxide is emitted to the atmosphere from human activities and the world warms, the role of the boreal forest and the permafrost that underlies it becomes increasingly significant.

I went north to look at wildness and possibility, and to learn what people there were thinking about their futures.

I. Mackenzie River Valley, Northwest Territories, Canada

For days, our three canoes and one highly piled raft had descended from our headwaters start in the remote Mackenzie Mountains of Canada's Northwest Territories. We'd plunged through rapids

and dug around tight corners, trading alpine openness for thick-
ening forest lit with wildflower blossoms. The mountain ranges—
Backbone, Redstone, Shattered, Canyon, Stony—rose around us
in craggy perfection as we flowed with the wild Mountain River
that cut through them, down, down, toward the mighty Mackenzie
River.

Then, on day ten, with dozens of miles yet to go, we floated past
a wooden post sticking straight up from a grassy area beside the
river. Aside from a couple of airplanes that had flown over and one
meadow where rocks had been redistributed in a way that suggested
a campsite, we had seen no signs of other humans along our course,
and the post—so smooth and straight and hatcheted at its end—
appeared as something entirely unnatural. I pointed to it from my
forward position in the raft. Our guide scowled. "So much for 'leave
no trace.'"

A few days later, in the town of Fort Good Hope fifty miles down
the Mackenzie from its confluence with the Mountain River, John
T'Seleie, the executive director of the Sahtu Land Use Planning
Board, mentioned that he and his son had recently taken a motor-
ized boat up the Mountain River to scout for sheep. "Did you see
the post?" he asked, the marker they'd left for future reference. That's
as far as they'd been able to get through the canyons and rapids, as
far upriver as he'd been in his fifty-six years. "Our people," he said,
"used to hunt the Mountain River." He told us how, traditionally,
the Sahtu Dene hunted in the mountains, then built boats of spruce
frames covered with moose hides and floated their loads down the
river, out to the Mackenzie and home.

Thus, a stick of wood transformed from an intrusive sign of human
presence to a cultural connection to land and history. It also begins
to tell the story of why as much as half the land in the Mackenzie
River watershed of Canada's Northwest Territories might one not-
so-far-off day be permanently protected for conservation purposes,
including carbon storage and ecosystem resilience to climate change.

More than a hundred million acres of protected lands—enough to cover all of Texas—would be the largest land conservation project in North America, bigger even than the expanse of national parks and wildlife refuges created by the 1980 Alaska National Interest Lands Conservation Act (ANILCA). If/when this happens, the protected lands will link past to present and future; that is, indigenous use and respect for the land will merge into a "buffering" of industrial development and the effects of climate change.

Let me go back, though, to the beginning of my Mountain River trip. This may be a story about the northern forest and its importance as the earth warms, but first, it's necessary to understand something of the *place*.

I'll admit that on the first day, when the third shuttle of float plane had left us at lake's edge, I felt about as deflated as the rolled-up eighteen-foot rubber raft our two Nahanni River Adventures girl guides were trying to lift in a fireman's carry. Were we really going to portage all those piles of "stuff"—the raft and three canoes, coolers of frozen steaks and oranges, cases of glass-bottled wine, the tents and the Dutch ovens and the library of natural history books—across most of a mile of brush and ankle-twisting tussocks to the beginnings of our river? My photographer friend Irene and I stared at a distant, single spruce tree that marked our course to the river, then looked at one another doubtfully. Was this fun? We had come for *fun*, hadn't we, as well as to document a wild river and the wilder country that surrounded it?

There was plenty to admire, no doubt about that. At four thousand feet, the July air was pleasantly cool and nearly bug-free. The dwarf birches were just leafing into a fresh green glow, and ptarmigan—still partially in white winter plumage—flushed from under our feet. Clouds hung on the angular peaks that towered around us, but the land—so close to the Arctic Circle—was lit with soft northern light.

"This is not fun," I admitted, a couple hours and portages later, as my compressed vertebrae ground together.

It didn't help that the three male members of our group (not counting the guy guide) all had announced their back and knee injuries at the start and taken up the lighter loads.

But a day later the ten of us had indeed moved the mountain that was our collective belongings to the thin thread of Mountain River close to its mountain source.

And the trip was, quite literally, all downhill from there, for twelve more days and more than two hundred river miles to the Mackenzie River. Once we packed everything into the covered canoes and the raft, we all remembered just why boat travel is so luxurious compared to, for example, acting as packhorses.

If the first day on the water was a little tricky, with shallows we had to drag through and a number of tight turns, we were all ecstatic to be deep in country unrivaled in its wildness. Despite its long history of use by the Dene, few people—some dozens of whitewater enthusiasts each year—find their way these days into the Mountain River's realm.

It took only a few miles of descent before we reached tree line and rode the waves past a mixed forest of spindly spruce and balsam poplar, the latter pungently sweet. Patches of pink—wild roses— shone from openings. Spotted sandpipers raced us along the shoreline, and, overhead, a kestrel shrieked as it tussled with a raven.

From there the days unwound slowly, filled with river challenges that required our constant attention and occasional scouting. We passed through narrow canyons, met with smaller tributaries, and chose between channels. The clouds cleared to expose towering mountains, a few still streaky with snow and one, distant, hung with a bit of rumpled glacier. We sought out ideal camping spots on gravel bars piled with driftwood for our cooking fires, and we hiked into woods and meadows. One day we explored a high tufa mound built of minerals (calcium carbonate in particular) precipitated from a spring bubbling from its top. The smell was sulfury, but the water, when I drank it, was fresh and cold.

The land surrounding us was both so majestically vast and so astonishingly intricate, from glowing peaks to polished pebbles, it was hard to match it to my small map, where the river was only a thin blue line through a finger of yellow. The map was one I'd picked up in Yellowknife, capital of the Northwest Territories and home to half its people. A product of something called the Protected Areas Strategy, it showed all the current and proposed conservation areas in the territory as a colorful patchwork. The yellow surrounding the Mountain River meant that the river and its corridor were an "area of interest," to be assessed and perhaps conserved at a future time.

On our fifth day on the river, we watched for a hillside that the guides knew from previous trips, where an ice patch lingered into summer and we could stop to fill a cooler. When we pulled ashore where the ice should be and looked up the draw, we could see nothing resembling ice or snow. Just in case the patch was around the corner, we beached our boats and hiked over a rocky outwash until we were staring up at sedimentary cliffs and the red mountains beyond. We wandered in circles, stretching our legs and admiring little blue flowers (blue-eyed grass, not a grass but a member of the iris family) growing on a bank, and then we went back to the boats. The missing ice could be nothing but a seasonal anomaly, part of the variation that occurs naturally from year to year. Or, it could be a sign of our planet's warming. Our guide kept saying, "I can't believe it's not here." I wondered if there were any more steaks in the coolers, and if they would go bad.

Each day the river widened, flowing through one mountain range and into the next, delivering us through more canyons and across whirlpools, alongside gravel bars bright with river beauty blossoms. The pencil-thin spruces, tilting from their shallow roots at the river's edge, gradually thickened, were joined by shivering willows, tamaracks, the white trunks of birches, an understory rich in juniper berries, delicate grass-of-parnassus flowers, pink paintbrushes, purple vetches, the occasional Arctic poppy.

On day eight we made camp beside an enormous freestanding hunk of sandstone known as Monument Rock and settled in for a layover and a chance to test our legs and lungs.

The next morning we plunged into steep forest that looked, from the water, like jungles of spindly and broken spruces. Inside, we easily found passages through the trees and the snarly alders, among beds of invitingly soft moss and scatters of lady's slippers already withering on their stems. A little higher, the forest opened to berry bushes—ripe blueberries and the astringent bearberries, cranberries still green—and then to talus slopes across which we clattered.

Below us, our tents and boats appeared as tiny colored dots in a broad river valley; we could see, as we could not have envisioned while careening along a single channel, the many braids of gray water twisting across the miles. Above us, a young Dall sheep grazed around a rock pile. Thunderclouds rolled in, and we stopped to snack near the highest of the stunted trees. "Look at this!" someone called out, and we all began pawing through broken rock and holding out examples of marine fossils—shells and corals that had been laid down on a tropical ocean floor millions of years ago.

Back on the river, we added our footprints to those of grizzly bears, moose, caribou, wolves, and sheep. We spotted a lone caribou—the woodland variety, more solitary than the barren-ground caribou that migrate in huge herds—clicking across meadows. We floated down on a grizzly swimming the river; it turned in front of us and returned to shore, where it shook off and ran into the brush. We passed a young caribou with spiky antlers and very alert ears, up to its knees in the river, and then, before we were swept past, watched a black wolf emerge from the willows behind its potential prey. Canada geese with their young paddled out of our way, and once a flock of sandhill cranes lifted past. Smaller animals, too—beavers and chipmunks, thrushes and sparrows—swam and chittered and sang around us as we paddled and camped and added to our collections of colored stones.

Toward the end, the air turned hazy and smelled like smoke from a distant fire, and that same day we passed forest burned a year or two before—blackened sticks leaning over a swath of glowing fireweed.

Always, the sound of the river was with us, rushing and bouncing us along or caressing our dreams as we slept. I listened and was lulled into its rhythms. I thought of the forces that make mountains and carve canyons and then grind rock to dirt that grows plants and forests. I thought about the age of our earth, evolutionary change, and the change that humans—so technologically savvy and so many— can make. I thought how frightening it is that, even in places with so little human occupancy, we can alter the conditions of life.

A magical place, yes, that Mountain River. In fact, all of the Mackenzie River Valley, way up there in Canada's northwest, is a marvelous and marvelously undisturbed landscape. The historical lack of development is not the result of any planning; it's simply that the area, with a watershed larger than all of Alaska, is so remote.

Biologically, the entire valley is extraordinarily productive, with rich soils and relatively mild temperatures. Warm air from the south flows north down the valley, making it the only place in North America where forest, much of it with good-sized trees, extends all the way to the Arctic Ocean. In recent decades, valley temperatures have been increasing dramatically; in the last century, according to Canada's Geological Survey, air temperature increases here have been the highest in all of Canada—more than three degrees Fahrenheit.

Only forty thousand people live in all of the Northwest Territories, and only a few thousand in the scattered communities that lie along the Mackenzie River, Canada's longest. There are very few year-round roads in this place; what commerce there is moves over water and by plane or, in winter, on ice roads.[1] (Ice roads, depicted on *Ice Road Truckers*, a reality TV show filmed in the Northwest Territories, are engineered over lakes and muskeg with bulldozers, packed snow, and water flooding.)

In 2007, though, as mineral prices soared, the mountains were filling with mining camps actively exploring for gold, copper, zinc, uranium, and lead. And the proposed Mackenzie Gas Project, an eight-hundred-mile-long pipeline designed to carry natural gas along the river's same route—only in reverse—from Arctic gas fields to Alberta, threatened (or promised, depending on one's point of view) to open up the country in major new ways.

Both the mining and the gas line were, indeed, not without controversy. In Yellowknife, before heading to the river, some of our group had met with Stephen Kakfwi, a Dene who, when he served as the territorial premier from 2000 to 2003, negotiated a governmental commitment to "Conservation First." This meant that, in regards to the pipeline, culturally and ecologically significant lands would be protected, first, before any route would be approved.

In a blue dress shirt and with his long, dark hair pulled into a ponytail, Kakfwi had been an imposing figure. He certainly knew the history surrounding Alaska's oil pipeline—the "deals" made to settle Alaska Native land claims and set aside public lands—and he expected Canada's own political exigency to link the issues of First Nations rights, conservation, and economic development. "We're deadly serious about it," he said about the "Conservation First" pledge. "We want a land use plan finalized *first*, before granting access to our land."

Indeed, in a recent poll, 90 percent of Northwest Territories residents had given the highest priority to protecting lands, water, and natural ecosystems before allowing development in the region. The number one concern of those polled—higher than social issues and the economy—was the environment. But money was certainly part of the discussion, too. "Why should our communities be dirt-poor while ExxonMobil makes billions of dollars?" Kakfwi asked us. He envisioned a tax system that would share pipeline earnings with communities.

Just as rivers join to grow larger and stronger, it is this confluence of political situations and other dynamics that has in recent years swelled the effort to conserve land in the Northwest Territories. Unresolved First Nations land claims and the desire of local Dene and Métis people to preserve hunting and other culturally significant lands are largely driving the movement. Both the federal and territorial governments have expressed interest in "balancing" development with conservation, and some members of industry have agreed to support a conservation plan in exchange for knowing where and under what conditions development *will* be allowed.

More than in the United States—more than I'd seen in Alaska—Canadians seemed to be thinking ahead, to a globally warmer future. Beyond indigenous rights and the usual reasons for protecting scenic and biologically significant lands lay a new conservation imperative brought on by climate change: the need to buffer. Throughout the Canadian north, a number of nongovernmental conservation organizations were working with governments and local people and promoting an awareness of the role that intact boreal forests can play in moderating the effects of global warming.

Jeff Wells, senior scientist with Pew Charitable Trusts' International Boreal Conservation Campaign, has said, "The boreal is to carbon what Fort Knox is to gold"—vital reserves and a virtual shield against global warming. Fifteen hundred international scientists signed an open letter to the Canadian government recommending that at least half the boreal forest be preserved in its natural state and that only ecologically sound and sustainable development be allowed in the rest. The scientists did not choose 50 percent randomly but based it on computer modeling of what it takes to maintain species across a landscape.

It was almost a flood—all those elements feeding, with new

urgency and complications, into the already decade-long planning process known as the Northwest Territories Protected Areas Strategy.[2] That effort, whose map with its yellow finger I'd carried along the Mountain River, was remarkable for applying both indigenous and scientific knowledge to land use planning. And it seemed to me to be a reasonable and responsible way to balance conservation needs with economic development.

It was not, however, a speedy process. Areas had been mapped, resources had been inventoried, community meetings had been held—but by summer 2007 there was little to show in the way of permanent protections for the lands in question.

"It's like a funnel," David Livingstone, the Northwest Territories' director of Renewable Resources and Environment, told us in Yellowknife. "There's a lot happening on the front end." The process was slow, Livingstone said, because it required inclusive involvement and consensus decision making. And, he insisted, it would not be driven by pipeline plans; there was "no quid pro quo."

As Livingstone unrolled maps for us to look at, I snuck a look around his office. Shelves were cluttered with rocks and stuffed birds, and more maps—including one of traditional hunting trails—covered the walls. A copy of the thick Arctic Climate Impact Assessment report held down one corner of his desk.[3]

The goal of the Protected Areas Strategy, Livingstone said, was to find a balance between environmental protection and economic development. "I'm absolutely convinced we can do both," he said with an emphatic nod. "It's all about managing human activity."

But, meanwhile, development activity had not stood still. The mineral boom taking place across the north involved parts of the Northwest Territories identified by communities for conservation but, for now, still open to other uses, including mining.

Later, when I spoke to Steve Kallick, project director of the International Boreal Conservation Campaign, he both praised the Northwest Territories' conservation effort as "the best of the bunch" and lamented the slowness of the process, which lost ground to development every day. "The government needs to move the conservation process and land claims faster or slow down the development permitting process," he told me. "We're in a race against time."

The irony could not be lost on anyone. On the one hand, a pipeline project that would result in more fossil fuel burning—especially if, as many suspected, all that natural gas would be burned to extract oil from tar sands in Alberta—and worsen greenhouse gas emissions and climate change. On the other, a landscape that holds carbon in its plants and soil. To save the latter, would we need to suffer the former?

On the river, I attempted to reconcile the age of mountains once laid down as river sediments and marine animal skeletons with the glacial pace of bureaucratic action and the knowledge that "balance" didn't mean the same thing to everyone. The world's economy needed mineral and energy resources, but the world's health needed some large places where entire ecosystems might be left in their wild condition, home to wildlife and natural processes and the few people with intimate ties to an older way of life.

Gillian, one of our canoeists, had a birthday, and we celebrated with cake and party favors—and a few small gifts we found with or around us. I presented her with a rock that, in its coloring and lines, resembled our evening's mountain backdrop, and the tiny, perfect cone from a black spruce. "A symbol of the boreal forest," I offered before we all hoisted glasses of wine.

That boreal forest is, we now know, key to the Mountain River's—and the rest of the Northwest Territories'—ecological importance. First, there's all that life—the megafauna down to the pollinating bees and the biting flies we met on our river trip. There are the, literally, billions of nesting and migrating birds. There are the rivers and lakes and wetlands that make that part of Canada a major source of freshwater. And then there's the carbon.

So much emphasis is placed on the burning of fossil fuels as the source of human-caused global warming that we sometimes overlook the role of deforestation. Deforestation—primarily the destruction of rain forests to convert land to agricultural use—accounts for 25 percent of global greenhouse gas emissions. (This compares to industry at 14 percent, transport at 14 percent, and aviation at 3 percent.) Most people recognize that China and the United States are the two largest emitters of greenhouse gases in the world, but few would be able to name the countries that rank third (Indonesia) and fourth (Brazil). Neither Indonesia nor Brazil has much heavy industry, but both have been cutting and burning their forests at record paces. It doesn't take a climate scientist to recognize that forests provide the single greatest opportunity to make cost-effective and immediate reductions to carbon emissions.

The carbon flux research I learned about on the Kenai Peninsula, near my home, was just one tiny piece of investigation into carbon cycling and balance going on all over the world, in wetland, forest, marine, and other ecosystems. Studies used standard technologies to measure, at different times of day and seasons and under various conditions, the amount of carbon taken up and the amount emitted. Some of what was being learned upset past assumptions. It used to be accepted knowledge that old, "senescent" forests took up less carbon than new, fast-growing forests, but studies had shown that, across the globe, old-growth forests continue to absorb more carbon than they emit and store the highest amount of carbon. In addition, natural forests store more carbon than managed forests.

In Canada, in response to requirements of the Kyoto Protocol to report on greenhouse gas emissions and removals from managed forests, a carbon budget model has been developed to help with forest management.[4] The model simulates the dynamics of forest carbon in various sectors—above- and belowground biomass, dead wood, litter, soil—and accounts for growth, tree harvest, fire, and other factors.

The reason the boreal forest holds so much carbon—Canada's alone is calculated to equal twenty-seven years' worth of the world's carbon dioxide emissions from the burning of fossil fuels—has to do with cold.[5] Decomposition, when it occurs, recombines the carbon with oxygen and hydrogen into carbon dioxide and methane. In the cold north, that decomposition takes place so slowly that little carbon is released and much more of it stays on and in the ground.

A very big question: What happens to all this carbon stored in the cold when the climate warms up?

The scientific community employs a number of competing models for projecting future carbon flux and actively debates just how warming will alter the balance. That is, under what conditions will forests continue to absorb more carbon than they emit, and what will it mean if/when the balance shifts and forests start adding to our carbon problem? Based on a Swedish experiment, researchers have hypothesized that, as the boreal forest warms up, it will shift from being a carbon *sink* (absorbing carbon) to become a carbon *source* (releasing carbon), until a new equilibrium between carbon fixation and decomposition is reached.[6]

Recent studies have raised serious alarms.[7] For one, tree mortality, apparently caused by stresses related to warming, has increased dramatically in recent decades in the western United States and Canada, changing affected forests into carbon emitters instead of sinks. Forest fires influenced by drought and fed by dead trees throw massive amounts of greenhouse gases into the air. Other research has demonstrated that soil microbes, more active in greater warmth, are emitting more carbon than trees are absorbing. A conservative consensus is emerging that the boreal forest has already become a smaller carbon sink than it has typically been and may be shifting into being a carbon source.

Forest dynamics and all the ways that warming might influence or be influenced by the boreal are tremendously complex. Consider: With warming, the boreal forest is expected to move northward (and upward), to replace treeless tundra.[8] The dark forest will absorb more heat than the snow-covered tundra and contribute to a positive (not in the good sense) feedback loop, the heating effects of which may be greater than any benefits that come from carbon absorption by the increased forest.

And this: Some boreal tree species are already near their limits, and may be pushed from the ecosystem all together. Forest ecologists theorize that the birches and white and black spruces that now dominate the boreal forest in interior Alaska could disappear from the landscape, replaced by aspen woodlands similar to those in Saskatchewan and Alberta, Canada, or even grasslands.[9] In an ironic twist, warming causes the death of some trees by freezing: Midwinter thaws melt insulating snow, and when the temperature drops again, tree roots freeze.

For now, the message from conservationists is, we must do everything we can to preserve forested—especially boreal—land, the carbon it holds, and the potential for holding future carbon. Humans cannot control the release of carbon by insect damage and fire, but we can certainly control industrial development that destroys the boreal forest and releases its carbon. Management actions can enhance carbon uptake and storage and allow the forest ecosystem to retain some of its natural resiliency. Some form of a carbon market, which would place a value on sustaining and enhancing carbon storage, might potentially—someday—generate a flow of wealth to Arctic regions.

Kallick, from the International Boreal Conservation Campaign, told me, "As a carbon storehouse or sink, you can't beat the boreal."

There's the forest and forest soils, and then there's the permafrost—the "permanently" frozen ground beneath an active layer of soil—that underlies so much of the boreal as well as tundra to its north, and even the Arctic Ocean.[10] As permafrost melts, carbon that's been locked up for a *very* long time is released to the atmosphere.

Just the upper three meters of permafrost across the Arctic store more than twice as much carbon as exists in the atmosphere today. Researchers are already seeing a thawing down to five meters and estimate that a huge amount of permafrost, including that in the Mackenzie River Valley, is now within two degrees Fahrenheit of thawing.[11]

Vladimir Romanovsky, a geophysicist at the University of Alaska, has pointed out that permafrost ground has been frozen for thousands and tens of thousands of years, and to return what has thawed to a frozen condition will require a new ice age.[12] Even then, newly frozen ground would not hold the carbon that's there today, because today's permafrost took thousands of years of a particular sediment-rich ecosystem to create. In other words, with permafrost thaw and the release of its carbon, there's no going back, not in any time period that's meaningful to us today.

Some of the most intriguing (and disturbing) carbon flux work has to do with methane (CH_4), the gas that forms from the decomposition of organic matter in the absence of oxygen. Although methane has a relatively short lifespan in the atmosphere (about ten years), it is a very powerful greenhouse gas, with twenty to twenty-five times the warming potential of an equivalent mass of CO_2. Since the 1800s methane in the atmosphere has more than doubled—principally as a result of human activities that include rice cultivation, livestock raising, and coal mining—to the point where it accounts for 27 percent of human-induced warming. Today, huge quantities are flared by oil wells to turn it into CO_2 (less immediately harmful but longer-lived in the atmosphere) and water.

The earth's stores of methane, in energy value, exceed all the proven reserves of oil, gas, and coal combined. Its release from thawing permafrost is creating a positive feedback loop of more warming, more melting, more warming. Moreover, the warming and melting causes water to pool into what are called thermokarst lakes on top of permafrost, and new research indicates that methane bubbling up through those lakes—not previously accounted for in climate modeling—could be a major emissions source. According to research by Alaskan aquatic ecologist and biogeochemist Katey Walter Anthony, fifty-five billion metric tons of methane could be released from beneath Siberian lakes alone.[13] That's about ten times what's currently in the atmosphere.

Recently discovered seeps from the shallow Arctic sea floor off the coast of Siberia suggest an additional source. The United Nations Environmental Programme has called these the "global warming wildcard."[14]

One evening of our river trip, I walked with Sue Libenson, media director for the Boreal Songbird Initiative,[15] along a mostly dry creek bed behind our campsite. A dozen Dall sheep were grazing a green mountainside toward which we wandered, and the tracks of moose and wolves were pressed into crumbling dirt. The reedy song of a thrush floated from the woods.

The boreal birds were, for the most part, busy raising their young in the quiet of the forest and wetlands, and we hadn't seen or heard huge numbers of them. The Boreal Songbird Initiative, a nonprofit organization dedicated to education about the importance of the boreal forest to North America's birds, makes the point that hundreds of bird species that winter in the United States depend on the boreal forest for their breeding grounds and that protection of those breeding grounds is in the interests of every American. Of the seven hundred bird species regularly seen in the United States and Canada, half rely on the boreal for some part of the year. Besides being beautiful creatures and valued by bird watchers and waterfowl hunters, birds are tremendously important within their ranges as pollinators and transporters of seeds.

"It's becoming more and more clear," Libenson said, "that these intact forests are going to be critical to adaptation as the climate warms." Large expanses of undivided and undisturbed landscape allow birds, other animals, and (more slowly) plants to move across distances and change elevations in search of food, water, and other habitat needs.

Libenson and I stopped to examine some purple vetch with its curly stem, and she told me about the work of Stanford's Terry Root.[16] Root, a member of the Intergovernmental Panel on Climate Change, has studied the relationship between temperatures and bird habitats and predicts that global warming will have a significant impact on the ranges of birds, including what she's called "a tearing apart of biological communities." That is, birds that leave one area and food source decouple the relationship and will end up competing with other species for new habitats and food sources.

In North America, southern species can head north, and low-elevation species can fly or climb higher, but in the mountains of the north there isn't much more room to move.

I was thinking about all this and the problem conservationists have always had with selling wilderness values to the general public. Really, how many people will ever care about an area, however spectacular in its scenery and wildlife, that's only visited by a few local hunters and recreationalists like us?

"I'm starting to get it," I told Libenson. "The arguments aren't abstract anymore. It's not about wanting to protect nature because it's the right thing to do. It's personal. It's the birds that come to your feeder in Ohio or Texas; they need a place to live in the summer, too. And the carbon. Everyone everywhere needs these trees as trees, more than they need more paper or more cleared land for development. Now we can appeal to pure selfishness."

It seemed, at the time, to be a kind of epiphany.

Later, I would learn about a study by the National Audubon Society that drew on bird sighting data from their Christmas bird counts.[17] Analysis of species sighted during the first weeks of winter showed that, over the last forty years and corresponding to temperature increases, birds have moved dramatically northward, toward colder latitudes. Of the 305 North American species identified, 177 had moved "significantly" northward and 60 had moved more than a hundred miles northward. The average northward movement of all, including those that had not moved or had moved southward, was thirty-five miles northward. Woodland birds like those of the boreal forest and the seedeaters that frequent bird feeders were the two bird categories most affected—with 70 percent of those species making significant northern moves.

I recall *never* seeing any American robins in Alaska in the winter —in the 1970s and 1980s. That's a species that now, continent-wide, is wintering more than two hundred miles farther north than it did forty years ago. The study found that southern states have fewer wintering robins now, while New Hampshire has five times more and Alaska has thirty-seven times more. Just recently, in February near my home, I watched a dozen robins flocking over a snowless lawn.

In Alaska, with its greatest-of-all-states winter warming, the trends have been dramatic. In the last forty years, nineteen species of winter birds have increased significantly in population and none have decreased significantly.

There are, of course, many reasons why birds alter their ranges, including habitat changes and interaction with other species. In Alaska, for example, Bohemian waxwings have taken to wintering in the Anchorage area. From a few dozen counted in the 1960s and 1970s, they have now become the most common Christmas Bird Count bird in Anchorage—twenty-two thousand in 2008. This population "explosion" is generally linked to the proliferation of mountain ash trees—popularly planted as an ornamental and loaded with berries. Other habitat changes, like lawns and bird feeders, also make parts of Alaska more agreeable to certain birds. But nothing except a warmer climate can explain the general continent-wide shift in range for diverse species.

The black-billed magpie, like the robin, is a species that has both grown in numbers in Alaska and extended its range northward. A highly adaptable bird that nests in bushes and preys on smaller birds and bird eggs, the magpie may well displace other species and disrupt the balance of ecosystems. They've become the mafia of my neighborhood.

Northern bird species that fill narrow niches, like those that depend on shore ice or tundra, both of which are shrinking, are at particular risk. They have no place to go. The Kittlitz's murrelet, a small seabird that typically lives near tidewater glaciers and feeds where glacial calving disturbs the water, is disappearing with our glaciers. Found only in coastal Alaska (and perhaps along the coast of eastern Russia), the species has declined by 80 percent in the last twenty years and is considered by the International Union for Conservation of Nature (IUCN) to be critically endangered.

Given all this, Audubon has a few recommendations. First, figure out where the key habitats are and protect or restore them. Then, expand protected areas and the corridors or flyways that connect them. Then, reduce the things we humans do to erode the natural resilience of ecosystems. That is, where possible, we should manage development for minimal disruption, prevent pollution and habitat fragmentation, and do what we can to not introduce invasive species to compete with native species.

Our last miles to the confluence with the Mackenzie River and a pickup by freight boats were a slow paddle and row across flat water. The mountains receded into the distance, even the foothills faded behind us, and the sky, dotted with cotton ball clouds, suddenly seemed immensely wide. At length we spotted the channel markers that guided boats around a set of Mackenzie River rapids, and the water of our wild river merged into Canada's longest. The far shore formed a band of light and darker green—the willows and poplars and spruces of more boreal forest. Beyond that, perhaps ten miles through the forest and wetlands, lay the route of the future gas pipeline.

I dipped my paddle and helped pull our heavy raft along. Our girl guides sang a hearty version of "There's a Hole in My Bucket," but I was thinking about that pipeline. Its construction will fragment habitat and destroy forest and wetlands. But in addition, conservationists and those who live along the river fear it will open up the entire basin to more development involving feeder lines, roads, and every kind of resource extraction, to further divide the land and harm wildlife and subsistence use.

Natural gas is, of course, a "clean" fuel, environmentally preferable to oil and especially coal. The insult of the proposed Mackenzie pipeline is that, rather than being used to heat homes, the gas was expected to be burned to produce oil from the Alberta tar sands. Those tar sands, in which thick oil is mixed with sand, clay, and water, must be heated to high temperatures to separate the oil and make it flow—a process that takes enormous amounts of energy and freshwater. The Alberta tar sands project, if it expanded according to plans, was expected to burn more natural gas each day than the pipeline could deliver. Importantly, tar sands development releases high volumes of greenhouse gases and other pollutants to the atmosphere. (With just 10 percent of Canada's population, Alberta already emits 40 percent of Canada's greenhouse gases.)

On the sandy shore of the Mackenzie we deflated our raft, set up the picnic table with its checkered cloth for a last time, and re-organized. Most of our group boarded the larger boat that had come for us, to be motored upriver to the oil town of Norman Wells and flights home. Four of us, who wanted more local perspective on the land conservation issues, piled our personal gear and ourselves into Edward Oudzi's freight canoe and continued downriver to the Sahtu village of Fort Good Hope, some fifty miles away.

Oudzi, a quiet, chiseled-faced man, piloted us over that smooth-as-a-lake broad river in leisurely fashion; the long, wooden canoe, much like those used by the old fur traders, was powered by a minimal 20-HP motor and overseen by an excitable black dog, Buck.

(Days later, we would run into Oudzi again, in the Norman Wells museum, where, as a cultural expert, he was furnishing a trapper's cabin with his handmade furniture and historically appropriate artifacts.) The brilliantly blue sky with its piled-up clouds and the river fringe of steely spruces reflected perfectly in the river reminded me of one of those mirror-image photos that can be hung either way to fool a viewer. On both sides of the river a broad "trim line" of sand and patchy vegetation showed that the water—and pans of scraping winter ice—sometimes rose another twenty feet.

There were no other boats on the river and little sign of any human activity at all. Twice I spotted the weathered wood of camps tucked back into trees. We stopped just once to stretch our legs, at a clear steam Oudzi called Bluefish Creek, its mud freshly tracked by a black bear.

Not far above the village, the landscape began to change. Tall limestone cliffs rose straight out of the water on both sides of the river. Shining whitely in the afternoon sun, they grew higher—two, three hundred feet high—and stretched along the river for miles as we passed below them. Oudzi took us in close, and we looked up at thousands of mud-made swallows' nests stuck under overhangs. We watched a beaver slip from a hollow near the waterline. Oudzi pointed out where Wichididelle, a culture-hero for the local Dene, had stretched out for a nap and left the impression of his giant head.

This much-photographed part of the river includes a section of rapids and is a traditional fishing and spiritual place for the Dene people. We'd passed the Rampart River, which flows in from the west and which itself drains a vast area of wetlands. All that land—everything on our left since about the time we started down the Mackenzie and stretching far back into the mountains, was another area, like the Mountain River, proposed for conservation. Referred to simply as "the Ramparts," it held "candidate" status and was valued for a whole lot of reasons: prime boreal forest, critical wetland for filtering water, key habitat for migrating and nesting birds, home to many moose and a few caribou, and long history of use—hunting, fishing, trapping, camping—by Dene people.

At the Fort Good Hope boat landing, we visited with an elder who said he used to trap marten and mink along the Mountain River in the 1950s. We watched a hunting party leave, and then found our way to our lodging. Smoke was rising from the teepee-shaped smokehouse next door, where our landlord was doling out chunks of moose meat to village women who came by with plastic shopping bags. Fort Good Hope, population seven hundred, has two stores, a baseball field, street lights, government offices, and a Roman Catholic church dating to the 1860s, but adheres to its Dene traditions and values in fundamental ways.

From a book in our Fort Good Hope B&B, I learned that, before fur trader Alexander Mackenzie came down the river in 1789 (looking for the Pacific and ending up in the Arctic Ocean), the river was known as Deh Cho, "Big River."[18] I learned that Fort Good Hope was established as a trading post in 1804 by the North West Company (which later became part of the Hudson's Bay Company) and that the Sahtu name of the village before that translated as "home at the rapids." The Dene who lived there called themselves "big arrowhead people" and were called by others "hareskin people."

It was in Fort Good Hope that John T'Seleie, the man who had placed the post on the Mountain River, talked to us about the development of a land use plan for the region. It was the intent so far, he said, that the Mountain River and its surrounds be managed for subsistence use and low-impact tourism. The future of the Ramparts depended on the Protected Areas Strategy, but that area had always had a lot of use by local people, who understood that taking care of its wetlands and wildlife meant the wetlands and wildlife would take care of them.

As the director of the regional land use planning board, T'Seleie tried to remain impartial about the choices yet to be made, but he was clear on one thing: the connection between land conservation and cultural preservation. The land was key, he said, "if we want to maintain hunting and gathering, which is the center of our culture." Maybe people didn't subsist on the land to the degree they once had, but the country—with its stories, its trails and landmarks, its spiritual places, and its wildlife—could help them know their past and guide them to a meaningful future.

T'Seleie was personally less concerned about the proposed gas pipeline itself—the route of which would pass within three miles of the village—than about what the pipeline and associated roads would do to open up the country and "make everything accessible to everybody." He was also, he said, worried about global warming. "The Arctic is really fragile," he said. "We need short, hot spells in July. If the insects don't come out at the right time, the birds suffer."

Elsewhere in the community, we heard more about the need to conserve lands as buffers against all kinds of change. Henry Tobac, a member of the working group that was collecting Ramparts information and making recommendations about the area's use and protection, told us, "Almost everyone has some connection to that area, even if we don't use it as much as before. We're not against development. We just want balance on the conservation end—to save some lands that we can use culturally." The people relied on the moose and the birds and the beavers all through that country—ancestral lands they'd never ceded—and they also wanted to know they could go there whenever they wanted, for any subsistence or spiritual need.

Over coffee in their home, Henry and his wife, Edna, both spoke about social problems in the community and the role that the land could take in addressing them. After twin tragedies the previous year—a boating accident that killed three and a plane crash that killed six of the funeral-goers—a grieving workshop was held out on the land. "For some, it was the first time they'd been in the bush in years," Edna said. "Culturally, it really helped."

A lot of change had come to the community in recent years, and traditional ways were disappearing along with the language. Now, climate change was adding to that. Winters were warmer and shorter, the Tobacs emphasized, with less ice on the river and for the ice roads. The storm that had caused the fatal boat accident the year before, flipping the boat as it was crossing the Mackenzie, had risen abruptly and with unusual force, something never before experienced by any elders.

Henry, who worked in community health, said his dream was to start a cultural institute that could help heal wounds that ran generations deep. He gazed out the window, past two of his boys chasing through the yard. "As aboriginal people we saw the universe as one big organic thing. The Western way separated everything, took the spirit out of it. People in Western society think about security, but for us it's always been about survival." After a pause in which he seemed to be considering just how much he ought to say, he added, "We need a place where we can go. All around, they're looking for diamonds, gold, oil, and gas, bringing more people, more dysfunction. Where does that leave us? We need a place to fall back on in the future if the world as we know it ends."

Edna had worked as a regulatory officer for the Sahtu Land and Water Board and noted that permits for mineral and energy projects were usually issued in a matter of days, while land conservation supported by local people was taking years to move forward. "The system," she noted with a shake of her head, "works in favor of industry."

The time came to leave Fort Good Hope on "the sched," the regularly scheduled plane that departs for points south each day. Reluctant to leave both the big-hearted country and the people, equally generous, who were so comfortably at home in it, I wandered around the small, crowded airport terminal while listening to travelers asking after one another's families and destinations. A newspaper clipping taped to the wall included a map of the world from the Arctic perspective, looking down on the North Pole. The article was called "Extreme Warming" and concerned increased temperatures in the north. Many fingers had rested on it, locating the place that was home until it was a dirty smudge.

The perspective, though, was one most of us seldom see: the north in the center, the rest of the world radiating out. And on that flimsy newsprint, a show of what was at stake and what was still possible. As the north suffers its disproportionate temperature increase relative to lower latitudes, it also offers a way to help regulate climate while respecting traditional cultures and conserving lands and resources for the future. The local good matches the national and international good in ways we've seldom seen.

O Canada, I thought with trepidation. Can your few people stand up to the power of corporations and the lure of economic development? For once, can the values of conservation and local planning be truly weighed in the balance?

One month later, Canada's prime minister Stephen Harper announced a major expansion of Nahanni National Park, home to a very popular canoeing river a few hundred miles south of our Mountain River. With the support of First Nations people and many others, the park, hailed as "the jewel of Canada's boreal forest and one of the world's greatest wilderness treasures," is now more than three times the size of the United States' Yellowstone National Park.[19]

And then, in November, the government agreed to protect another 25.5 million acres of the Northwest Territories' boreal forest. This included the Ramparts area of such concern to those good and hopeful people of Fort Good Hope. Nearly four million acres there—half again the size of Yellowstone—is now reserved for a future national wildlife area. It's closed to new development while management plans, allowing for local use, are finalized in the next few years. And then, the Canadian Wildlife Service stepped forward to sponsor the Mountain River corridor, along with three others in the region, as another future national wildlife area.

Elsewhere in Canada, the provinces of Ontario and Quebec embarked on planning processes in line with protecting at least half of their northern lands, and Manitoba was working toward the creation of a ten-million-acre World Heritage Site. Among Ontario's announced goals were benefiting First Nations communities, conserving habitat for sensitive species, and "fighting climate change by ensuring that the boreal landscape keeps its capacity to act as a giant carbon sink." Quebec's premier Jean Charest announced that, in addition to establishing a series of parks and forest reserves, his government would create new carbon sinks by planting one hundred million trees on 250,000 acres to capture carbon equivalent to that emitted by thirty-two thousand cars. In Manitoba, the goal is to protect—along with carbon-rich land—freshwater reserves, wildlife habitat, and aboriginal culture.

Meanwhile, rising cost estimates for the proposed Mackenzie pipeline coupled with a global glut of natural gas made that project's economics a bit more questionable, and the pipeline's promoters were pursuing government funding and guarantees. At the end of 2009 a federal review panel threw its support behind the project—but with a long list of recommendations it said should be fully implemented to protect the environment and communities. Among the 176 recommendations was one that asked the federal government "to develop and implement, as soon as possible, legislation and regulations to reduce greenhouse gas emissions in Canada to meet or exceed existing national targets."

II. Fort Yukon, Alaska

Before visiting the village of Fort Yukon in Alaska's interior, 145 air miles north of Fairbanks, I knew it for three claims to fame.

First, it was the home of Alaska's lone congressman (for thirty-five years), Don Young, who had once been a tugboat captain on the Yukon River and a fifth-grade teacher at the local BIA (Bureau of Indian Affairs) school, and who was married to a local Gwich'in woman. He was also a strenuous denier of climate change and, on a campaign visit to my hometown in 2008, had lambasted environmentalists and Democrats for perpetuating the "myth of global warming."[20] He asserted that warming and cooling patterns are cyclical and, because they have happened six times over the planet's history, were nothing to worry about, and then he declared that the unusually cool summer proved that the environmentalists were wrong.

Second, Fort Yukon held the record for the highest temperature ever recorded in Alaska—one hundred degrees Fahrenheit. (This, by the way, is the same as the highest temperature ever recorded in Hawaii.) Fort Yukon's winter temperatures, some claim, are the coldest in Alaska—although the state's official coldest temperature of minus eighty degrees was recorded at a place called Prospect Creek, a little to the west, and Fort Yukon's official coldest is only minus seventy-five degrees.

And—Fort Yukon's third claim to fame—the previous March, a polar bear was shot there. That bear had wandered 275 miles inland from its usual coastal habitat, to a village where no one had ever seen the species before. Its journey was the longest inland trek ever recorded for an Alaska polar bear.

My flight from Fairbanks to Fort Yukon, in a twin-engine Piper Navajo, took forty-five minutes. Three of the ten seats had been removed to make room for freight, and I peered around grocery boxes to get a look at the rugged White Mountains—was that fresh snow in mid-August?—and then the blue line of Beaver Creek, where, years before, a friend and I had once spent a frigid Thanksgiving with friends of hers who lived there as fur trappers.

The landscape below me reminded me of my trip to Canada's Northwest Territories the summer before. Here was more boreal forest, including not just stunted trees but also rock-sided mountains, river valleys, and wetlands. Fort Yukon, as a community, also paralleled Fort Good Hope in many ways. Besides its location on a major river—the Yukon is Alaska's longest—and being named for a fort established by nineteenth-century fur traders, Fort Yukon lies at roughly the same latitude at its Canadian counterpart (eight miles above the Arctic Circle compared to twenty-five miles below). The populations are comparable—about six hundred mostly Gwich'in in Fort Yukon compared to seven hundred Dene (Athabascan Indians, like the Gwich'in) and Métis ("mixed," descended from the unions of European trappers and traders and First Nations people and officially recognized as aboriginal) in Fort Good Hope. Both communities are "remote," without road access (if you don't count winter ice roads). Fort Yukon is surrounded by millions of acres of federal lands protected since 1980 as the Yukon Flats National Wildlife Refuge, while Fort Good Hope lies adjacent to the newly protected Ramparts wildlife area. The people of both places depend to a large degree on local food resources, and job opportunities are limited.

There are, of course, significant differences between the communities, too. Alaska's Natives have for almost four decades been "shareholders" in regional and village corporations created by the Alaska Native Claims Settlement Act, while aboriginal land claims in Canada are still being adjudicated. And Fort Yukon serves as a busy "hub" for the other villages in the Yukon Flats area; as such, it's home to regional services including a massive new state-of-the-art health center.

Both villages, though—like so many other Native communities —have undergone dramatic social and cultural changes in recent decades and now face additional challenges brought on by climate change for which they and their ancestors are minimally responsible.

As I watched mountains fall away to lowlands, I envisioned the border of the Yukon Flats National Wildlife Refuge, drawn in thick yellow on the map I carried, and then the chunk of that refuge land—some 110,000 acres—that surrounded Beaver Creek and was proposed for a controversial land swap. Under the proposed trade, the land would be given to Doyon, Limited, the Native regional corporation, to be developed for oil and gas, in exchange for other Native-owned lands. I looked at that country that would be transferred out of refuge status; it was hilly and pocked with myriads of high lakes. I looked again at my map and saw the trade land connected by future roads to the Dalton Highway farther west; of the two proposed routes, one would pass through a recommended wilderness area and the other through the national recreation area surrounding the part of Beaver Creek that's designated as "wild."

And then we were out of the hills and flying over the flatter part of the flats, a wetland basin where old and older oxbows were filled with variegated vegetation like the swirls and crescents in a paisley print. I looked down at dozens of little lakes and saw how many were surrounded by rings of newer, paler growth, where green was moving in from the edges.

The lakes were shrinking, drying. Although the current summer had been cool and wet—the newspaper that morning had reported that July temperatures in Fairbanks had averaged 60.6 degrees Fahrenheit, almost 2 degrees below the long-term average, and the rainfall had nearly set a record—the trend for several years had been to warmer and drier weather. In 2004 and 2005 wildfires had ravaged interior forests; the 2004 fire season was the worst in Alaska's history and burned an area the size of New Hampshire. (Firefighting is a major source of summer employment for Alaska villagers; I'd read that half the men in Fort Yukon had worked on the 2004 fires.) The fires were so hot those two years they burned up organic material in the soil and thawed permafrost a long way down, radically altering the environment to which new growth will return. The fires burned even into tundra, destroying the slow-growing lichens on which caribou depend.

From the plane, I watched the wide Yukon River flow into view, thickly braided around numerous islands, and that other great river, the Porcupine, merging with it from the north. And then, as the plane began to bank, my eyes settled on the village at the junction—tiny in all that landscape, little boxes of buildings.

As previously arranged, I was met at the airport by Craig Gerlach, an anthropologist with the Resilience and Adaptation Program at the University of Alaska Fairbanks, and Bruce Thomas, the natural resources director for the Council of Athabascan Tribal Governments. CATG, a quasi-governmental organization that has its headquarters in Fort Yukon, represents the ten area villages in efforts to protect tribal lands and resources while supporting economic development. If that "balanced" approach could seem a little contradictory to me, I appreciated that, at least, there was a structure and process for making those decisions on a local level. Thomas and Gerlach were working together on plans to create greater food security, in the face of climate and other changes—including frighteningly high energy costs—faced by the villages.

And off we went, bumping down a dirt road in a CATG truck, to look at a spot for a garden.

One might think that north of the Arctic Circle would be an unlikely gardening spot, but in fact growing food—especially root crops like potatoes—has been a common practice in Fort Yukon for more than a century. If the crops and the gardening techniques were introduced by traders, missionaries, and government officials in a colonial attitude of "civilizing" Native people, it's the people themselves who adopted and adapted them into their own diets and practices. And although "farming" never became a successful Arctic enterprise in terms that government agency people would recognize, garden foods meet local needs.

Over the two short days I spent in Fort Yukon, everywhere I went I saw gardens behind and beside houses, as well as one community garden near the river. Mostly I recognized robust potato plants, but there were among them other root crops like turnips and rutabagas, greens like lettuce and chard, and even, at Thomas's mother's house, a couple of struggling corn stalks. At the new health clinic, the director spoke about plans to establish gardens around the building to provide healthful, local foods to counter the poor store-bought diet that was causing so much ill health among residents. The boreal soil may be thin and acidic—and underlaid with permafrost, about six feet down—and the growing season decidedly short, but the long days of sunlight and bursts of intense summer heat spur amazingly rapid growth. And, with climate change, the season and possibilities seemed to be expanding. In Alaska as a whole, the growing season had lengthened by more than fourteen days over the last fifty years.

The place we drove to on the edge of town had been a private potato field years earlier. Thomas and Gerlach walked over it, discussing what it would take to get it back into production. It was still largely an open field—dirt with bunches of parched grasses around cranberry patches. Some taller bushes with white berries—silverberries, I think—were growing up in spots but wouldn't take much to pull out. The day was lovely—blue sky overhead and temperatures that must have been in the sixties—and there were no bugs, a special blessing in a region notorious for its biting insects. We all stopped to look at fresh moose prints pressed into the sandy earth. Thomas, a big man with a small, graying mustache offset by bushy, black eyebrows, was surprised and excited by them; there weren't many moose on the flats these days.

Around us the forest was thin and scrubby, with ladderlike spruce trees pricking the sky over tangles of young birches. It had not been long since most of the spruce forest adjacent to the river had been felled to feed the steam-driven riverboats that had coursed along the Yukon. But I remembered, too, the words of a forest ecologist at the university in Fairbanks, that climate change was very likely to shift Arctic vegetation zones in dramatic ways.[21] The dominant spruces and birches of the boreal forest were already stressed by higher summer temperatures and drought—growing more slowly and becoming more susceptible to budworms, leaf miners, and other insects.

Gerlach, a tanned and bearded man who looked like he was probably a lot happier scraping at soil samples than lecturing in a classroom, was pleased with the location and with Thomas's plans to bring in someone with equipment to clear the field. The idea was to provide not just healthful and local food for the community, perhaps involving a marketing co-op and sale through the store, but to develop a small export industry; Thomas had already spoken with military procurement people about potentially supplying the base near Fairbanks. "It's about helping people with food they can have control over," Gerlach said.

The gardening project was not a climate change project per se, but Gerlach and Thomas both were well aware of the connections. Different weather patterns, warmer winters, drought and fire, shifting wildlife populations—Thomas had seen these all himself. They were among the many changes facing Fort Yukon and the other Yukon Flats communities, and they challenged access to the land and the food resources to be wrested from it. In the old days, the Gwich'in had been nomadic, moving among food sources and substituting one for another in times of change and shortage. These days, with villages fixed to the landscape around modern infrastructure, other expressions of flexibility and innovation were needed. The gardening project was one aspect of a larger initiative in which CATG and the university were partnering.[22] To quote the academic language, the project was designed to address the "synergistic effects of climate change and land use," with a goal to "build capacity for coping with a changing climate and mitigation of impacts from those changes."

Gerlach had been working with Fort Yukon, as well as other villages, since 1993, and valued Fort Yukon—otherwise known by its Gwich'in name, Gwich'yaa Zhee, "house on the flats"—because of its history of doing for itself. Within a larger Alaska culture of dependence on "transfer payments" and government assistance, local leaders expected greater self-reliance. Fort Yukon had, Gerlach had explained to me earlier, "an unusual combination of people—some visionary young guys who listen to visionary elders—and they've got some capacity to make things happen."

Community leaders were trying, in as many ways as they could, to plan for an uncertain future in which they hoped to sustain both culture and economy. They looked to build houses with local materials and labor. The gardening project was expected to bring multiple benefits. Gerlach told me, "They know this place can't last with the price of food and fuel. The goal is to provide the community with high-quality food and make it a business opportunity."

It was not just a potato patch he and Thomas were plotting. There were plans for greenhouses to grow vegetables like tomatoes and cucumbers for local use. There might be a livestock component, too—hogs and Shetland sheep, both of which could do well in the Arctic. The idea was to produce healthful food, at home, to supplement the wild foods that people traditionally relied on but that were often hard to attain and might become harder in the future.

Biofuel was another project. Thomas told me, with a big smile and one hand pointed at the forest, that the village corporation had just received a major federal grant to begin this. The plan was to establish a village business that would harvest and sell wood, to replace diesel energy for both heat and power in the village. This would involve home wood stoves, wood boilers in public and commercial buildings, and eventually a hybrid power plant that could burn both wood and diesel. Local resources would be used, within a sustainable forestry plan, and local people would be employed. Here were multiple layers of sustainability—ecological, economic, and social—with a goal of replacing as much diesel and fuel oil as possible and essentially converting Fort Yukon to running on wood. Wood burning puts carbon into the air, but efficient systems minimize pollution, and sustainable harvest practices could make the effort "carbon neutral."

The biofuel project, if it succeeded, could be a model for other communities. It could demonstrate that similar conversions to wood might be possible throughout interior Alaska and elsewhere—anywhere where enough wood could be sustainably harvested.

And then there were the bison. I had noticed that Thomas was wearing a ball cap with WOOD BISON RESTORATION PROJECT written on it. Once there had been wood bison—larger cousins to the plains bison of the American West—in these parts.[23] Historians and biologists had thought they'd been gone for hundreds, maybe thousands, of years, that they'd been prehistoric like the woolly mammoths and the giant beavers. Only when interior Athabascan elders spoke of their own elders who remembered the bison did others come to understand that the species had survived until 1900 or so. These days, archaeological evidence supports the existence of bison in Alaska for some thousands of years—possibly as long as four hundred thousand years—and the theory that they disappeared from a combination of drought-related habitat change and hunting.

And now that climate change is altering the landscape again, researchers and wildlife managers believe that reintroduction of the

animal, from herds that survived in Canada, is particularly timely.
If the forest indeed transitions to something like grasslands, bison
might well flourish in interior Alaska. Moose, which depend on
woody shrubs like birches and willows, might, in contrast, survive
poorly. Matching wildlife to available habitat and providing a sub-
stitute food source for local people was a conscious climate change
strategy of those behind the plan.

Indeed, one of the stated goals of the project is to "provide an
opportunity to monitor the long-term ecological effects of a large
grazing mammal as global climate change occurs, possibly shifting
northern ecosystems toward grasslands."

To these ends, the state of Alaska had recently purchased a herd
of fifty-three wood bison from Canada and added them to a smaller
herd confiscated from a rancher who'd illegally brought them to
Alaska several years before. The animals were being kept at a wildlife
center near Anchorage, in quarantine, to be sure they were healthy
and wouldn't introduce disease to the wild. The plan was to re-
introduce the species to two or three places in interior Alaska, where
its presence would be good for the habitat and provide food for local
people along with hunting opportunities for hunters generally. The
Yukon Flats around Fort Yukon was one of the three areas proposed
for the reintroduction.

(Elsewhere in Alaska, there were already about a thousand roam-
ing plains bison, not native to Alaska but introduced from Montana
in the 1920s. These support small permit hunts for mostly urban
hunters.)

Unfortunately, for Thomas and others who were excited about the
bison restoration project, it was at least temporarily stalled for the
Yukon Flats area. Doyon, the Native corporation with oil drilling
ambitions, had argued that the animals, once reintroduced, might
qualify for endangered species protections. They didn't want that
possibility to get in the way of the proposed land exchange and
their development plans. So, for now, the first herd was designated

for Minto Flats, west of Fairbanks, and a Yukon Flats homeland lay sometime in the future, if ever.

Thomas was clearly annoyed by this wrench in the works. The villages and the wildlife refuge had had an often rocky relationship, but finally they'd been working on something together, something that benefited both. Now the refuge had backed away. "It's Fish and Wildlife's mission to protect the lands and resources," Thomas said. "So why were they against the bison project but in favor of oil and gas development? What the hell's that about?"

That was a good question, one I'd heard expressed in a variety of ways, even back in Fairbanks. The proposed Doyon land exchange would trade scattered corporation lands around the Yukon Flats villages for that block of higher land I'd flown over, coveted for its oil and gas potential. The oil field there was thought to hold some-where between 173 and 800 million barrels of oil, not that much compared to estimates that started at 5.7 billion barrels for the pres-ently off-limits coastal plain of the Arctic National Wildlife refuge directly to the north.

The Yukon Flats National Wildlife Refuge, at eleven million acres, is the third-largest refuge in the nation and was created in 1980 primarily to conserve fish and wildlife (including 150 mostly migratory and nesting bird species) and their habitats in their natu-ral diversity. Those lands were also set aside to protect water quality and quantity and provide for the subsistence uses of local residents. It's hard to see how oil drilling is compatible with any of that. The refuge manager (recently replaced) had decided that consolidating lands within the heart of the refuge would be in the public inter-est—although those lands weren't under any threat and in fact were highly prized by the villages for their subsistence resources.

The refuge lands that would go to Doyon included deep lakes and moose habitat, both of high ecological value. Moreover, the removal of those lands from the refuge would divide the refuge into two pieces, and access roads and pipelines would cut into it further. Doyon, as a money-making corporation, certainly wanted the trade for the financial benefits that would accrue from leasing oil and gas rights. As a *Native* corporation, it might not have been as sensitive to its local shareholder concerns as some of those villagers would have liked.

In 2004 the trade just about slipped through as a congressional rider—appended by Alaska's senator Ted Stevens—before local opposition and alert members of Congress slowed the process and insisted on an environmental impact study. A draft of that had been issued the previous January, with a final one—and a decision about the trade—expected within months.

In Fairbanks, I'd shared a pizza with Pam Miller, a longtime and passionate activist for the protection of arctic lands. Currently working for the Northern Alaska Environmental Center, she has the mild-mannered look of a librarian until she starts talking, and then you know she has both encyclopedic knowledge and a dogged commitment to cause. She had so much to tell me she could hardly eat. Interior Alaska, Miller insisted, was "the untold story of climate change. The magnitude of losing the boreal forest is as big as losing the sea ice—but it's more subtle."

The Northern Center had worked closely with residents of Fort Yukon and other villages in the region to make sure that local people got heard and that the public process wasn't subverted by political and economic considerations. The proposed exchange was playing out a situation all too common throughout Alaska today—conflict between the corporations set up by the Alaska Native Claims Settlement Act in 1971 as profit-making enterprises, with Alaska Natives as shareholders, and village-based tribes, whose interests have more to do with maintaining cultural values and the lands that have always supported those values, which include subsistence use. As more shareholders leave the villages and live elsewhere, sometimes in other states, the interests of those shareholders tend to shift away from the well-being of the villages to the size of their individual dividend checks.

"Village elders," Miller said, "have that long view of the land, and that undergirds the opposition. They say, 'This will harm the land.'" With the trade, they'd be losing tribal lands—"and they're not happy about it." She handed me a flyer with a quote from Fort Yukon elder and former chief Clarence Alexander: "Maintaining our cultural and Native ways and keeping our Native lands intact will be most beneficial to all of us into the next century."

It was the tribes that had pressed for the recently completed draft environmental impact statement (EIS). That massive document had, among other calculations, projected that a summer oil spill in the traded area would reach the Yukon River, 148 miles distant, in forty-nine hours. Miller asked, "Do we really want to add another risk to the precarious salmon situation that's facing global warming?"

An original justification for the trade was to protect bird habitat closer to the river, by placing Native lands in that area into the refuge. But now, as the lakes were drying, it made more sense to Miller and others to protect the high-country deep lakes and wetlands for waterfowl displaced from the warmer and drier areas. An additional concern was the oil and gas industry's need for massive amounts of water.

"Fish and Wildlife didn't do any analysis of climate change in the EIS," Miller said. She listed for me what had *not* been considered: the all-important salmon already subjected to warmer water, the increase in forest fires and resulting air pollution, the ecosystem changes related to warmer temperatures. "It's basic," Miller said. "It's simply ironic that the agency whose job it is to protect the refuge is proposing to remove areas for oil and gas development in a refuge that's already suffering from climate change. The issue goes right to the heart of our need to make the transition to future energy solutions. This adds insult to injury. People far away will continue to burn the oil while the people closest to the source are already paying the price."

A few weeks after we spoke, and after my visit to Fort Yukon, the U.S. Fish and Wildlife Service announced it would delay its decision about the trade for a year, primarily to allow more time to appraise the value of the lands to be swapped. Almost a year later, backed by one hundred thousand public comments opposing the trade, the Service called the whole thing off. By that time, the soaring price of oil had changed the equation, and even Doyon wasn't sure it wanted the trade; instead, it was talking about drilling on lands it already held within refuge borders.

There in the future potato patch, Thomas, Gerlach, and I walked around, kicking at dirt clumps and peering at berries. Thomas took pictures of the field, and I took pictures of him taking pictures. Food was a problem, Thomas conceded. For the previous five years the weather was so hot in the fall, Thomas said, "the animals weren't moving." The state had done nothing to adjust the hunting season, and so hunters were forced to go out in the hot weather, and if they were successful it was hard to keep the meat from spoiling.

When the men were satisfied with the location and what might be created there, we piled back into the truck, and Thomas took us by the CATG building so that I could meet the executive director, Ben Stevens. Stevens has the same name as the son of Alaska's then senator Ted Stevens; Ted Stevens had just been indicted on seven felony charges for accepting gifts from an oil service company, and his son, a former state senator, was also under investigation for corruption.[24] I asked Stevens if he was ever confused with the other Ben, and he told me about once meeting with Senator Ted and that the senator (joking, he assumed) had him sit on the other side of the table so that people "wouldn't think he had an illegitimate son."

This Ben, who's originally from Stevens Village, farther down the Yukon, has an Athabascan's dark hair and penetrating brown eyes.

I thought he might be forty at most, one of the younger generation of Alaska Natives who went away to college (in his case, Colorado) and then, eventually, came back to the region with, as he put it, "the tools to help the people." At CATG, he was in charge not only of the natural resource programs, but health and education, "trying to fill the gaps where other entities end." He explained to me that the goal for all ten communities in the region was sustainability based on innovation and self-reliance, guided by a strategic plan that was, right then, focused on short-term projects to create "synergy" for the longer term. One wall of his office was covered with photographs and other expressions of community health—pictures of babies and sports teams, award certificates. "I started it, and now people keep coming in and adding to it," Stevens said.

I asked about how climate change fit into CATG's work. Stevens leaned back in his chair. "People here are concerned about survival, where their next meal is coming from, how to be ready for the next frost." Addressing climate change was not even on a back burner, he said; it was "several burners back." It was not that people weren't concerned about changes in the weather and seasons. "The meadows are drying up all around—I've seen that with my own eyes." And he'd heard plenty from the elders, who complained they could no longer predict the weather. "They used to say, 'Let's go tomorrow.' They could tell by the light in the sky what the weather would be. But now they can't tell the difference."

Stevens went on to name other changes: The lakes were drying up, which affected the muskrats people depended on for food and fur. There had been huge wildfires in recent years, and the smoke had lain in the river valley. "In 2004 and 2005, you couldn't see across the river." The air quality was so poor that people, especially kids and elders, couldn't go to fishcamp but had to stay home, indoors. And when that polar bear wandered into town, yes, people associated that with climate change and were concerned about changes in animals' behavior.

What about that land exchange? CATG, which operates by consensus, was neutral on the land exchange, since some of the village chiefs supported it and others did not. It was another "back burner" issue, Stevens said, though he acknowledged "a tremendous amount of opinion out there. If I had to guess, I'd say most villagers are opposed. Opening up the country has never been good for local folks."

In the outer world, Fort Yukon was known as the center of opposition to the exchange. The village chief, Dacho Alexander, had been quoted in the newspaper as being disappointed with Doyon's approach: "They're acting like any other corporation."[25] I had wanted to see him while I was in Fort Yukon, but he was out of town. The tribe's executive director was also not to be found, the office locked up tight. But that flyer that I'd picked up in Fairbanks, put out by the tribal government of Fort Yukon, said, "Doyon Land Swap is Bad Business" and asked, "Why are we giving up our land so BP, Exxon, or another oil company can get rich and U.S. Fish and Wildlife Service can buy our Native lands?"

At the Natural Resources Building, where Thomas worked, I looked at photos of the dead polar bear displayed on a bulletin board. In one photo the dead animal was lying on snow-covered ground, bleeding from what looked like the red wound of a slit throat, with someone in black clothes lifting one leg in the air. Three other pictures were of its big paws being held in gloved hands; the paws were fur-covered top and bottom, with little circles of black palm and toe pads exposed. I was surprised at what a small, pathetically scrawny animal the bear was, only about the size of a large dog. But it was undeniably the polar species, evolved to live on sea ice and so clearly lost in the wilderness far from any kind of landscape and prey it should know.

Upstairs, Thomas showed me a wood bison skull he said had been dated to forty-three hundred years old. It was only the top half of the skull, from the eye cavities north, but it included an impressive set of pointy horns—rather, the bony core, white and porous, of the original horns. The bone sutures looked like a squiggling river, broad up the middle of the forehead and then dividing across the top, as into tributaries. These wood bison—like the ones Thomas hopes to see reintroduced to the flats—are the largest land mammals in North America, with males averaging about a ton in weight.

Maps were hung all over the walls—part of another CATG project, using a sophisticated Geographic Information System (GIS) mapping technology to identify traditional land use around each of the villages. I studied one, noting old settlements, sacred sites, areas relied on for hunting and berry picking. The maps and their information were confidential—owned by the tribes, which did not necessarily want the world to know their special places—but would be used in some form for making future decisions about land use, including those driven by climate change.

I was introduced to Adlai Alexander, a former village chief, who pointed to one of the maps and a lake that had completely drained when permafrost melted. "We adapt to that," he said. "We can tolerate whatever Mother Nature dishes out." He mentioned some notorious accounts of people who had come to Alaska and died because they didn't have basic survival skills—Chris McCandless, the young man featured in *Into the Wild*, who starved to death, and "the bear guy" who was eaten by a bear. "They were stupid," Alexander said, and told me about a local example, a man who'd come to Fort Yukon and chartered into the mountains, where he ran out of food and then shot himself. Alexander shook his head. He was getting ready for caribou hunting; he would take a boat upriver in September to where the caribou would be.

In the afternoon, Gerlach and I walked the dusty road to the river. We passed the cemetery, set into a birch grove, with white picket fences surrounding most of the graves. We looked for and found the grave, with its huge concrete cross, of the revered missionary Hudson Stuck, "First Archdeacon of the Yukon," who died in 1920. We also paused before the grave, heaped with plastic wreathes and flowers, of Jonathon Solomon, the highly respected traditional chief of the Yukon Flats and winner of the Goldman Environmental Prize, who was outspoken about Native land rights right up until his death in 2006.

We walked past an area of dead spruce trees that Thomas had told us a forestry expert had said died from drought. A gray jay (a.k.a. camp robber) darted from one of the live trees. We looked at congressman Don Young's new log house, its windows boarded; the congressman hasn't actually lived in Fort Yukon since going to Washington thirty-five years ago but sometimes visits.

At the river, what looked like a brand-new fish wheel sat onshore. Fish wheels, used on the Yukon for both subsistence and some commercial salmon fishing, are made from spruce poles and wire mesh, with two big baskets turned by the river's current. Scooped-up salmon slide down a chute into a box that fishermen empty periodically. The design is ingenious: effective, powered by the river, made from the simplest materials. It's also ancient, tracing back to China and employed through much of the world before being brought to Alaska by gold stampeders at the end of the nineteenth century. Native fishermen readily adapted it to the Yukon and a few of Alaska's other big rivers. Most recently, I'd seen the same design transferred to an experimental hydrokinetic project producing electric power from river current for the village of Ruby, downriver on the Yukon.

Things were quiet along the river. The bank was pocked with the nesting holes of swallows, but the birds were absent—already flown south. A half dozen flat-bottomed riverboats rested on the shore. Gerlach was surprised there were so few and that, on such a beautiful day, with the broad river stretching out like a mirror, there was no one around, no one coming and going. As we watched, a single figure in a heavily loaded canoe drifted past—likely one of the recreational "floaters," mostly Europeans, who travel the Yukon every summer.

"I think," Gerlach said, "people are really not wanting to burn fuel right now." Indeed, the summer's salmon fishing had been dismal, with most commercial fishing on the river shut down because of low runs, and even subsistence use curtailed. The reason for several years of poor salmon returns wasn't clearly established, but most people blamed the Bering Sea trawl fleet that unintentionally intercepted salmon along with the target pollock species. The biologists thought other factors were likely in play as well—perhaps poor survival of young salmon before they migrated to sea, or disease, or predation, or changes in oceanographic conditions and climate.

It struck me then, as I breathed in the clear air, that I'd seen nothing in Fort Yukon to tell me that this was a place with a long, deep dependence on the fat-rich Chinook and chum salmon that travel the Yukon to their spawning grounds. Nowhere in town had I observed racks of fish drying or smoke rising from a sweet-scented fire or any other sign that people were eating or putting up fish.

Those who were doing without their usual fish catches and income were also coping with the high cost of gasoline, which had risen in the village to $7.76 a gallon. Heating fuel was even more expensive. In some of the neighboring villages, health clinics had closed for lack of fuel, and the generators that provided electricity were being turned off at night. I thought of the brand-new health center. It had real-time video cameras and monitors in all the treatment rooms for "telehealth" connections to the other clinics on the flats as well as to hospitals in Fairbanks and Anchorage—but what if they couldn't afford to even keep the lights on?

For village Alaska, the "energy crisis," not climate change, was the story, and the concern, of the summer. Although the state of Alaska, along with Saudi Arabia and other oil-rich nations, was profiting handsomely from high oil prices—with a $12 billion surplus for the current year—individuals and communities, especially in the "bush," where transportation costs factor in, were suffering. The state legislature had just approved a $1,200 "resource rebate" for every Alaskan resident, but, still, everywhere I'd been recently, people were fretting about the coming winter. Some predicted a mass exodus from villages into the cities, with all the attendant social and cultural disruptions.

To rural people having to choose between food and heating fuel, "climate change"—if it brought them warmer temperatures—might not seem a bad thing.

At the village AC (Alaska Commercial Company) store, a small jar of peanut butter cost $7.59, a loaf of white bread $6.19, and a half gallon of milk $6.49. A bulky item like paper towels was $18.95 for eight rolls, and a heavy item like watermelon wasn't even marked, but rang up—when Gerlach bought the smallest one, the size of a basketball—for $30. In general, because of freight costs, store food in rural Alaska costs two to three times what it is in urban Alaska, which itself is considerably more expensive than in the rest of the United States.

Fort Yukon people still get much of their food from the river and land, but if the salmon runs continue to decline and the moose disappear and fire blackens the berry patches, food security will indeed be a big issue. One can argue that no one in bush Alaska needs to eat watermelon imported from California or fresh milk from Wisconsin cows, but if local foods become harder to find, or require farther travel to reach, something needs to fill the void.

As we walked the empty road back from the river, Gerlach and I talked about what he called "the bigger story of change," the awareness in the villages and particularly among the elders that things weren't right: *The world's not working right.* Strange weather and animal behavior were part of it, but so were—and more dramatically—the loosening of cultural underpinnings on which people have always relied, new social issues, food issues, a whole host of environmental problems. Television, the Internet, Western education and resource management systems, alcohol, the shift away from subsistence into a cash economy, reliance on government programs and funding—these all had changed the order of things and eroded the traditional value system. If the weather was acting crazy, that was just one more expression of the world being out of whack.

"It's a hungry country out here to start with, all up and down the river," Gerlach said. "But now they're constrained by everything. The adaptation these people were so good at only worked when they were highly mobile. But then the government forced people to settle in permanent communities, and now they're locked in."

In his work with communities, Gerlach emphasized what academics call "place-based design solutions" and what Gerlach characterized as bottom-up decision making. What he tried to do was introduce examples from elsewhere—"this is how other people do it," whether the "it" is community gardening, livestock raising, food storage, water management, or anything else that helps communities with their needs. Then the question is, "What do you think works for you?"

We met up with Thomas again and watched a dark cloud move across the sky. Thomas told us a story, a true story from his life: "Once I stopped on the river to visit an old woman at her fishcamp. We were just sitting on the bank of the river and visiting, and a big storm was coming over. There was a huge black cloud. There was thunder and lightning. That old woman got up and went into the brush. She cut a forked stick—like for a slingshot—and then made a ball of grass and shot it at the storm. Just in that spot the sky cleared, just over us. It didn't rain on us, but it rained all around."

I didn't doubt that this had happened. Thomas had been there; he had seen it. I was less sure what it meant to him, although he seemed open to the idea that that woman could have changed the behavior of clouds. My scientific mind told me that shooting at a cloud was not going to make it move or withhold rain, but I also knew that indigenous cultures have a more encompassing view of relationships and believe that human behaviors can influence weather, just as they influence plants and animals. In Alaska whaling cultures, whales "give" themselves to hunters who treat them with respect. In the traditional Dena'ina Athabascan culture from my part of Alaska, certain plants grow only when they are used for food and their nonedible parts are returned to the soil. What we call "supernatural" is part of an older wisdom that comes from living in deep dependence on the land and what it provides. Not everyone adheres to the old beliefs these days, but a general acceptance of unusual natural phenomenon—with two-way response, people to weather and weather to people, in Thomas's case—underlies much of Native life.

I recalled a conversation I'd had earlier with Terry Chapin, an ecologist at the university in Fairbanks (and the first Alaskan to be elected to the National Academy of Sciences). Chapin's work has evolved from a focus on plant adaptation to look more broadly at ecological and social systems and their vulnerability and resilience to change. He told me that he'd heard more than once in community workshops statements like, "It's all because people landed on the moon. Ever since then, everything's different." At first, he said, this kind of comment seemed off-the-wall, but when he thought about it—and when he heard that similar sentiments were being expressed by Native peoples in Russia and elsewhere—he interpreted it differently. What it meant to him was, when people fail to show respect for nature, there are unforeseen effects that change everything. The thought behind the statement was deep, and perhaps not so different from what I believed myself. If humans don't live in harmony with the rest of the natural world, the natural processes are going to do things that are not favorable to people.

In the unoccupied Department of Fish and Game office in the State Building, Gerlach and I heated frozen fried chicken in the microwave and opened a bag of wilted salad greens—some of that expensive fare from the AC store. We were willing enough to drop a little money into the local economy, but we were also well aware that local people, especially the younger ones, were eating more of this same store food these days, and less subsistence fare—even as the price of store food was skyrocketing. The transition from healthful local foods to unhealthful overprocessed foods was taking a toll on the health of rural Alaskans throughout the state.

I cut up a hard tomato that had traveled a great distance to get to Fort Yukon, and Gerlach dug into his duffel for an advance copy of *Where Our Food Comes From*, the newest book by the ethnobotanist Gary Nabhan, whom Gerlach knew as a friend and fellow traveler in the world of understanding food in a community context.

As an anthropologist, Gerlach's approach to food centered on the broad spheres of nutritional ecology, community health, and in interior Alaska, the restoration of traditional food systems. Food, Gerlach stressed to me, is so much more than calories and nutrition. In rural Alaska, food is very much about shared harvests, celebrations, and maintaining traditions—about strengthening social networks and kinship ties. Societal roles and culture at its deepest levels are all expressed and valued through the getting, preparation, and sharing of food. Often, when he visited Fort Yukon, Gerlach was invited to homes for dinner, where he appreciated not just the moose stew or salmon steaks but the also inclusion in local life.

In his academic work, Gerlach makes the point that the Alaska food system, in general, is "overconnected." That is, the store-bought foods in rural Alaska come from supply systems in urban Alaska, and almost everything in urban Alaska is imported from outside Alaska. Thus, rural food supplies are vulnerable to even the smallest changes in weather, economics, transportation, and energy costs. I knew this was true even in my town. When avalanches occasionally close the road to Anchorage, store shelves are quickly emptied. When fuel prices go up, so does the cost of everything in the stores.

On the other hand, the ability to obtain traditional subsistence foods—what Gerlach calls "country foods"—was also running up against new challenges. One of Gerlach's particular complaints is the slowness with which regulatory agencies respond to ecological and social changes. When climate-related changes in weather and seasons affect the safe times to travel on river ice, the migrations of animals, or the ability to keep meat cool, management rules and regulations need to be adjusted. But government bureaucracy has so far lacked the mechanisms for anything like a timely response.

Gerlach said, "Some of these climate changes—we thought we might be seeing them by 2050 or later. Well, we're seeing them now. We need real-world solutions to address these problems, right now."

That evening I played Scrabble with Ginny Alexander and two of her friends. Ginny, one of the few non-Athabascans in the community, had come to Fort Yukon years ago as a teacher. She was the mother of the current chief, and she ran the only bed-and-breakfast establishment in town. We snacked on Bugles and baby carrots from the store, and in between turns I paged through Ginny's "plant book," a journal of precise watercolor paintings she'd made of local wildflowers. An ethnobotany of sorts, the book not only identified each plant and noted when and where it had been seen or collected, but listed what Ginny knew about it and its food or medicinal uses.

Ginny flipped pages to point out several plants she'd seen recently for the first time and thought had not been part of the flora until recently, when conditions had changed. She was plainspoken about the weather or climate changes she'd seen and the ways she'd adapted. Always, she'd swept the dry snow from her steps with a broom; only two winters ago had she had to buy her first shovel, because the snow was now wet and heavy.

"The snow is wetter," she told me, "but the rain is wetter, too. It's true. The rain used to be light and fluffy. Now it gets you wet."

In the past, Ginny had always hung plants and sometimes meat in the house, to dry in a few days, but this year her plants had taken a full week to dry out.

Outside, Ginny showed me a willow with brown, shriveled leaves—a new condition brought on by disease or insects, she didn't know. She told me about a new, bright red bug that she'd never seen before, and that the usual bees seemed to be missing. In the backyard, her potato patch and lettuce were flourishing, and she proudly pointed to two struggling lilac bushes and an apple tree she was nurturing.

Apples in the Arctic? I remembered when my neighbors in Homer first planted apple trees, and nobody thought they'd ever get any edible fruit. Now lots of people had apple trees, and you could even buy local apples at our farmers' market.

The next day I visited with other older women in Fort Yukon. Thomas's mother, a recent widow, was most concerned with heating her home through the winter and was planning on closing off rooms. She was looking forward to a grandson coming to cut wood for her woodstove. The biggest effect of climate change? That was easy, she said. It made people depressed.

I'd heard this before, elsewhere—that not being able to predict the weather, to know what was coming and to plan around that, and to face conditions of wind and snow different from what they'd known all their lives caused people to be restless and unsure. That change unsettled people in a way that could cause them to lose heart.

Doris Ward was another elder who'd seen a lot of change, of all kinds. In her home, where the walls were covered with family photos and dozens of blue ribbons she'd won for her beadwork, this white-haired woman with swollen hands lamented the loss of the old ways. "Young people don't care which way the wind blows," she said. "Life is too easy nowadays."

Doris no longer got out on the land much, but she was well aware that recent winters had been so warm the river wasn't freezing properly, and it wasn't safe to cross. People on their snow machines had been falling through the ice; this had happened to her own son-in-law. But summers were a problem, too. Where were the salmon? And when you caught them, if you hung them to dry, the way people always have, they spoiled. Younger people were putting up their fish in jars now.

While we talked, Doris's grandson sat at the table eating caribou meat a relative had sent from Barrow—and he looked as though he was pleased to have it. When she was growing up, Doris said, her family had "lived out," way up along the Porcupine River. There had been a lot of TB in those days, but her family had stayed healthy from living out. She'd never gone to school and didn't move to town until her oldest child was eleven.

Doris wasn't sorry that someone had shot that polar bear, hungry as it was. It had come right into town and was eating a lynx carcass left beside a garage. She'd always been nervous around bears—the local grizzlies and blacks—especially when she was berry picking with children. Leaning forward on her stool, she offered me some advice: If you're berry picking and see a bear, lift your shirt to show you're a woman, and the bear will leave you alone.

The CATG truck wouldn't start. Thomas got out, took a shovel from the truck bed, opened the hood, and pounded something with the butt of the shovel's wooden handle. He got back in the truck and told us the battery terminal was loose and he needed to knock it back together.

It's not an unusual situation anywhere in the north to have mechanical problems, and neither is it unusual for anyone to throw open a hood and apply some kind of fix, however crude or temporary.

In Fort Yukon and most of Alaska, if your vehicle doesn't run, you don't call AAA or even your local garage.

In this instance, Thomas's remedy struck me as a sort of metaphor. If the weather or the climate breaks down, or the usual systems don't work, Thomas and his colleagues weren't going to wait to be rescued. They would be as northern people always have been—creative, innovative, self-reliant, flexible, adaptive. It they didn't have a shovel, they'd find a stick, and if they didn't have a stick, they'd make a rock work. They'd figure out a way.

Gerlach and I took a last walk to the river, to see if anyone might be coming in from fishing. A pale blue bus pulled past us, and we waved to the rows of smiling tourist faces pressed to its windows.

Like so many rural communities hoping to build an economic base, Fort Yukon was trying to encourage visitors. With neither hotel nor restaurant, the community seemed to me a little short on the necessary infrastructure. The Fort Yukon tour, offered by Warbelow's Air Ventures in Fairbanks, appeared to be mainly aimed at marketing the Arctic Circle. Its other options included riding along on the mail plane, wildlife viewing (guaranteed moose and sheep or your money back), and (especially for Japanese tourists) a visit to the village of Beaver, established by a Japanese explorer/miner/trader in 1906 after he walked from Barrow with a group of Eskimos.

For $319 per person, though, tourists could leave Fairbanks at 7 p.m., fly across the Arctic Circle to Fort Yukon, bounce around on a bus tour of the village with a local guide, dip their hands into the Yukon River, and return to Fairbanks by 11 p.m.

I was skeptical that American tourists, so accustomed to comfort and Disney-style entertainment, would find much to love about Fort Yukon, but the faces at the bus windows were wide-eyed and laughing. When I met the tour guide later, he said the visitors, from around the world, always told him his tour was the best they'd had anywhere in Alaska. He said they couldn't stop pressing money into his hands.

I had my own concerns, too, from a carbon budget point of view, about flying such a distance for a one-hour tour. I imagined new promotions: *Burn up extra fossil fuels! Add more greenhouse gas emissions to the atmosphere, and help warm the earth even faster!*

Warbelow's newest tour, just added to the schedule, made its own links to climate change and might even be described as "global warming tourism," akin to cruises being offered through the newly opened Northwest Passage and trips to look at retreating Greenland glaciers. Their advertising read NEW! POLAR BEAR EXPEDITION! SEE POLAR BEARS! SEE THEM BEFORE THEY'RE GONE! On the new tour, visitors fly to Kaktovik, on the Arctic coast, during the fall whaling season and watch polar bears feed on the whale carcasses left onshore by hunters.

PART THREE

Sea Ice and Ice Bears: Barter Island

On Thanksgiving morning in Kaktovik, my teacher friends and I took a long walk along the beach facing the frozen Beaufort Sea. I say "morning," but it was 11 a.m. when we set out, when the day was approaching its brightest, and we got back at about 1:45, just as dusk was settling back down over the land and in time for the community feast. In the Inupiaq language, the word for November translates as "the month when the sun goes down for the winter," and three days earlier—the day I'd arrived by plane from Fairbanks—had been the first day the sun had failed to reach the horizon.[1] It would be the middle of January before the sun would rise again.

I had never been so far north in the winter and was almost disappointed to discover that the world of darkness I imagined at seventy degrees latitude actually contained a lot of light. The reality was that the sun, crossing below the Brooks Range mountains in its gentle arch, provided plenty of daylight between lengthy twilights. The reflective snow cover added to the brightness; in fact, rainy winter days in my hometown, eight hundred miles to the south, seemed darker.

If it was not dark, it was also not very cold. Temperatures on the north coast of Alaska are generally warmer than in the interior, but the difference is the fierce winds that can add a "wind chill factor" well below zero. On this day the temperature was a positive six degrees Fahrenheit, and there was no wind. As we started out in our puffy parkas and snow pants, a very light snow was falling—not flakes really, but tiny ice particles.

Pete and Elaine Velsko were friends I'd worked with, thirty years before, at a salmon hatchery. Although they'd spent many years in the Arctic, they'd only come to Kaktovik in August and were still exploring the island, as enthused about following animal tracks as we'd all been back at the hatchery to watch pink salmon courting in the creek and to stir up bioluminescence when we checked the bay for plankton blooms.

The compact village (originally Qaaktugvik, "seining place"— reportedly named after an event in which a drowned person's body was recovered with a seine net) of three hundred Inupiat sits on the northeast side of Barter Island, an inverted triangle that itself lies in the Beaufort Sea just off the coastal plain of the Arctic National Wildlife Refuge. Sometimes described as the most isolated of Inupiaq villages, it's the only coastal community east of Barrow (by 310 miles) and the Prudhoe Bay oil fields; the Canadian border is only 63 miles farther east. The island has a long history of off-and-on inhabitation and was central to trade among Inupiat from all along the northern coast, who rendezvoused there with inland peoples and eventually whaling ships as well. In 1889 a Captain Stockton cruising the coast reported no permanent settlements. He wrote, "The country is sterile, affording but little upon which to live, the sea also having little or no animal life in its waters. The Eskimos give to this part of the Arctic ocean a native name which signifies 'the sea where there is always ice.'"[2]

From the teacher housing behind the school it had taken us just a few minutes to reach the beach. Now, the snow under our feet was dry and gritty with fine sand and tightly packed by the wind. I had to stop to admire the beauty of it: the way snow and sand had been mixed by the wind, then the layers scoured so that a texture like wood grain was revealed, the sand forming darker, swirling rings through the lighter snow.

It was hard to say just how much snow Kaktovik had, since it didn't stay where it landed; wind blew it until it piled up against structures, like the snow fences placed around the village, and the school, where a drift in the back was ten feet tall. The North Slope is generally considered to be a desert, and Kaktovik's annual precipitation is just five inches, including twenty inches of snow.

In the flat light of overcast sky, our view to the north was shades of gray and white—the foreground of windswept beach where snow and sand were mixed and scoured into ridges and hollows, the frozen ocean beyond rising to an indistinct horizon and more grainy distance. It was hard to tell where the shore ended and the sea began, and the topography of jumbled ice and pressure ridges was indistinct, blended into a smoother version of itself. A little to the east we could just make out the hangar at the airport, located on a spit that extended to the "bone pile," the place where the remains of bowhead whales hunted each September are left to be scavenged by bears.

"The local people think we're nuts," Pete said through his frosting beard, referring to villagers' warnings about bears and advice that they should always carry a gun when away from town. A quietly competent man who tends toward self-effacement, Pete carried not a gun but a GPS receiver around his neck, just in case the visibility shut down and we needed help finding our way home.

"We never see anyone out here," Elaine added. "They hunt, though. Depending on the season. Right now they go to the mountains for sheep." In her enunciative, schoolteachery voice, *sheep* captured a few extra *e*'s, like something wildly exotic.

Indeed, the afternoon before, we'd seen a freight sled parked in town—piled with hunks of purple meat. Sheep soup was on the menu for the Thanksgiving feast. That morning, as Elaine had baked rolls from her mother's recipe and I'd made a Jell-O salad with crushed pineapple and sour cream—one of my mother's Thanksgiving standards—villagers had also been cooking up the traditional foods they'd be sharing at the feast.

We scanned the beach and the sea ice for any movement. The ice had fastened to the land in October, earlier than the previous year, when there'd been open water into November. The polar bears that had been onshore around Kaktovik—dozens of them that had typically spent their days on the barrier islands just offshore and swam to the spit near the airport to feed at night on the whale carcasses—had headed off weeks earlier to the pack ice for their winter diet of seals.

There were still a few bears around, though. The morning I arrived I caught a glimpse of one by the snow fence near the airport, and a couple of nights before that, one had been in town; Pete and Elaine had seen the tracks just beyond their living room window.

Pete turned in a circle. "It's a good idea to look behind you every now and then. A polar bear could be following you."

He wasn't kidding. Polar bears have been known to follow people, out of curiosity or—some say—to stalk what might become prey. In Kaktovik, though, despite the number of polar bears that fed at the bone pile and sometimes entered town, there had never been any incidents in which people, or even pets, had been harmed.

We hoped we might see a polar bear—yellowish against the white—at a distance, or an Arctic fox, which were generally plentiful around town. Wolverines, those shy but fierce members of the weasel family, had also been spotted recently—three shot by hunters in recent weeks.

Where the snow was less polished and a little crustier, we soon came upon tracks. They were weathered into soft edges and partially filled with snow dust, but the heel and toe pads, and the ridge between the paw and its toes, and the claw marks were still distinct. We were headed in the direction from which the bear—not a huge one, but with paws as long as my boot length and nearly as wide—had come, and so we didn't worry that we might catch up to it where it had settled in for a snooze.

Polar bears have long been icons of the north, and it's quite understandable that they're now seen as ambassadors for climate change— "canaries in the coal mine," if you wish. They are at once frightening (the world's largest carnivores found on land) and cute (especially the roly-poly cubs). There's hardly an environmental organization today that doesn't feature them as part of its donation pitch, and they're used to sell everything from Coca-Cola to diamonds.

The people of Kaktovik have a long—as in thousands of years— history with polar bears. They learned from bears how to sneak up on and hunt seals; they used the fur for warmth and the meat for food. They respect *nanuq* as a fellow creature of great strength and intelligence. *Nanuq* knows how to get down and spread his weight on the ice so he won't break it. *Nanuq* covers his black nose with his tongue or a paw when he sneaks up on seals.

Although polar bears in Alaska are protected under both the Marine Mammal Protection Act and, since 2008, the Endangered Species Act, exemptions are made for subsistence hunting by Alaska Natives. For the Beaufort Sea population of perhaps fifteen hundred (out of a worldwide population estimated at twenty thousand to twenty-five thousand), an agreement between the Native people of Alaska and Canada provides for an evenly divided quota of eighty bears per year. Few Kaktovik residents actively hunt the bears anymore; instead, as a bear biologist expressed it to me, the village people are "very bear tolerant" and "have a very low harvest." The people like to see them, and then they like to talk about what they've seen. I heard a lot of bear stories during the week I was in Kaktovik, and though some of them had to do with bears being shot, none of them were about setting out to purposely hunt one.

One day the school principal invited me to drive to the dump and the airport (the two endpoints of the very short road system) to look for wildlife. We didn't see any, but we did stop to roll down windows and visit with elders Isaac and Mary Akootchook, who were making the same tour. On an interview recording the postmaster loaned me, Isaac and two of his brothers spoke about having bear cubs as pets when they were boys. Daniel Akootchook said that *nanuq* knows your heart, and "if you have a kind heart, they won't do anything to you." "In old days," Isaac said, "as soon as we saw a polar bear, we shot it. Now, everybody like to see. We're living with them." Later I noticed a photo on the bulletin board at the borough office; it was an old Akootchook family photo, with two of the boys holding bear cubs on their laps as though they were cats.

As we continued our hike west that day, following the single set of bear tracks overlaid with dainty fox tracks, the bluff rose beside us from beach to higher ground, perhaps twenty feet above us. Here, recent coastal erosion was obvious. During the summer months the land had been undercut by waves. Now, huge slabs of solid, frozen earth, some as large as houses, were broken and tilted toward the beach; others were completely cut loose and had fallen to be pummeled by tides. This is the story all along the northern coast of Alaska—the land, and often the communities that perch on that land at the edge of the sea, being eaten away.

The warming climate contributes to this erosion in two main ways. First, the permafrost is thawing, loosening the earth and making it more vulnerable to rain, gravity, waves, any disturbance. Second, the loss of sea ice—its earlier retreat from the coast in summer and its later return in fall—leaves the coastline open to the action of the Beaufort Sea, especially the fall storms. The storms themselves may be stronger, and sea level is rising. (Until recently, most sea level rise was attributed to thermal expansion—that is, the fact that warmer water takes up more space than colder water—but recently the melting of glaciers and ice sheets has surpassed thermal expansion as the major source of rising seas. The melting of sea ice itself does not contribute to sea level rise, for the same displacement reason that ice cubes melting in a glass of water don't cause the glass to overflow.)

Erosion, of course, has always been a factor along this battered coast, and it would be hard to say exactly what portion of it can be attributed to climate change. We do know, though, that coastal erosion has been accelerating. A U.S. Geological Survey study of the Beaufort Sea coast found that, along a forty-mile stretch between Barrow and Prudhoe Bay, the considerable erosion of twenty feet of shoreline per year in the 1960s and 1970s had increased to twenty-eight feet per year in the 1980s and 1990s and then to forty-five feet per year since 2002.[3] The fastest erosion corresponded to the period of the greatest sea ice loss.

In 2007 the amount of Arctic sea ice at summer's end was less than ever before recorded—23 percent less than the previous record low set in 2005 and a million square miles less than the average from 1979 (the year satellite photos began to track sea ice coverage) to 2000. A million square miles, just to give that some perspective, equals six Californias. The year 2008 was somewhat cooler; sea ice covered more area than in 2007 but still less than any previous year. However, researchers at the National Snow and Ice Data Center found that the 2008 ice was actually less solid, with more broken floes—suggesting a weaker and more vulnerable ice pack altogether—and it set a record for its rate of retreat.[4] (The pattern would continue; the extent of sea ice in 2009 would be the third-lowest recorded.) The greatest loss of ice has been north of Alaska and Siberia.

Just a few years before, when I'd first started paying attention to sea ice loss, modeling predictions that the Arctic could be ice-free in summers by the end of the century were alarming enough. A few years later the Intergovernmental Panel on Climate Change revised that to midcentury. Now, as we watch a frightening acceleration of the melting, leading scientists project that summer ice could be gone as early as 2013. The feedback loops of open water absorbing more solar heat to melt more ice and slow the freezing of new ice, resulting in more open water, more heat absorption, less ice, more open water, and on and on, were outpacing the scientific models and raising increased concern about "tipping points." As it's sometimes put, in the simplest of terms, *the warmer it gets, the warmer it gets*.[5]

I knew these numbers: White sea ice reflects about 80 percent of the sun's heat, blue water absorbs about 90 percent.

And these: Twenty years ago, 80 percent of Arctic ice was at least ten years old; in 2007 only 3 percent was that old.

And this fact: The Arctic has been ice-free in summer before, but, according to the National Snow and Ice Data Center, the last time scientists have confidence that it was was 125,000 years ago (a period known as the Eemian interglacial age).[6] At that time sea level was thirteen to twenty feet higher than it is today and forests grew on the North Slope.

There may well be no turning back from an ice-free Arctic and the loss of ice-dependent species like polar bears, walrus, and seals. Granted, polar bears (thought to have diverged from brown or grizzly bears during an earlier period of glaciation) did live through the Eemian age, and some researchers have hypothesized that the species could survive again, perhaps by eating bird eggs. But polar bears require the kind of fat energy they get from seals and could never survive on a diet of berries and squirrels, and back in Eemian times they didn't have to face today's multiple stressors: spatial conflicts with human communities, oil and gas and shipping activities, toxins that compromise their health. And the climate change, then, likely did not occur with the same rapidity we're experiencing today; just how quickly can a species shift its basic requirements?

In any case, the loss of sea ice is far more than a local issue of concern to those who live in the Arctic and rely on its resources. The heat soaking into blue Arctic waters will continue to warm the rest of the world, disrupting weather patterns, increasing sea level, and potentially changing ocean circulation in disastrous ways. Finely evolved organisms and food webs everywhere will confront new conditions for their lives and interdependences.

I had seen photos of the exact coastline we were walking, taken the previous summer and in 2005.[7] The 2005 photos showed an air force erosion protection project undertaken along this beach, with groins and giant sandbags. The 2008 photos are of a July storm battering the bluffs with fierce, frothing waves. The after-the-storm photos show some tilted posts in the water—useless remnants of the erosion project—and old, rotting garbage—plastics, pop cans, and unidentifiable slime—falling from the top of the bluff. The dump site there, from the old village and the military site that lies just back of the bluff's edge, has been eroding for years, polluting the ocean, as the air force has tried to hold back the sea and clean the land.

As I looked at the slumping coastline that reached into the distance, it was clear to me that no engineering feats—no seawalls and protective barriers—were going to hold back the unleashed forces except in very limited and temporary situations. A new assessment from the U.S. Geological Survey estimates that global sea level is likely to rise by as much as four feet by the end of the century.[8] Only geoengineering on a massive scale—perhaps, as proposed by an Anchorage engineer named Dominic Lee and promoted by our former governor Walter Hickel, building canals from the Mediterranean Sea into interior Africa to flood below-sea-level lands with a giant new lake—would maintain coastlines in some semblance of their current selves.

Pete had joked before we started that those collapsed chunks of bluff would make good bear dens. Pregnant females would, in fact, be denning now—out on the ice or on land, dug into snow drifts—to birth their one-pound cubs. (The only polar bears that den and enter a form of hibernation are pregnant ones, which lose up to

two-thirds of their weight while fasting and nursing in the den.)
Now, ahead of Elaine and me, Pete was on his knees, peering under
an overhang. When we caught up to him, he pointed to fox tracks.
"Look where it was lying down in there."

The tracks both entered and exited the overhang. In the back of
the shelter, a smooth space on the icy ground showed where the
fox's body heat had warmed the slightest depression.

"What can they be eating out here?" Elaine wondered. On the ice,
foxes typically follow polar bears and clean up the remains of seals
the bears catch at their breathing holes. I imagined that foxes drawn
to town cleaned up around Dumpsters and dog dishes.

All along the exposed edge of the land, permafrost ice wedges,
like enormous canine teeth, bit through the frozen earth. I had read
about ice wedges but never seen them before. When we came to
a classically shaped one, like something you'd find in a textbook,
I stopped to photograph it. It was as long as I was tall, and nearly
as wide at its flat top, which formed a line against the active soil
layer, about eighteen inches below the top of the bluff. I pictured
in my mind the process I'd read about: In winter, the permafrost
soil contracting, forming cracks. In spring, water seeping into the
cracks and then freezing into wedges, wider at the top, narrowing
down the crack. In summer, the active layer of the soil and the top of
the wedges softening, melting. Winter again, cracking again, water
seeping again, the wedges growing. All of that taking place across
the frozen tundra, out of sight. Only here could we see them, and
they wouldn't last long. Exposed to the air, the ice wedges would
melt in summer, further weakening the face of the bluff.

Looking at the wedges, I couldn't help wonder how long these
particular ones had been forming, and how long the soil around
them had been frozen. I indulged myself in a fantasy of finding
mastodon or mammoth bones—even a frozen part of a long-extinct
animal—eroding out of the bluff, just as similar items have been
uncovered along the cut banks of northern rivers or dug out by

miners. I knew that a more likely find would be something human—
a grave or perhaps an ice cellar—from the time, not so long ago,
when people lived in sod houses along the coastline. Today's village
elders had lived in those houses formed of driftwood and earth. I'd
already heard stories, bitterly told, of being forced to move for the
construction of a Distant Early Warning (DEW-line) station after
World War II. (During the Cold War, these manned radar stations
formed a line across the high Arctic for detecting Soviet bombers;
their construction and operation employed village people but also
brought in work forces from elsewhere—and required landing fields
for the delivery of materials and supplies. Because national defense
was at stake, local people had little say in the matter.) The people of
Kaktovik had been forced to move twice—once to make room for
the runway and again, a few years later, to get out from under the
expanded airport's flight path. We were under the flight path now.

It was the airport, now, that was in need of relocation. Barrier islands
seaward of the airport somewhat protect it from wave action, but
the runway, with its eastern end just one to two feet above mean
high tide, was exceedingly, and increasingly, vulnerable to flooding.
Normal tides on the island are less than one foot, but storm surges
can raise the sea level by as much as six feet.

Nora Jane Burns, the North Slope Borough liaison in Kaktovik,
had shown me photos of the flooding the previous July, when a
good portion of the runway was underwater and scheduled planes
couldn't land for a week. (A smaller plane was able to land with
necessities after a few days.) This is a problem in a place that otherwise has no access except for supply barges that arrive once a year,
in August.

An environmental assessment was still under way to help determine which of three airport alternatives would be chosen—from
raising the existing one to moving to higher ground currently occupied by the landfill to moving off island. The off-island location

favored by the village council would require six miles of new road and a bridge and was the most expensive (something upward of $40 million, most of which would be paid for by the Federal Aviation Administration). The "preferred alternative" in the Barter Island Airport Master Plan was the landfill site, which would mean finding a new place for trash, on an island that has little high ground to begin with and appears to be ever shrinking.

The bluff we were walking beside eventually became lower and less steep, and we climbed up to the high ground, a point of land with driftwood arranged like a bench for sitting. This was a picnic spot people came to in summer, Elaine said. Back toward the village, the giant golf ball structure of the DEW-line station rose up off the tundra. It was not actually a DEW-line facility anymore, though everyone called it that. In 1990 it had been updated as part of the U.S.–Canada North Warning System, a more advanced long-range radar surveillance system.

Pete nodded toward the golf ball. "See that, and you can't get lost."

I suspected that, between fog and blizzards, there were plenty of days when the golf ball would be no help at all.

A sort of gravel road, generally obscured by snow, led across the tundra, back to the DEW-line station and then to the village, across Department of Defense property. We debated whether to follow it and possibly trespass, possibly lose it under our feet and sink into drifts and hollows, or whether to return the same sure way we'd come. None of us like retracing our steps, so it wasn't much of a debate. The snow was thin enough, and firm enough, and we only sometimes wove like drunken sailors trying to find the track again when we lost ourselves on the tundra. We remembered to look up from our feet, to watch for foxes—or anything that moved.

In the low light, the snow-covered land stretched away in shades of blue white, smoothed and contoured by the wind. Where the wind had scoured to the ground, shades of gray formed blooms and bands, and dried wind-whipped grasses and lousewort endured. And over all—the huge sky, the same color as the land and frozen sea but with a pink glow where it met the island on its south side. The land-sea-sky felt enormous, open in a way that was inviting rather than intimidating.

There was a reason for people to live on this island at this edge of the continent—and it was not just for bartering with the Yankee whalers who eventually showed up. There's a reason they live here still. It has to do with the life the Inupiat draw from the land and sea, the riches of food and spirit, and their own talents to embrace nature's forces with impressive resourcefulness. I pulled Arctic air into my lungs and kept searching the landscape for movement. I imagined, in summer, the flight and cacophony of geese and plovers all around, blue waves crashing against the shore, the carpet of waving wildflowers that would stretch into the distance.

When we reached the DEW-line property, it was easy to see where a massive cleanup, from the buildings out to the edge of the eroding bluff, had taken place during the summer. There was still fencing around the area, and the ground had been torn and scraped. Signs warned against trespass. This was just one of numerous cleanups that have been conducted around the site in recent years—of soil contaminated with petroleum products and PCBs, old fuel barrels and junk, and dumps. And this site is just one of many military sites in Alaska where similar cleanups are being conducted, where hazardous materials are being eroded, thawed out, or otherwise released into the environment.

We were approaching the village now, with its towering fuel and water tanks, rows of streetlights, the multiwinged school building across the street from the original one-room school built from DEW-line scrap, the fire station, clinic, community center, store, the new senior housing, and all the rest—the infrastructure of a modern, "permanent" community. "Permanent," because how long-lasting can Kaktovik be when its streets run right to the edge of the sea and the highest point on the whole island is only a hundred feet? If—when—the sea does rise, they'll have to clean up more than an old dump site, have to move more than an airport. And not only here in Kaktovik. According to a 2003 Government Account-ability Office report, 184 out of 213—86 percent—of Alaska Native villages were experiencing some level of flooding and erosion. And that's just Alaska. What about the rest of America's coasts, with their major cities?

What about the rest of the low-lying world?

These thoughts were more than my mind could hold, and I turned back to Pete and Elaine, to check the time, to talk about the food waiting for us at home and the feast we were about to attend.

Minutes later, minus a couple layers of clothing, we hurried down the road to the community center, converging with elder ladies tow-ing wheeled picnic coolers and clusters of shiny-faced schoolkids who shouted their greetings.

Just inside the hall, a sea of huge rubber totes and black plas-tic bags full of chunked-up whale meat and *muktuk* (fat with skin attached) were pushed together in an enormous yet neat assem-blage. I have to say they were quite beautiful—the blocks of meat two or three pounds apiece, like a kind of marble, a deep red with streaks of black, and the *muktuk* with a pinkish opacity and its layer of black skin. They were frozen, frosty with cold, but the smell—not bad, not exactly appetizing, enticing in a (to me) foreign, somehow fruity way—permeated the room.

These were the gifts of the successful whaling captains, to be dis-tributed to all the village households.

Beyond the totes, tables in the center of the room were lined with covered soup pots, trays of fried fish, bags of fry bread. Chairs were arranged all around the perimeter of the room and in rows at the far end. We placed our offerings on a table and moved to the back of the room, exchanging "Happy Thanksgivings" and handshakes as we went. Devilish little boys I'd seen at school were now wearing white shirts with vests and ties, and the older girls were carting around younger siblings on their hips. People I'd just met introduced me to their mothers and fathers, cousins, and neighbors.

When everyone was seated, elder Isaac Akootchook (who I learned was also the retired Presbyterian minister and who looked to me like a Shakespearean friar, with his gray hair cut straight across his forehead) led us in prayer. Partly in English and partly in Inupiaq, we gave thanks for the food that came from the land and the sea. Then the servers, a group of young adults working in pairs, brought around the pots and platters to everyone in their seats. First came the soups—sheep, goose, duck, and caribou, ladled into our held-out bowls—and the breads. Then came the ham, turkey and stuffing, coleslaw and macaroni and Jell-O salads, a compote made from dried fruits, a huge bowl of crowberries, cans of pop.

Everybody ate and ate, and took seconds, and then, when the soups and other foods came around for a third time, opened their coolers and filled containers to take home. Elders smiled, children played, babies were passed around, everybody ate some more. My bowl of sheep soup had chunks of meat in a rich broth, the fry bread with raisins was warm, and the compote reminded me of meals I'd had in Russia. I wondered who had picked all those crowberries, and I thought of fall on the tundra and what it would be like to be part of a berry-picking party, seated among plenty, fingers turning blue.

The servers came around again, this time lugging the bags and boxes of *muktuk*, then whale meat, whale tongue, and the highly desirable pieces of whale flipper. Each recipient was asked the size of his or her household, and shares, parceled out accordingly, went into the various coolers.

This is Inupiaq tradition—sharing throughout the community by the whaling captains, regardless of who may have helped (or not) with the whaling or the work that followed. Shares had been distributed after the September hunt, and the next occasion would be at Christmas.

As if we all hadn't had quite enough to eat, the *ulus* (crescent-shaped knives used by Eskimo women) came out and tastes of *muktuk* were sliced up on plates or on cardboard atop coolers. As a snack, *muktuk* is cut very small. The pieces are not much longer or wider than matchsticks, the whitish whale fat with the black skin on one end like a match head. I watched one little boy with his own small *ulu* cut and salt a piece and hold it out to his mother. I watched others dipping theirs into a pool of ketchup. When Austin, one of the boys I knew from school, offered me a piece, I was glad for it and a second one, too. Despite my full stomach, the salted fat and soft chew of skin filled a certain craving, not unlike the one I might have for a sweet at the end of a meal.

The fire chief, George, was showing Pete something on his camera, and Pete waved me over. "This was two nights ago," George said and turned the viewer to me. The picture was of a polar bear standing at an open Dumpster, its front paws on the rim and its head reaching in. "Someone threw some whale scraps in there."

A couple of evenings later, Pete and Elaine plugged their video camera into the TV to show me polar bears—specifically polar bears feeding on leftovers from that fall's whaling. The first of the three bowhead whales allocated to Kaktovik (by international and Alaskan whaling commissions) in 2008 was taken on September 6, towed to shore, and stripped of its fat and meat. That night, when the bones and scraps had been hauled to the bone pile on the spit, Pete and Elaine joined others in the community to watch the bears feast. The scene was illuminated by headlights, while people got out of their cars and trucks to stand just fifty feet from the powerful animals.

On the video, three white bears work over the bones and the mounds of waste. They're beautiful animals—thick bodied and narrow headed, bellies already bulging, impossibly plush fur rippling with every turn and every extension of long, reaching necks. One has a dirty face, and another wears a research radio collar around its neck—a white band that glows like a reflective strip on a child's jacket. They seem utterly intent on eating, equally indifferent to the lights focused on them and the people moving around and talking. The video picks up the murmuring of appreciative voices, someone saying, "There's one lying down over there."

In recent years Kaktovik has become famous for its polar bears— for the opportunity to see them close up, at the bone pile. Tourists come from afar after whaling season for precisely this opportunity. I remembered the advertising I'd seen back in the summer—SEE POLAR BEARS! SEE THEM BEFORE THEY'RE GONE! Several photographers and photographic guides who live in Kaktovik now make their livings from the easy accessibility of the bears, as do Art and Jennifer Smith, who operate a business specializing in "embedded natural history media productions" and in 2009 would release a documentary film, *Ice Bears of the Beaufort*.[9] Two "hotels"—trailer or trailerlike structures with a lot of character if not class—cater to the increasing number of visitors.

This polar bear tourism, which might rightly be considered one species of "climate change tourism" is not without its challenges and controversies. Was it not at least ironic for wealthy people to fly thousands of miles and spend gobs of money to see creatures that their well-traveled and materialistic lifestyles are responsible for threatening? A friend of mine who operates high-end hiking and rafting tours in the Arctic Refuge recently added a Kaktovik polar bear tour. The biggest challenge, she'd found, was getting there in foggy September. But the bear viewing, when they did get there, was fabulous. She laughed when she told me how, the first day, they'd been so careful about approaching the bone pile and bears— stopping their rented vehicle a long way off, without lights, whispering. Then the locals had arrived, roaring up with bright lights and loud voices, and the bears never even looked up from feeding.

(In fact, though, individual bears react differently to such disturbance, depending on such things as past experience with humans, nutritional status, and approach distance and speed; some are more tolerant than others, and it's never a great idea to crowd them. Data collected by bear researchers has found that at the Kaktovik bone pile—and elsewhere—bears are frequently affected and sometimes displaced by human viewers.)

Elaine's video, as we watched it that night, captured more whaling and more bears. As the date in the corner showed us progressing into and through September, we watched three bears swimming smoothly across the lagoon next to town, flocks of ravens perched on whale bones while bears moved around them, an Arctic fox with some summer brown still in its coat, a collared mother bear with two small cubs, six or seven bears all feeding together. "The most we saw out there at one time," Elaine said, "was thirteen bears."

We watched, on the video, as a collared bear moved to the side and exposed an odd-looking square patch, the size of a sheet of paper, on its haunch. I leaned toward the TV. "That looks like it was shaved." I remembered something I'd read: Researchers had taken muscle samples from the bears' rumps to see whether fasting bears were getting their energy from fat stores or muscle, and they had inserted small thermometers under their skin to monitor body temperature and see if they were in an energy-conserving state known as "walking hibernation."

"The villagers don't like that, the collars and the other research." Elaine sipped her tea. "They think it's disrespectful to the bears, and sometimes the collars get too tight on their necks."

By all accounts, there are more polar bears around Kaktovik now than there have been in the remembered or storied past. The reason for this is not an expanding population but a shift in habitat use. It's that shift—related to the loss of sea ice—that researchers are trying to understand.

Polar bears are categorized as marine mammals and evolved to live primarily over the ocean, on sea ice. They survive in punishing physical conditions by eating the fatty seals they capture at breathing holes or at the edges of broken ice. But now, with more open water in summer, a longer melt duration, and younger and thinner ice, the bears have lost much of their habitat.

In Canada's Hudson Bay, where the loss of sea ice has led polar bears to spend longer periods onshore, those bears generally fast while they wait for the return of the ice and their access to seals. The well-studied bears there have gotten smaller and thinner and have demonstrated poorer reproductive success and survival.

The Beaufort Sea situation so far is less dire, although comparisons between data collected twenty years ago and today show that more bears in the southern Beaufort Sea are now going without food and for longer stretches of time, that fewer cubs are surviving, and that adult males weigh less.[10] A study completed in 2007 by the U.S. Geological Survey concluded that, within fifty years, two-thirds of the world's polar bears, including all those now living along and off Alaska's coast, will likely be gone. The only place in which a remnant population is projected to survive is the high latitudes of the Canadian Arctic and northwest Greenland, the last area projected to hold summer sea ice.

Since the early 1990s, scientific surveys and observations from local residents have suggested that bears are increasing their use of land during the open-water season. In addition, scientists have found that since 1998, more females have been denning on land instead of on the ice. Researchers now estimate that, for the southern Beaufort Sea population, up to 8 percent are using the coast during summer. Before this last decade, it was rare to see any polar bears on land in summer.

One Alaska study, based on weekly aerial surveys since 2000, confirmed that the number of bears on land increased when sea ice was farthest from shore.[11] Bears congregate onshore near high densities of ringed seals, their primary food source once they regain the ice, and in areas closest to the ice edge. The part of the Beaufort Sea coast with both the highest ringed seal density and the shortest distance to the pack ice edge is at Barter Island. The scientists have theorized that, if the summer ice pack continues to decline as predicted, more Beaufort bears will come ashore in anticipation of reaching seals from the land-fast ice that forms in the fall, as opposed to staying out on the pack ice and waiting longer for it to extend, from the other direction, over the continental shelf and the seals.

Of course, the whale carcasses onshore are an inviting source of food. There are more carcasses in Barrow compared to Kaktovik, but more bears at Kaktovik, as many as sixty-five seen eating at the same feeding site at one time. Thus, the bears at Barter Island not only avoid fasting by feeding on whale carcasses, they position themselves for seal hunting once ice re-forms in the fall.

A University of Wyoming study involving bears fitted with GPS collars was a two-year program designed to understand just how the Beaufort Sea bears are coping with longer ice-free seasons. How are bear health and survival being affected? What strategies are bears employing to access habitat and food?

In the first part of the study, twenty-nine bears along the coast were captured in August 2008, and twelve were fitted with radio collars. Two months later six of the collared bears were recaptured. (The other collars were programmed for automatic release in November.) Measurements and samples were taken from the bears, to determine how they fared over the period onshore. One of the biologists involved, Eric Regehr of the U.S. Fish and Wildlife Service, told me shortly after his return from the recapture effort that his "impression was that the bears on land were pretty fat and healthy."

(Later, the second year's research, which used an ice-breaking ship to reach the summer ice pack two hundred miles north of the coast, involved collaring eleven bears and recapturing four of them later in the season.[12] The comparison between how bears were doing on the ice and how they were doing onshore would take longer to complete, but the researchers noted with concern the scarcity of seals available to the bears when the sea ice is so far out, over deep water. They also found the thinness of the ice a safety issue—for both themselves and the bears.)

Susi Miller, a biologist with the U.S. Fish and Wildlife Service, said to me about the capture work, "That research has given us much of what we know about bears, but we have to be sensitive to concerns in the Native community. We have to be handling the bears only when we absolutely can't get data any other way."

A Kaktovik resident warned me, "If you worry about the bears, you better also worry about the seals." Ringed and bearded seals, the two largest parts of the polar bear's diets, are also "ice-dependent species." The lairs where ringed seals birth on the ice are collapsing now earlier in spring, leaving the young vulnerable to the cold as well as to predators, including ravens. Bearded seals forage for invertebrates on the sea floor—habitat they cannot reach from ice that's retreated far over deep water. Walrus, too—not near Kaktovik but farther west—need ice as a platform for resting and bearing young. In recent years young walrus have been abandoned by mothers that had to swim hundreds of miles from the shrunken, distant ice pack to find food in shallower seas. Walrus have also crowded onto beaches, where they're more vulnerable to predation by humans and bears, and to trampling one another when panicked. In October 2007 an estimated 6,000 to 10,000 walruses came ashore in Northwest Alaska, for the first time in recorded history. Then again, in 2009, some 3,500 walruses were spotted along that same coast, and a few days later 131 of them—mostly young animals—were found trampled to death. Aside from the risk of trampling deaths, researchers questioned the feeding success of so many animals confined to small areas; one biologist likened it to putting all the cattle from a farm onto one little pasture.

Polar bears, seals, walrus—they're the megafauna at the top of the whole ice-dependent ecosystem. The Arctic food web begins with algae that grow on the underside of the ice. Tiny shrimplike amphipods and other zooplankton feed on the algae, then are fed on by Arctic cod and other small fish, which are then fed on by seals and seabirds. Bowhead whales also feed on zooplankton—up to three thousand pounds of them per day, each. The equation's pretty simple: no ice = no algae = no zooplankton = no "higher order" animals, all the way through the food web.

There aren't a lot of eyes watching what happens in and over Arctic waters, but troubling reports have been floating in of exhausted polar bears seen swimming far from any ice or shore. Elaine had captured with her video three bears—a mother and cubs—swimming almost effortlessly one after another across the lagoon by the bone pile. With their big paddle-shaped paws and their buoyant fat layers, polar bears are capable of crossing up to a hundred miles of calm open water. But they can't swim forever or in rough seas, and there have been reports, too, of bloated humps of drowned bears drifting through Arctic waters.

Alaska's polar bears had, just months before my visit to Kaktovik, been listed as threatened under the federal Endangered Species Act. I knew how environmentalists felt about this—surprised that the Bush administration would list *anything*, no matter how clear the case might be, and then angry when they read Interior secretary Dirk Kempthorne's order and realized how limited the protection would be. And I knew how the state of Alaska, which likes its oil and gas industry, felt. The state, despite having no polar bear biologists of its own, had argued that the bears were doing fine and immediately announced that it would sue to overturn the listing.

The listing got mixed reviews in Kaktovik as well. While Fenton

Rexford, the tribal administrator, criticized it as unnecessary, hunter and wilderness guide Robert Thompson called the listing "essential." My sense was that two main issues were wrapped around individual responses. One was nervousness about whether there'd be a new layer of regulation and perhaps restrictions concerning subsistence hunting, and the other was attitudes toward oil development.

Rexford, a whaling caption who'd held many leadership positions in the village and region, was both wary of outside interference in local matters and in favor of economic development—specifically opening the Arctic National Wildlife Refuge to oil drilling. (He'd once appeared on PBS's *NewsHour* as a local expert, to explain that Kaktovik had prospered from Prudhoe Bay oil tax revenues—prosperity that had brought running water and flush toilets to the village in 2000.) Rexford is well aware that climate or weather, and particularly the sea ice situation, has been changing, though he's not sure how much of that change can rightly be attributed to global warming associated with greenhouse gas emissions. He might or might not have been kidding me when he told me about an icebreaking oil tanker that had come through in 1969, when the industry was testing the possibility of moving Prudhoe Bay oil by tanker as opposed to building an eight-hundred-mile pipeline; that, he said, could be a reason the sea ice was now more fragile.

Guide Robert Thompson was perhaps Rexford's polar opposite. An activist who opposes oil development—onshore and off—in the Arctic, he was hooked up by the Internet to national environmental organizations, traveled frequently to conferences as an Inupiaq speaker, and wrote editorials. I had known of his involvement with an Alaskan Native grassroots network known as REDOIL (Resisting Environmental Destruction on Indigenous Lands) and was glad when he offered to stop by teachers' housing one evening to talk.

Thompson, a sturdy, middle-aged man with a professorial talkativeness, understood the polar bear listing as an essential part of the larger picture—the changes we need to make to move from a fossil fuel–driven economy to renewable energies and sustainability. The first thing he said to me was, "Look at polar bears. Some people say, 'I don't think they should be listed. There's lots of them.' There's lots of them because there's *no ice* for them to get onto out there. If you look around you and see that there's twenty bears out at the bone pile, you might think there's plenty, you don't have to be concerned. But it's a little bigger than that. Look at the satellite photos."

Noting that nine hundred thousand people had written letters or e-mails or signed petitions supporting the listing, Thompson compared the place of polar bears in the sea ice situation to that of caribou in the Arctic Refuge. "The polar bear's the poster child for the climate change issue. We need something for people to rally behind." The essential part of the listing, for him, was the protection of habitat, which would include onshore denning sites as the bears spent more time ashore. "You don't just list it and say it's listed and carry on with oil development or whatever."

The effort to get the polar bears listed went back to 2005, when a number of conservation groups first petitioned for the designation, based on the loss of sea ice habitat. There have since been five more petitions for ice-dependent species—walrus and four seal species; these determinations are still being studied and/or litigated. Conservationists have wanted, with such listings, to bring attention to global climate issues—and more, to force our government to address climate change and reduce carbon emissions. When the polar bear listing (as a threatened species, not yet endangered) was finally announced in May 2008, Kassie Siegel of the Center for Biological Diversity, one of the petitioners, said, "Even the Bush administration can't deny the reality of global warming."[13]

The celebration was short-lived. Interior Secretary Kempthorne, forced into the listing by the science and federal courts, added a caveat that the listing would not "set backdoor climate policy"—that the ESA could not be used to regulate greenhouse gas emissions. He stated that no new regulation of either industry or subsistence hunting in Alaska would be necessary. He specifically ruled that oil and gas development allowed under the standards of the Marine Mammal Protection Act would also be allowed under the ESA. Only one change to the status quo was anticipated by Interior officials—polar bear trophies could no longer be imported from Canada to the United States.

Indeed, it's hard to say just what the ESA listing will mean for the bears, not until we've had years more of litigation. Conservationists have challenged the rulings that oil and gas development can continue in bear habitat and that emissions are immune from controls. And, Alaska has its own lawsuit, which insists that projections for sea ice loss are only hypothetical.

When I asked Susi Miller, the polar bear biologist, what she thought the ESA listing meant for the bears, she said, "I don't think we'll stop the ice from melting." She was hard put to say what might be different, except that the listing had made people more aware of climate change. The Fish and Wildlife Service would continue to work with the oil and gas industry to minimize potential conflicts with the bears, and she thought they'd be taking a hard look at critical habitat—specifically key denning and feeding areas and the role of barrier islands. She hoped there'd be some funding for new research and the development of a long-term conservation plan.

Almost a year later, the Obama administration would propose 200,541 square miles of critical habitat for polar bears—7 percent of it barrier islands and onshore denning sites and the rest sea ice in the Beaufort and Chukchi Seas. The designation would not stop oil and gas or other development but would require consultation with the Fish and Wildlife Service. The announcement was made the same week that the Interior Department approved a plan for exploratory drilling in the same, critical-habitat-designated area of the Beaufort, a move environmentalists called "schizophrenic."

Thompson, on his third cup of coffee, told me about his plans for installing a wind generator at his house, about the difficulties of cleaning up spilled oil in broken ice, and that, when more droughts and food shortages resulted from climate change, "we'll make it, but the person who buys from the store, they could be in dire straits."

I asked finally, as delicately as I could, about hunting—or, more accurately, polar bear shootings. I had heard that three polar bears had been shot in the village recently—bears that were staying around and considered potentially dangerous—and that Thompson had shot two of these, one of them in his yard. "People don't just go shoot them," Thompson said. "Nobody's abusing the privilege." He estimated that, in the last twenty years, no more than two or three were taken each year in and near Kaktovik. "What we're looking at is protecting the habitat. It's not just for the polar bears, it's for the whales and all the other animals."

Thompson turned the conversation back to oil development. "We've been told for years we had to support ANWR [that is, opening the coastal plain of the Arctic National Wildlife Refuge to oil development] so they don't go offshore." While the inland Gwich'in Athabascans have steadfastly opposed drilling on the coastal plain, calving grounds of the caribou they depend on, the people of Kaktovik have generally been okay with oil development on land but adamantly against it offshore. Although the refuge is, quite literally, their backyard and they eat caribou, too, their Inupiaq culture is based primarily on what the sea provides.

Aside from environmental effects, one big difference between onshore and offshore development is that local governments and the state of Alaska receive taxes and other payments from the first, but only the federal government makes money from the second.

If administrator Fenton Rexford held a viewpoint of someone in authority who needed to worry about public services, and Robert Thompson was an activist concerned about the global environment, Marie Rexford was largely traditional in her views. Marie, sister-in-law to Fenton and an artist known for sewing traditional women's clothing out of unusual fabrics (like the *atikluk*, or overdress, she'd worn at the Thanksgiving feast, with sailboats and lighthouses on it), met me one day at the Waldo Arms Hotel, one of two establishments in Kaktovik that serve food. Surrounded by historical and wildlife photos, maps and big baleen fronds etched with whaling scenes, all the material culture that makes the hotel-café almost a museum, she lamented to me the intrusive nature of some of the polar bear research. ("We keep telling them, why don't they just go to the elders. The elders have all this knowledge.") And then she told me about growing up in Kaktovik and the changes she's seen over the years.

Marie told me how "weird" it was not to see sea ice in the summers anymore, about the erosion of the barrier islands on which people had always camped to escape bugs and mice, and about catching a new kind of fish and having to take samples to the Fish and Game people to identify because no one had ever seen them before. A few years earlier the caribou herd from Barrow had come to Barter Island for the first time anyone could remember, and then an ice storm covered the tundra and prevented the animals from digging their way to food. Many had died.

Marie had been a part of a whaling crew but wasn't going out anymore, was letting the younger people go instead. The last time she'd gone, she said, was "hard for women." When I looked puzzled, she explained: It had to do with the sea ice, that there wasn't any, and so there was no ice to get out on, away from the crowded open boats, when they needed to relieve themselves. (I had to smile when brother-in-law Fenton later told me that whaling was actually easier with less ice, because "it wasn't in the way.") Elsewhere across the north, whaling is typically done from the ice edge, in open leads, and lack of ice is a serious problem for those hunters.

We talked more about whaling: There used to be eight crews in the village; six had gone out this year. Marie said, "We lost two people this year."

"Do you mean the boating accident?" I had heard about this earlier, when it had happened in the summer.

"It was not a boating accident!" Marie was emphatic about this. "We never had an accident like this in this village."

Haltingly, Marie told me about the family—related to her and, it seemed, everyone in Kaktovik—that had been traveling along the coast by boat. They'd camped on a barrier island, leaving the boat in a protected area behind a point and taking a four-wheeler to a higher spot. A big storm—the same one that had flooded the airport and undercut the bluffs at Kaktovik—blew up.

Marie paused to wipe her eyes with a napkin. I murmured something about how sorry I was, but I was thinking how similar this story was to the one I'd heard in Fort Good Hope a year earlier, about a sudden fierce storm that swamped a boat on the Mackenzie and drowned three villagers. The weather used to be something the elders were good at judging, the dynamics of the water something they knew, the land a solid state. Now the world was different, less predictable, more dangerous.

Choking back tears, Marie described how the family had gone back to get the boat, only to find that the storm had cut a channel through the island. The older man tried to wade across, sank into a soft area, and was knocked down by waves. "The big waves got him. His son was trying to help him, and he got washed out." Both were swept by fast currents into the ocean and drowned while the wife of one, mother of the other, watched helplessly. It was several more days before she and a grandchild were able to reach the boat and motor back to the village, just the two of them pulling into the lagoon on a beautiful summer's day. "It was the first time this happened," Marie said again, and blew her nose. "We couldn't believe it."

I hated to probe at such obvious pain, but I had to ask: "I'm wondering, though, do people associate that storm with changes in the weather and climate? Was it because the sea ice was so far away that there were big waves?"

"I think *so*," she said with emphasis. "Not enough ice out there. That's how we're losing our barrier islands. They're going underwater."

As is the case everywhere in the rapidly changing north, environmental and societal changes are hard to separate from one another. At one point while we talked, Marie lamented that she'd been "born too late," that she wished she'd lived in an earlier time when people were more nomadic, traveling on the land instead of staying home and watching TV. When her six kids were finished with school, she wanted to move into the mountains, to allotments her family has there, and live a life more connected to the land. "At least I have my hunters," she said, referring to her sons and a young grandson, "when I can't go anymore." But she also thought that oil development was necessary to the economy, and she was looking forward to the $4,000 dividend the Arctic Slope Regional Corporation would be paying every shareholder in December.

We talked about art. As an artist, Marie made—in addition to clothing—caribou skin masks, drawings on baleen, purses, and note cards. I asked if she thought "climate change tourism" could provide more of an economic opportunity for Kaktovik, if people concerned about polar bears made it a travel destination. She was not much interested in tourism, she said. She had all the art market she wanted from people already passing through the village as they visited the Arctic Refuge and who were sometimes a problem when they camped on private land. She'd worked, very briefly, for one of the operations that brought tourists to see bears at the bone pile. "It was really boring for me," she said, to stand there for hours and answer the same questions over and over.

Marie was reluctant to talk too much about the future, to speculate on what climate change might do to her village and the lives of her children and grandchildren, or to suggest what things might be done differently to prevent the worst from happening or to adapt to what was happening, or would, or might. "How can you tell the future?" she asked. "You cannot, because it's always going to change. Elders say, 'Be careful what you say. What you say can happen. You have a powerful mouth.'"

Later, Marie's words kept returning to me. I knew I was always pushing, trying to learn from others what they knew and what their expertise could teach the rest of us about what it takes to cope with climate change, what we could learn from traditional cultures about adaptation and resilience. I had learned less well to understand that the success of northern people has also come from acceptance of what can't be controlled and from a knowledge that people are not in charge of the natural world, but a part of it, susceptible to its rules rather than being its ruler. It would be a hard thing, in the Inupiaq culture, to believe that humans had altered basic conditions of life on earth and that we should think about the future we have wrought and how we might live in it. It was a step even beyond that to consider what we should do to reverse the harm.

On Sunday, Elaine and I attended the Presbyterian church service, in the simple wooden building with a velvet Jesus on the wall and an altar with its one lit candle. (It was First Advent Sunday.) I was not normally a churchgoer, but I'd long been intrigued with the way Alaska Natives have married traditional spirituality and practices with the Christian beliefs and rituals brought by missionaries. To be sure, missionaries, like teachers and government officials, had done much to denigrate and destroy Native culture, but Native people didn't so much assimilate as adapt, actively choosing what worked for them as they shaped modern lives around age-old values. I had found that, in villages, I could learn something about strength and resilience by attending church.

The ordained minister, Mary Ann Warden, was a large woman in her sixties, dressed in sneakers and slacks and wearing a beautiful beaded necklace with a cross and a dove over a plain blouse. Warden had grown up in Kaktovik but, like so many of her generation who were now in leadership positions, she'd lived elsewhere and been well educated—in her case earning degrees in criminal justice and sociology as well as an MA in divinity. She'd returned to Kaktovik only a few years earlier, when her uncle Isaac retired from the ministry.

On this Sunday the theme was awakening, and Warden spoke (in English for the morning service—an evening service would be in Inupiaq) of the religious sense of being awake and ready for the return of the Lord, and then she'd spoken more particularly about the value of being awake generally, paying attention to the world around us. Hunters, she reminded us, would have to be awake, but so would the family at home. We wouldn't know when the hunters might return, but we would cook up a big pot of soup and have it ready for them at any time.

The other part of the service I most enjoyed was the "prayers of the people," when congregants offered prayers to specific people in need. There was a prayer for a woman who was having all her teeth pulled the next day, for Uncle Daniel who had a pain in his shoulder, for the family that had gone to California to get medical treatment for a child.

When I spoke with her later, Warden, like so many others, told me she was seeing different kinds of birds than she had as a child, and that the ground was melting. I was curious about her religious view; did she teach that whatever happened was in God's hands or that humans had a responsibility to care for the earth? She was emphatic on this point: Presbyterian and Inupiat values were the same regarding the environment. "Our people have deep roots in taking care of the land," she said. She remembered her grandmother collecting "mouse food," the seeds stored by lemmings in their burrows, to feed her own family; she would always put something back for the lemmings, so they wouldn't go hungry. "And we never polluted the land." But there were other teachings, too: "A long time ago they said the island might fall into the water," so perhaps what the elders had said was coming true.

In Kaktovik, the whale bone pile is purposely located on a far spit past the airport, away from the village, and away from the beach where the whales are brought ashore and butchered. We tried to drive there one afternoon, but the road was drifted over and the bears were gone, anyway. Only the massive rib and jaw bones stuck up in the air like an old shipwreck.

The idea with the bone pile was that scavenging bears would stay there and not wander into the village, and when they left they would swim to the barrier islands beyond or the ice itself, when it came. This worked, for the most part. The bears had feasted in September and October and then left on the ice. Still, and as much as residents and tourists enjoyed seeing the bears, the bears could be a danger. Two decades ago in Point Lay, another North Slope village, a young couple walking through town in the middle of a December night was attacked by a polar bear, and the young man was killed. In Kaktovik, a sign in the post office warns BEWARE OF POLAR BEARS! DO NOT LEAVE CHILDREN UNATTENDED OR FOOD IN THE OPEN, and one door of the school is always left unlocked so that anyone can escape into a vestibule for safety.

I visited Nora Jane Burns, the village liaison for the North Slope Borough, in her office in the Borough Building. Partway through our conversation, when she showed me photos on her computer of the airport flooding, she also showed me her screen saver picture. It was a photo of herself in the village in the 1960s: a little girl, apple-cheeked, her face circled with a wolverine-fur parka ruff, and piles of snow all around.

Among Burns's duties was to coordinate the community bear patrol. For the sixteen darkest hours each day/night (when the truck was running, which it wasn't right then), a member of the patrol drove up and down and around Kaktovik's few streets, watching for bears and listening for the sounds of barking dogs (the usual bear alarm). Any bears that were where they shouldn't be were run off by the vehicle or by firing "crackers" into the air to frighten them. The idea was primarily to keep the community safe, but also to protect bears by discouraging them from coming into town, where they might learn bad eating habits, become too comfortable around people, and be shot. Bears that were still around this late in the season were considered to be dangerous; they were usually in poor condition and especially hungry, looking for an easy meal. Soon they would either go away or be dead, and the polar bear patrol would cease for the season.

The bears were running out of ice, Burns said, but a big factor that brought them to Barter Island, in her opinion, was the food supply. "The new generation of bears is attracted to whaling. They know how to live off the land." The real problem, and the need for the polar bear patrol, was that "people aren't putting their shares up." They were leaving whale meat and *muktuk* in their yards or un-secured storage places, and bears were attracted to that food source, just as they were to the bone pile until that was picked clean. More grizzly bears were showing up, too, from inland; someone had shot one recently. Grizzly bears are considered to be more aggressive—indeed, they'll run the larger polar bears off the bone pile—and villagers have no tolerance for them at all.

(This habitat overlap between species was something new, with grizzlies moving northward to the coast and polar bears moving to the coast from the ice. In 2006 on Banks Island in the Canadian Northwest Territories, a hunter shot an odd-looking bear that, with DNA analysis, turned out to be a hybrid between the species—with a father griz and a mother polar bear. The hybrid has been called a pizzly or grolar bear.)[14]

Aside from the patrol, there was also a polar bear committee just getting started. Its purpose was education and preventing bear problems. One project under discussion was the purchase of sturdy, bear-proof containers for residents to store their shares of whale meat in. Another was establishing a safety zone around the bone pile, to keep people from getting too close to the bears. They'd discussed blocking that road altogether so that people couldn't drive right up to the whale bones, and they had raised the idea of bull-dozing the whale remains into the ocean instead of leaving them on land.

That, Burns said, was controversial. First, because nobody knew what the loss of that food source might mean to the bears—whether they would disperse, go hungry, or come into the village even more. And second, because bear watching had become very popular.

There had to be limits, though, or someone was going to get hurt. Burns, in her stylish blue-rimmed glasses, looked very stern. "Right now people go right up to the bears. If you're going to be a guide, you have to follow some rules." One man, a local who had started a guiding business, had walked up to and touched a sleeping bear, and a video on YouTube ("Polar Bear Tag") showed a photographer being chased around his vehicle by a bear.

Burns worked with the U.S. Fish and Wildlife people, like Susi Miller, who visited frequently from Anchorage. Relations with the federal agency "used to be real bad, but they're getting better. Now they ask questions and get advice, instead of telling us how it is." Miller and her colleagues had assisted residents with text for posters and pamphlets; a poster on the wall in Burns's office read YOU ARE IN POLAR BEAR COUNTRY and listed proper behaviors.

Now, at least, the community whale meat was being stored in old steel-sided shipping containers and people were more careful with their trash and about "airing" their meat in their yards to age it.

Alaska isn't the only place to have polar bear patrols. In fact, such patrols began in Chukotka, Russia, on the northern coast that faces

the Chukchi Sea, assisted by the World Wildlife Fund. Later, I
would meet Chukotkan hunters from those patrols, when they visited Alaska to share their experiences in managing human–polar
bear interactions. At a presentation given by brothers Sergey and
Vladilen Kavriy, Vladilen told how they began to see major climatic
changes in the 1990s. Both walruses and polar bears, which should
have been living on the sea ice, began to come ashore. "In the 1980s,"
Vladilen said through an interpreter, "ice was along the coast all
summer. Now it's very far offshore." At Cape Vankarem, close to
three villages, huge numbers of walrus—more than thirty thousand—began to haul out on the rocky beach. "This is not a natural
habitat for them," Vladilen said. "They stampede in this environment" when disturbed, and they can be disturbed by anything, "even
the sound of an unusual bird." Trampled animals were scavenged by
bears, which then also came into the villages.

The Umky (from the Chukchi name for the polar bear) Patrol
was initiated in 2006 by villagers to protect the walrus, the bears,
and the villagers.[15] The general goal, Vladilen explained, "is to protect
nature and to teach people to live harmoniously with nature." The
haul-out area was guarded by a "keeper," someone to keep people
and dogs away, and hunters learned to hunt the walrus they needed
for food with spears, quietly and carefully from the edge of a group,
to prevent stampeding. The local people proposed that the haul-out
be formally protected, and the regional government did just that in
2007.

Today, the Umky Patrol moves walrus carcasses from the haul-
out to a place farther from the village of Vankarem, where the bears
(as many as two hundred) feed as they migrate down the coast.
"Fat and happy," they then pass by the villages. The patrol keeps
an eye out around the villages and scares away bears that come too
close; its members teach safety lessons, escort children to school,
and generally educate people about bears and how to live among

them. Hunters also work with biologists to locate and protect bear denning sites and to collect traditional knowledge and other data to help with bear conservation.

During school hours in Kaktovik, I spent much of my time at Harold Kaveolook School, named for the first Kaktovik teacher, who came from Barrow in 1951 and personally built the first school building out of DEW-line scraps. With sixty-odd students from kindergarten through high school, the current school felt spacious on the one hand and intimate on the other. The class sizes were small, the classrooms cheery, the entire building well equipped—with a wood shop where Pete taught, a library that also served the community, a gym, and even a small swimming pool that doubled as a water supply for fire safety. The teachers, who complained to me about the not-designed-for-rural-Alaska No Child Left Behind requirements, did their best to make education relevant to their students.

There were certain motifs to the artwork hung on the walls, bulletin boards, and lockers. Whales. Polar bears. Inupiaq names. Northern lights. Turkeys.

On my first day, Elaine's first- and second-graders were dizzy with excitement over the Pilgrims, the first Thanksgiving, and the paper turkeys they were constructing for table centerpieces.

Another day, the third-, fourth-, and fifth-graders, avid writers, shared with me stories they'd written about their lives and the things they most enjoyed. One had written about fossils and wanting to be a dinosaur scientist, several others about helping with whaling and then helping the researchers take samples from the dead whales and how they'd gotten to hold a whale's eyeball, which felt "gushy." There were stories about wolverines and how "tourists go crazy for polar bears," and about making the northern lights move around by whistling and humming. One very excited boy read to me about his first seal hunt and how he'd presented the seal to elders. I was struck with how many of the stories exhibited pride of place, and how many were grounded in both Inupiaq culture and Western science, exhibiting no contradiction between eating an animal and wanting to study it. Scientists who worked in the region very often volunteered talks at the school, and it seemed that some of that had rubbed off.

The junior high students were fidgety, but we talked about writing and about doing research for books, and they told me, very matter-of-factly, that the ice was disappearing and salmon, formerly sparse in the Arctic, were showing up more frequently in their families' nets. Later, in the library, I paged through the photo book *The Last Polar Bear* with some of those same kids.[16] They called out the familiar images: the bone pile, bears feeding, the village on a clear day with mountains in the distance, eroding coastline. They told me the land was washing away.

"What do you think will happen?" I asked.

"People will move away."

"Where will they go?"

"Canada."

"Fairbanks."

They didn't seem to have thought about the whole village—Kaktovik—moving, only that individual families would leave for other communities, perhaps where they already had family.

I talked to the high school science class about science writing and heard from them a litany of changes they'd observed—the waves washing across the runway, permafrost melt out on the tundra, an ice cellar filling with water. They told me about poor polar bear cub survival. They told me these things as though they were facts of life: what they knew to be true, a reality they lived with. They told me, without judgment, who had killed the recently killed bears, and they told me that one of their uncles had made a Disney film about polar bears.

The high school English class had recently written letters to U.S. representative Michele Bachmann (R-Minnesota), and copies were posted on the classroom door. Bachmann, after an American Energy Tour by members of Congress, had described the coastal plain of the Arctic as being buried in snow and ice most of the time and "covered in complete darkness" for three months of the year, without wildlife or other values worthy of protection.[17] The indignant student letters said things like "Readers of your comments would assume that no one lives in this supposed wasteland" and listed some of the animals—whales, seals, caribou, polar and grizzly bears, foxes, lemmings, and birds—that live around the village and are "vital to our culture." They'd been asked by the teacher to limit their letters to misstatements of fact made by Bachmann, and so they didn't express opinions about oil drilling on and near their lands, but what was clear from their letters was the hurt of having their place and lives misrepresented, their pride in who they were and the bountiful place that was their home.

At school one day, I talked to Flora Rexford, the twenty-two-year-old Inupiaq culture teacher (and daughter of Marie) as she was tidying up her room after her last class. With a big poster of a polar bear face looking down on us, Flora rolled up butcher paper sheets she'd been using to teach Christmas carols in Inupiaq and wiped away the dust from reindeer antler carving. She'd recently interviewed Kaktovik's elders for a university professor documenting climate change. "The biggest concern from all the interviews is how much smaller the island's getting," she told me. The elders were alarmed that the erosion was taking graves and historic sites. That is, it wasn't just land that was disappearing; it was cultural history, knowledge of the past.

Flora herself was clearly concerned. In the summer she'd worked on a cleanup project, collecting trash that had blown onto the tundra. She could hear water running and at one point broke through the surface and fell into a hole up to her armpits. "The TV says that in ten years we'll be underwater. I don't know if that's true, but if it is, it means the whole community will have to move." If the worst happened, if civilization collapsed, she wanted to be prepared and to know the old ways. "I want to learn to survive here on my own, just in case."

If Flora represented the young generation that was staying home, dealing with climate change on the local level, her cousin Allison Warden, who visited from Anchorage over Thanksgiving and was, with Flora, one of the servers at the feast, represented those who had taken their cultural knowledge and personal experience out into the world. Allison, a performance artist who had lived in New York and Seattle before returning to Alaska, created an acclaimed one-woman show she called *Ode to the Polar Bear*. I hadn't seen it, but I'd heard a lot about it as she performed it around Alaska (standing ovation at the Last Frontier Theatre Conference) and in Seattle. Later, when I did see it in Anchorage, I appreciated the way she impressed upon her audience the reality of melting sea ice and its consequences for bears and Inupiat, while also conveying Inupiaq values. By playing four separate characters—a bear, a dreaming girl, an old woman, and a hunter—she wove together a number of stories, "all true," all heard from her family and other elders, about polar bears and what people have learned from them. In her view, the bears were moving, following the ice east toward Greenland, and the Inupiat, too, will adapt, as they always have. After all, she said, elders had long told stories about Alaska once being a tropical land; they taught that the palm trees would return.

In my last days in Kaktovik, I thought often of the young people I'd met. We're all stakeholders in this changing world, of course, but for some the stakes are higher. I thought about the boy whose seal hunting had given him both pride and a respected place in his family. I thought of the young girl who had said with great non-chalance, "They'll move to Fairbanks." I thought of the tiny children eating *muktuk* at the Thanksgiving feast, and one little girl, out in the middle of the community center floor later that night, danc-ing with the women while the men struck their traditional circular drums and sang in Inupiaq. I thought of the high school science students who understood how melting permafrost released carbon dioxide and methane, and who might stay in the village and try to live a subsistence life or might go out to college and might or might not come back. I thought of Flora, serious with the importance of her culture, and Allison, who adhered to traditional values even as she embraced experimental art. All of them will live in a world vastly different, in so many ways, from that of their elders. They may see within their lifetimes physical changes that, in earlier eras, took place over thousands of years. All of them will have to decide how, and where, and for what, they'll live.

Just before Christmas, when I was home again, Elaine sent me some photos she'd made from her video of bears feeding at the bone pile. The enclosed note, after news of weather, ravens, foxes, and the other teachers, read, "Someone shot another bear. They brought it in Pete's shop to skin it. I held its paw for a while and apologized to it . . ."

PART FOUR

When a Village Has to Move: Shishmaref

In the plywood skiff with the big outboard engine, we wound our way up Tin Creek. It was nearly mid-August, the scene all around us pulsing with birds: green-winged teals tipping in the side sloughs, the white-fronted geese locals call speckle-bellies overhead, gulls keeping pace beside us. Tony Weyiouanna, driving the boat, knew the channel—knew where to find the deepest water—as only someone with years of close acquaintance could. The lowland country all around us was huge, and I was easily turned around in it as the creek bent one way and then folded back on itself, winding into low, treeless hills. Miles off, Ear Mountain with its two top bumps like rodent ears rose against blue sky. Somewhere out there, a crew was digging holes, evaluating the mountain as a source of gravel for a road, airstrip, and new village. And back behind us, twelve miles across the shallow inlet everyone called a lagoon, lay the barrier islands that lined the coast and the one called Sarichef, on which was located the village of Shishmaref, population 608.

If there is one place in America most identified with global warming and climate change, that place has to be Shishmaref, Alaska. The Inupiaq community struggling for its very existence has been portrayed around the world as an early victim of climate change. The opening chapter in Elizabeth Kolbert's landmark book *Field Notes from a Catastrophe* is called "Shishmaref, Alaska." Reporters have come from dozens of news outlets, from *The New York Times* to *National Geographic* and *People* magazine, from the BBC, National Public Radio, and CBS and ABC News.[1] They've come from Germany, Japan, France, Sweden, and Holland. Al Gore's documentary crew came, and Gore has referred to the people of Shishmaref as "the first climate refugees." A group of scientists and evangelical religious leaders visited, accompanied by PBS reporters who filmed the visit for a *NOW* program called "God and Global Warming." A Dutch film and a separate Dutch photo book are each titled *The Last Days of Shishmaref.*

The story that has been told and shown, exhaustively now, is of the Inupiaq village on a small sand island on Alaska's northwest coast, eroding from storm waves no longer blocked by sea ice, and made more vulnerable yet as the permafrost that formerly held the land together thaws. As at Barter Island and elsewhere along Alaska's northern coasts, waves have a longer "fetch" across open water and storm surges pick up more energy. In 1997 a fall storm took 125 feet from the northern side of Shishmaref's island, dropping buildings into the sea and necessitating the move of a dozen homes as well as the National Guard Armory. Storms since have continued to erode the shoreline, and emergency seawall protections have been but a temporary "fix." The entire island is four and a third miles long and only a quarter mile wide, with the high point twenty feet above sea level. In 2002 residents voted to relocate the community and in 2006, following a study of alternative sites, voted to move to the area known as Tin Creek, on the mainland.

Shishmaref is not alone in its exigency. That Government Accountability Office report from 2003 identified 184 of the 213 villages in Alaska as being affected by erosion and flooding, and the situation has only worsened since.[2] Shishmaref is one of six villages on the "immediate action" list. It is also the one that has been most public about its situation and need.

Weyiouanna, the principal architect of Shishmaref's public

campaign, had brought me to Tin Creek to take a look at what he hoped—if the soil and other studies checked out—would be the new village location. He snugged the skiff up against the bank, and Fannie, his wife, jumped out with an anchor to secure us to shore. Weyiouanna, a kind man with a bushy mustache and the beginnings of gray in his dark hair, was born in Shishmaref and has lived there all his life, except for some time at college and in Nome. Since the late 1980s he's been a tireless advocate for relocating the village to higher ground—not because he or anyone *wants* to move, but because they know they must. From 2001 to 2007 much of his time as the village's transportation planner was devoted to an organization called the Shishmaref Erosion and Relocation Coalition, in which role he used his considerable computer, communication, and personal skills to bring Shishmaref to the world's attention.

But Weyiouanna was tired. It had been a long effort, and it seemed to him now that the local people were losing control. More state and federal agencies than he could count were involved in multiple layers of studies and planning, and it was not at all clear how or when a move would actually occur, whether the preferred site would even be approved, and how any of it would be paid for.

"We seem to be going backward," Weyiouanna had told me at his house earlier in the day, when I'd met him and Fannie for the first time. He'd been sitting at the kitchen table and sharpening *ulus* while Fannie set out a pile of sourdough pancakes and the younger members of the Weyiouanna household—they have four teenagers—drifted in and out. They'd all gotten home from their camp on the mainland just hours earlier, and the Ziploc bags of salmonberries they'd gathered—gallons of them—were piled in the entry, ready for the freezer. (Salmonberry is the local name for *Rubus chamaemorus*, otherwise known as cloudberry and, in Inupiaq, *aqpik*. It's the second-most important traditional subsistence resource in Shishmaref, after the bearded seal.) Weyiouanna is also an artist, and some of his whalebone carvings looked down at us from a high shelf.

Weyiouanna searched the kitchen for the right stone for his *ulu* sharpening, then told me that, although he'd given up the transportation planning job and his lead role with the coalition for a part-time position as the village's grant writer, he couldn't turn his back on the dire situation, the future of his family and community. It was just very frustrating to have so many entities involved in such a confusing and uncoordinated way and so little progress, and now the media had lost interest and was on to other, fresher stories. Senator Ted Stevens, so successful at delivering federal funds to Alaska's villages, had lost his seat, and who knew how that was going to play out?

Now, at Tin Creek we disembarked onto tundra lit with the feathery heads of cotton grass, and Fannie and her niece Brenda set out with berry buckets. Weyiouanna and I started uphill so I could get a better view and sense of the country that might be Shishmaref's new home. The tundra growth was wound tight to the ground and into hilly tussocks, intertwined with grasses, willows, Labrador tea, lichens, gemlike blueberries we paused to pick and eat, and an occasional single gold *aqpik* berry. Despite the advancing season, the landscape was still green, with leaves just beginning to suggest the yellows and reds of autumn. We staggered over the dry, prickly tussocks as they twisted and toppled under our feet, and I thought of what a biologist in Nome had told me—that the tundra surface was drier than usual, not for a lack of rain but because, as the "active layer" of ground deepened over thawing permafrost, there was more soil for the moisture to soak into.

"What's that dark thing?" Weyiouanna pointed toward the creek and a patch of willows, upstream from the boat and from where Fannie and Brenda were leaning over their yellow berry buckets.

I raised my binoculars. A caribou with smallish antlers was staring back at us.

Weyiouanna took his own look. "This is a closed area," he said, as though he wished it were not and he could go get the rifle from the boat. Caribou are a major subsistence food for his family and most others in Shishmaref. While bearded seals, the village's main source of protein, are threatened by the loss of sea ice, caribou, too, are having a time of it as snow conditions and vegetation change with the climate. Here on the Seward Peninsula, the now treeless expanse of tundra is expected to transition into spruce and deciduous forest within the next hundred years. A forested landscape would no longer support certain species, like caribou. Winter icing, elsewhere in the north, has already collapsed some caribou populations by blocking their access to nutritious lichens, and warming is also increasing the numbers of biting insects that drive caribou to exhaustion.

As we continued to wind our way uphill, we began to see over the land beyond the creek, to the water that was the lagoon and then across the twelve miles that separated us from the chain of barrier islands and Shishmaref. The islands out there are true barrier islands, long and narrow and almost continuous, with a few breaks that open to the Chukchi Sea. They're made out of sand and, like all barrier islands, are hugely dynamic. That is, they're constantly being reworked by wind and waves. Although the mechanics of barrier island origins are still debated, their development is linked to the end of the last ice age; when the glaciers stopped melting and the rapid rise in sea level slowed, the islands formed. Scientists note that rising sea level causes existing islands to move shoreward, typically by a process called "rolling over," when waves top an island and carry sand to the lagoon side.

The mirage effect over the water caused the islands to lift in the distance, and the village of Shishmaref looked like a shimmering line of tiny, boxy shapes, minimalist in such a massive landscape. *What a crazy place to build a community*, was all I could think. Who in his right mind would ever put six hundred people and all their modern infrastructure on a sandbar?

No one, of course, had made any such intentional choice. One thing led to another, until we have today's situation. Although Shishmaref's people claim four thousand years of habitation on the island (known as Kigiktaq—"island"—before explorer Otto von Kotzebue, working for the Russians, came along in 1816 and began renaming places), that habitation was nomadic and seasonal. Seals and other marine resources were, then as now, a mainstay of the Inupiaq food supply and culture. Eventually, because of the natural harbor in the shelter of the island, Shishmaref became a supply center for gold mining activities. A post office was established in 1901. Then came the school, the Lutheran church (on the highest ground in the center of town), the electrical system and fuel to run it, the government housing, and on, and on. Like so many other coastal places in Alaska, the location made it easily accessed by barges for unloading all the construction materials and fuel and now packaged foods and TV sets that barges bring.

And always, there was erosion—"natural," if you will, and increasingly related to the reduction in sea ice and the thaw of permafrost. For more than three decades now, as more and more infrastructure was piled onto the sand, there's been talk of moving. In 1974, the estimated cost of relocating the community to the mainland was $1 million. In 2006, an Army Corps of Engineers study set the estimated cost of moving at $179 million.[3] Anyone can do the math; for 142 households, that's more than $1 million each. Who's going to pay?

The alternatives are scarcely less costly. The Corps estimated that the village could be "colocated" to either Nome or Kotzebue for about $93 million. To stay in place on the island but shield it with seawalls, at least for a while—$109 million.

Weyiouanna and I sat on the hummocky tundra while he pointed in one direction and another. We were somewhere on the grounds of the potential relocation site, the one selected by the community after a reconnaissance study had evaluated such things as space requirements, room for growth, and access to the sea. Over the hill lay Goose Creek, an important area for waterfowl hunting and the collection of greens, and beyond that rose the Serpentine Mountains, above the river where the Weyiouannas and other Shishmaref families have their hunting and berry-picking camps.

Since spring, a road study had been under way, drilling into the tundra to test the underlying materials and ice depth to determine the best route as well as likely development costs. The road—to cover about twenty miles—would go from the edge of Shishmaref Inlet across village corporation land and part of the Bering Land Bridge National Preserve (perhaps the least visited unit of our national park system) to the granitic Ear Mountain, from which rock and gravel needed for construction would be mined. The village site would lie partway along the route, approximately where we sat. Just the exploratory work on the road was costing some millions in federal highway funds, and the road itself was expected to be in excess of $30 million. Other studies were clocking wind speeds and directions at a potential airport location, to determine where a runway might be built and whether a cross-runway would also be necessary.

The tundra, the sky, the skipping-by small birds and the flocks of ducks over the river, the deep quiet, the sweet smell of the crushed plants beneath us—it was hard for me to sit in such a place and to anticipate a construction zone or a village. My mind stuck on the current village, with its poorly built government houses, four-wheelers parked by the post office, children playing, meat and fish hanging, smell of sewage, and steady drone of the power plant. But the new village would be built with a plan, and that plan would include new technologies and concepts of sustainability.

Weyiouanna talked, and it was clear he held a particular, perhaps even utopian, vision in his own mind. In the new village, houses would not be crowded on top of one another, and they would be built for energy efficiency. They would have plumbing and pump-out sewage tanks instead of water barrels and "honey buckets." There would still be a need for fuel tanks and fuel, but at least some of the electricity would come from wind or other renewable sources. There would be a new clinic and new school building. The village, in a safe and permanent place, might become a service hub for the rest of the region, might build an economy from that. Most of all, in Weyiouanna's vision, Shishmaref's people would be together and would still have access to their traditional lands and resources. Without the constant worry of living on a disappearing island, and with room to grow, young people and their families would stay in the community, would embrace and carry on the culture. Those who had left would want to return.

"I want us to use as little fossil fuel as we can," Weyiouanna said. He had told me earlier that both gasoline and fuel oil were presently priced, in Shishmaref, at $7.50 per gallon. "Subsistence is an important part of our lives—we don't have an economic base. It's important that, in our planning, we ask, 'How can we be more efficient in using resources?'" The ongoing studies were moving the project forward, however slowly. They would help identify the best, cheapest, most sustainable way to do the job. As the village grant writer, Weyiouanna was doing what he could, including applying for funds for small-scale projects, some wind and solar.

Below us, Fannie and Brenda were still picking, just feet apart, and I imagined they were talking together, too, the way that women do, everywhere, when working with their hands. Beyond them, sunlight glinted from the boat's windshield.

Shishmaref can show the way, Weyiouanna stressed. Shishmaref's relocation should be seen as a demonstration project to show how communities and government agencies can work together to both respect the cultures and needs of the relocating communities and be cost-effective. He didn't say it, but Weyiouanna's implication was clear: Shishmaref's climate-induced need to move was only among the first of the flood to come.

Could a new Shishmaref actually be a model of energy efficiency and renewable energy? The idea was not so far-fetched. On my way to Shishmaref I'd stopped in Nome, which was making a name for itself in renewables and already planning to export technology to the surrounding villages. On Banner Hill, just north of town, a private venture of the regional Bering Straits Native Corporation and the local Sitnasuak Native Corporation has installed the largest wind farm in Alaska. Banner Wind's eighteen wind generators are capable of feeding nine hundred kilowatts of power into Nome's electric grid, replacing about a quarter of the expensive diesel generation that was otherwise the source of the community's electricity. While the capital cost of the wind project—$5.5 million—was significant, the Native corporations were taking advantage of tax incentives and the sale of carbon offsets, otherwise known as "green tags."[4] The wind power was sold to the local utility for less than the cost of their diesel production, allowing the utility to lower costs to consumers. Banner Wind expected to make a profit, which would flow to shareholders, the Native people of the region. And half the profits were committed to the development of renewable energy projects in the villages around Nome.

All was not perfect with this plan, however. The farm had begun operating in early 2009 but soon ran into problems with high winds and icing. When I drove out to Banner Hill, the turbines were not moving. They looked like a work of environmental art, the eighteen of them strung along the ridge, grouped and spread out, blades frozen into contrasting, aesthetically pleasing positions. They'd been shut down for three months, since May, and I'd read in the paper that the wait was for the manufacture of new parts.

The day of my visit was warm and sunny, with just a breath of wind, and I was lucky to find Bob Hafner, the local person in charge of the project's installation and maintenance, at the foot of a tower. Hafner, a very fit-looking guy in a white Harley-Davidson T-shirt, was happy to talk to me while his assistant climbed the hundred-foot tower. The project for the day was installing aluminum planks at the top of towers, to use as platforms when, later, they'd be working on blades and turbines.

"I'm a fix-it guy," Hafner told me, before describing in detail the reason for the shutdown. There had been a problem with the pitch of the blades, which overproduced in the high winds, and with the anemometers, which frosted up and didn't register the wind speeds. The blades had spun too fast, the controls for shutting down in high winds didn't work, not enough oil reached the shaft to lubricate and dissipate the heat, and there was a whole lot of wear and tear on the parts. But the blades would be repitched—"washers are being cut as we speak"—and other modifications made to deal with icing, and Hafner was confident the whole farm would be back up and working by October. Getting replacement parts had been made difficult by the manufacturer's financial problems. Entegrity Wind Systems, a Canadian company with a Boulder, Colorado, office, was trying to make things good but had laid off workers and was facing bankruptcy. According to Hafner, America's erratic government policies had messed them up.

I stood back while Hafner hauled on some lines to lift the plank to his assistant near the top of the tower.

"It's a big experiment," Hafner said. "My challenge is to help prove that we can make it work." There'd been a lot of interest—from the media, but also from the surrounding villages. From the village point of view, there was a certain amount of skepticism; years ago a number of wind generators had been sited in villages, but the technology then wasn't what it is now, and the ability to maintain them didn't exist locally. Most of those early models hadn't operated very long before being mothballed. "The technologies are different now," Hafner emphasized. "And they know they can't continue to pay the prices they're paying now for electricity. It's all diesel out there. We have to change our mind-set and get off oil. Wind technology is proven and scalable to the villages."

Indeed, a state study in 2008 had found that, for more than one hundred Alaska villages, wind power was both technically and economically feasible.

I walked the rest of the way up the hill, under all eighteen of the turbines, accompanied by a flock of yellow wagtails. From near the top I watched a single musk ox meandering in the distance, down in the valley. From the top itself I looked across at an enormous open-pit mine I realized was the controversial NovaGold Rock Creek mine I'd heard so much about. It was shut down, at least temporarily out of money and business, its equipment idled and its tailing pond full against an earthen dam. One of the reasons there'd been so much interest in wind power in Nome was that NovaGold, in full production, was set to use as much electricity as all the rest of town.

Back in town, at the Bering Straits Native Corporation headquarters, I met with Jerald Brown, the corporate VP and the man credited with the wind farm and other renewable energy initiatives. The wind project, he said, was driven by economics. "It's a matter of survival, to be able to stay in the region." The goal was to build a large enough farm to require a support staff, and then to use that staff to support wind projects throughout the region. The type and size of generator was chosen to fit village needs. Support staff and materials would be located in Nome, and villagers might come in for training and take their skills back home. In the future, they would likely switch to a different manufacturer, but "a turbine is a turbine," and they would develop solid expertise to keep them running.

The BSNC headquarters itself is a model of renewable energy. A visitor doesn't expect, walking down Front Street in a place where the sun barely clears the horizon in winter, to find a building covered with solar panels. But that's another demonstration project, and one that seems to be both working and cost-effective. Installation of the ninety-three panels on the building's roof and south face in 2007 cost $175,000, but, according to Brown, the panels have generated more than 10 percent of the building's electricity (on an annual basis), and the project is on target for a ten-year payback. The corporation has also started an alternative energy branch, with a retail store that sells LED lights and other products and a staff that installs solar hot water heaters and panels for homeowners. Brown told me, "We're trying to do the same for others," including the National Park Service and the National Guard, both of which have large facilities in Nome.

On the Tin Creek hillside, it was early evening and the sun was lowering toward fall.

Once, Weyiouanna said, someone at a conference had asked him why so much money should be spent for so few people.

It was a question any of us might contemplate. I waited for Weyiouanna to say more, and when he didn't I had to ask, "What's your answer to that? What did you say?"

Weyiouanna looked off into the distance. Finally he said, "I asked a question back. 'How many communities in the Lower Forty-eight subsist off their land?' I tried to say that our uniqueness is our subsistence. We're trying to pass that on to our kids. We've lost so much. Subsistence is the last thing we have, and we need to keep it intact for the future."

I didn't have the heart to ask how the road and airport studies were going. I'd heard from people in Nome that the road studies had found poor soil conditions and permafrost problems. As well, there were serious issues about the shallowness of the lagoon and the ability to get fuel barges to the mainland, and then challenges to get fuel, by pipe or truck, to the village site. Everything would be expensive. There was no Alaska village yet that expected to find a way to live without imports of fossil fuels.

The problems Shishmaref faced—along with the rest of Alaska's eroding villages, and much of the world—were so much more than climate change. They were tied to all kinds of environmental, social, and cultural changes. Perhaps above all, they were economic—the costs of energy, a lack of jobs and job skills, the challenge of trying to live modern lives without an economic base. Massive amounts of money had been flowing into Alaska's villages for years; the university's Institute for Social and Economic Research estimated that $1.4 billion in federal and state grants, subsidies, and wages each year went to the more than two hundred far-flung Alaskan villages. Just getting the mail out to Little Diomede Island in the Bering Sea requires a long helicopter flight. I had read in the news that the tiny town of Takotna in Alaska's interior, population fifty-something, was getting a new airport costing $18.7 million in federal funds. The Denali Commission, established by former senator Ted Stevens, existed to channel federal funding to rural Alaska and worked on the premise that every village was entitled to a basic level of health and safety. Enormous strides had been made in providing water and sewer systems and in building modern health clinics. But the commission's funding, $140 million in 2005, was expected to fall to $50 million in 2010. There were limits to what was reasonable—or possible—for the expenditures of public funds.

I looked out at the ocean and thought about elevation. The country all around us was tundra plain, none of it along the coast very high. Ear Mountain, where the rock and gravel would come from, rose to twenty-three hundred feet, but the Tin Creek site where we sat was not at all high—perhaps something more than a hundred feet. I remembered maps I'd seen of different sea level rise scenarios; with more global warming and more glacial and ice cap melt, those graphic depictions showed the coast of western Alaska being inundated for miles inland.[5] Most villages, built for good reasons by the sea and along rivers, would be flooded out.

The sun was losing some of its heat as Weyiouanna and I stumbled our way back over the tussocks to the creek, stopping for handfuls of blueberries along the way. This had not been a great berrying spot, but Fannie and Brenda had collected enough blueberries that Brenda was happily looking forward to adding hers to pancakes.

We motored back out the creek, racing with ducks, past a pair of sandhill cranes posing on the tundra like something from a Japanese print. We had another stop to make, at the next creek over, where sour docks grew in plenty.

Goose Creek, when we arrived, appeared to be well named. The banks of the creek and the adjacent lowlands were littered with goose poop and feathers, and flocks flew over us in scrawling lines. After anchoring the boat, we took pillowcases and walked away from the creek, across dried mud imprinted with caribou hoof prints, past scatters of Arctic daisies and Jacob's ladder, around thick stands of marsh fleabane and their dense yellow flowers turning to woolly cotton balls. I lingered behind, taking photos, while the other three beelined for the nearest reddish field.

Sour dock (*Rumex arcticus*), a member of the buckwheat family, grows on a tall red stalk with red bracts surrounding the small, dense flowers. The stalks, higher than anything else in the meadow, were easy to spot, but it was the arrow-shaped leaves at their bases we had come to pick. Cooked like spinach, they're very high in vitamins. The Inupiat traditionally fermented them with seal oil, often adding berries, and relied on them as a vegetable all winter long. Today, still an important food source, they're chopped and cooked, then frozen in Ziplocs.

This was the first Weyiouanna sour dock gathering of the year, and Fannie was unhappy to find the leaves already splotching into red. I joined in the picking, searching out the younger and greener leaves, pausing to sample a leaf. It tasted okay—maybe a little tough, a little sour. I wouldn't want to eat a salad bowl of raw greens, but I imagined that, cooked up and seasoned, they'd be as tasty as any spinach or kale. Fannie told me she usually added some sugar to them just before serving.

Each of us lost in thought, we worked from patch to patch, along a bank, past a slough spilling with ducks. We picked for more than an hour, through the sea of red, while the sun lowered into the kind of Arctic sidelight that brings everything green into fresh brilliance. Our pillowcases fattened. I've always liked gathering food (as opposed to either growing or purchasing it), with the sense of the earth (or the sea) freely providing, the so-clear connections among soil, sunlight, water, life, and health. I like, even love, the repetitions of motion and Zen-like state that softens the mind. Most of us don't live that way anymore, but surely there's something to learn from those who do, and value in maintaining their ability to do that, in the places they know and care for. In Alaska, we call it *subsistence*, a word wrought now with political meaning and conflicts over rights to resources, a word that reduces a way of life to something that sounds deprived.

All the rest of the summer and fall, back home and everywhere else I traveled, reddish dock plants I'd never noticed before would spring to my sight from meadows and roadsides. They reminded me of Shishmaref, Tin and Goose Creeks, the faces of people who welcomed me into their homes and homeplaces, cultural values we should hope to maintain.

When the pillowcases were full enough, we lugged them back to the boat and sat on the boat's benches to share the snack foods we'd brought along. My foods were a three-ounce bag of beef jerky from the Shishmaref store ($10.99), a green apple I'd carried from home (that is, from the Homer Safeway), and a liter bottle of water from the Shishmaref store ($3.81). My hosts pulled from their ice chest a dish of chopped bearded seal—some dark meat, some bits of intestine—soaked in seal oil, a spread of silver salmon to put on Pilot crackers, chopped sour dock also packed in seal oil, *agutak* or "Eskimo ice cream" of whipped caribou fat and seal oil, Spam, and store-bought cookies. I sampled the seal meat, sour dock, and *agutak*; the distinctive taste of seal oil is something few Westerners (myself included) take to, though it's easy to understand why it's been such a critical preservative and energy-packed food in northern cultures.

I was sorry that none of the Weyiouanna teenagers had come along with us. They were, Weyiouanna told me, having pizza that night at home. And salmonberries. Fannie said she had no sooner put the berries into the freezer than they were taking some out again.

Truly, the numbers of agencies and layers of actions (and inactions) involved in trying to rescue Shishmaref from its life-threatening erosion problem were hard to fathom. There was Shishmaref itself, with multiple units of tribal and Western-style governance and the Erosion and Relocation Coalition that brought those together; the regional Bering Straits Native Association; and Kawerak, Inc., a nonprofit arm that provided family and community services. There were many state agencies, dealing with transportation and infrastructure, health, emergencies, energy, planning, and community development. The federal Army Corps of Engineers had a major role in erosion control and the building of seawalls, and FEMA was expected to respond to disasters. Alaska's congressional delegation, especially former senator Ted Stevens, had provided budget earmarks to pay for capital projects, and the Denali Commission brought additional involvement and funds. Many university people—scientists and social scientists—had been assisting with studies. For years these efforts had been uncoordinated, piecemeal. The village, with such limited resources of its own, had struggled to work with all those entities while also trying to maintain some control and autonomy over decision making.

In 2006 the Alaska legislature created a Climate Impact Assessment Commission and charged it with a number of duties related to assessing the effects of climate change in Alaska, including identifying examples of flooding and erosion, figuring costs for addressing them, and developing policies to guide infrastructure development in areas susceptible to erosion and flooding. This commission was intentionally confined, by political circumstances, to looking at *results* of climate change; it was not to consider causes or what might be done to mitigate those causes. In its 125-page report, issued two years later, a very measured tone pointed out that change occurs all the time and that climate change will have both positive and negative effects in Alaska. (Among the positives might be more open water for shipping and oil and gas development, and more agriculture and tourism opportunities.)

Commission members were weathered out of a site visit to Shishmaref but did visit another eroding coastal village and did take public testimony from around the state. And the report does, finally, contain a litany of challenges, with emphasis on the many communities threatened by erosion and flooding. It made a series of recommendations, principal among them having the administration carry on the effort. Before then governor Sarah Palin veered off into the national arena and partisan Republican causes, she made some strong declarations about the need to address climate change and appointed a subcabinet to pick up on the legislative recommendations and develop a comprehensive strategy.[6] In a "Dear Alaskan" report of July 2008, she (or her press people) wrote that her "team" was preparing an Alaska Climate Change Strategy. "The strategy is to serve as a guide for a thoughtful, practical, timely state of Alaska response to climate change. It is to identify priorities needing immediate attention along with longer-term steps we can take as a state to best serve all Alaskans and to do our part in the global response to this global phenomenon."

That subcabinet did carry on, with more than a hundred volunteers serving on various committees and the whole effort generally falling below the radar of most Alaskans. Four advisory groups tackled mitigation, adaptation, immediate action, and research needs. The reports of these groups are detailed and substantive, but, aside from some state budgeting to address the most immediate

needs, to date there has been little implementation of their recommendations. Without leadership from either the administrative or
legislative branches, the good work is destined to do the electronic
equivalent of collecting dust.

The group that got the most attention and praise and arguably
made the most substantive progress was the Immediate Action
Work Group, which addressed those communities, like Shishmaref,
in present danger. The group's achievement was to bring people
together from all relevant agencies and all levels of government, for
a coordinated response. For the six most at-risk villages, it identified actions and funding levels needed to prevent the loss of life
and infrastructure. It also recommended a set of policies to advance
more of the same kind of coordinated data collection and planning.
Recommended policy number three reads, "Assistance to communities in peril must utilize comprehensive integrated planning and
viable, future-oriented solutions with funding that allows for sustainability whether the community remains in place, uses a migration strategy, or needs to relocate."

Earlier, I'd spoken on the phone with Mike Black, the deputy
commissioner of the Alaska Department of Commerce, Community and Economic Development, who cochaired, with a representative of the Army Corps of Engineers, the Immediate Action
Work Group. Black was careful, in our conversation, not to over-
state Alaska's commitment to the villages whose coastal locations
are threatened. "The state's commitment has been to prepare a
statewide strategy. Appropriations are not a commitment." In
2008, when Alaska's bank accounts had swelled from sky-high
oil prices, then governor Palin and the legislature had agreed to
spend millions of dollars to address some of the most obvious
and immediate needs relating to erosion and flooding. The state
appropriations helped pay for seawalls, a barge landing, a planning process—and were meant to help attract additional federal
funding. For Shishmaref, the federal government came through

with more than $10 million for the first two phases of new seawall construction.

I pressed Black on the question of responsibility: Did the state and federal governments have a responsibility to protect or relocate threatened communities? "Not necessarily," Black told me, other than that the governments owned infrastructure in the communities—schools and such—that represented investments they needed to protect. "It's not a government responsibility to relocate communities. The government may or may not participate if communities choose to relocate."

The approach taken by the state had changed in one significant way, Black explained. When the Corps of Engineers had initially considered the problem, they'd assumed that entire communities would be relocated—re-created at new sites. That had resulted in the enormous cost estimates that made the job seem all but impossible, or at least unaffordable. "The state position is to consider if there's a safe site to move to in a flooding event, and allow the community to move to the site if they choose to." In other words, have an evacuation site and plan, so that if, for example, fall storms flood a village, the people can escape temporarily to a safer place, one with a minimum infrastructure. Black called this "pioneering infrastructure." "Then if individual households wanted to move to the new site, they could, over time, build new houses there." Schools, clinics, utility systems, and the rest would follow, as desired, needed, and funded.

The state was not going to dictate where or how people should live, Black emphasized. "It's about providing opportunities." The state did not have a stated commitment to keep people together in their communities or to help maintain their unique cultures.

"Environmental change is not an Alaskan phenomenon," Black said, "but we do have some unique aspects." Alaska, he said, had the opportunity to show the rest of the world something about adaptability. "Native villages can be a lesson to everyone. They survived hundreds and in some cases thousands of years in an inhospitable climate. Adaptation should be our strength."

When I'd first arrived in Shishmaref, I'd walked through the town to orient myself: from the Emergency Services building where visitors stay ($125 per night, no running water, a sign in the kitchen that reads THE SINK IS OUT OF ORDER—USE THE WINDOW) to the Lutheran church and its cemetery, past homes surrounded by the snow machines and four-wheelers that are the tools of modern travel and subsistence, around the occasional chained dog and the odiferous bins into which "honey buckets" were emptied. The "streets" were more like dirt trails, and more sand than dirt—a fine sand at that, as fine as pastry flour. On the lagoon side of the island, viewed across open tundra, dozens of skiffs rode at anchor. It was early morning, and there weren't many people about, but everyone I met was genuinely friendly, recognizing me as a visitor and asking who I was.

I turned next to face north, to confront the Chukchi Sea, wild with frothing whitecaps even on a windless day. From the abrupt end of a sand street, I looked across part of the new seawall—giant rock boulders I'd heard had been barged from a quarry near Sand Point in the Shumagin Islands, about eight hundred miles away—at the huge yellow bucket top of a heavy-equipment excavator working on a section farther along the beach. This was phase two of the federally funded work—750 feet of new revetment being added to the 600 feet completed the previous year behind the school and teacher housing, close to the community's huge diesel tanks and electric generators. Buildings, including one of the village's two stores and its fuel tanks, lay just feet away from the back of the new seawall. I walked to the gap between the two seawalls and over some rocks to the beach. There, the remains of some earlier, less successful armoring looked pathetically unsubstantial: bunches of rocks sunk into the beach and scattered, hunks of twisted metal, shreds of fabric that had once held rocks and sand. None of that earlier effort, clearly, had withstood for long the force of storm-driven waves.

I walked past the big blue school—by far the largest building in town, and a stone's throw from the sea—to where the phase one seawall ended; the shoreline there was badly eroded, with the remains of buildings and trash scattered over the beach. The main town infrastructure ended, and the bluff farther west was lined with simple tent and driftwood structures and drying racks—the places where people landed and processed their seals and fish, all right at the edge.

The next two seawall phases, under design, would, in part, help protect the washeteria and its sewage lagoon farther to the east. But there was no funding, as yet, for that substantial investment, some $20 million.

Besides cost, the problem with seawalls is that they don't really prevent erosion; they relocate it.[7] I know enough about coastal erosion processes and seawalls to know that wave energy will erode downward in front of a seawall, leaving no beach for sand on which to subsequently rebuild, and will deflect to the sides of a seawall—into the gaps I was looking at there in Shishmaref. I had personal experience. At my fishcamp on Cook Inlet, for years every summer my partner, Ken, and I, by hand, reinforced and added to barriers in front of the cabin that in 1972 had been built well back from the beach; the beach got steeper, the erosion increased on either side, and at last, one fall after we'd left, waves breached our barriers and tore them—concrete and rebar, bolted timbers and the side of an old boat, heavy rocks and sandbags—apart. We lost the cabin. And in Homer, a professionally engineered seawall built to protect a city road and neighborhood failed immediately, was repaired and re-inforced, and still requires constant maintenance.

Some months earlier, when I'd been in Fairbanks, I'd met with Dan White, director of the Institute of Northern Engineering at the University of Alaska. He'd told me, "Engineers solve problems. If you give me enough money, I can find a solution." He'd cited the success of the Dutch in engineering a way to live below sea level. For Alaska's eroding coastal areas, it was entirely possible to build huge seawalls to protect communities, at least until the longer-term problem of sea level rise would defeat them—or require additional engineering. But White was quick to acknowledge that just because something was possible didn't mean it should or would happen. He'd said, "It's always an issue of money."

Back at the community center across from the post office, women having a smoke on the porch told me that when they were girls the beach on the north side was long and gradual and they played out there. Now there was no beach at all, just ocean coming up to the steep seawall, which fell off, one said, "like a cliff." They told me they were afraid, and that their elders had said the island was sinking. They described a big storm a few years before, how frightening the crashing sounds were, how they could feel the pounding through the ground. One had left her house in the middle of the night and taken her family to a relative's house farther from the sea. Whatever happened, though, they wanted the village to stay together and not to move to cities. They knew the news: Nine homeless men, most of them Native, had died outdoors in Anchorage that summer, mostly from the effects of alcohol, though one had been beaten to death by teenagers who stole his beer.

The day following our boat trip, in the basement of the Lutheran church, I sat in on a meeting of the Shishmaref Erosion and Relocation Coalition. Thirteen members—drawn from the village (tribal) council, the separate city council, and the Native corporation—sat around a couple of long tables to conduct their regular business—approving minutes, reviewing a profit and loss statement, and planning for visits from government agencies. Since Weyiouanna had resigned as the transportation planner, Brice Eningowuk had taken over that post and, along with it, served as staff to the relocation committee.

Eningowuk is a handsome young man with army-short hair, rectangular glasses, and a ready smile. He did in fact do a stint in the army, between enrollments in the University of Alaska, and he was still working on a college degree in rural development. He'd told me earlier that relocation planning was a big part of his job, but he had other duties and wasn't giving it the same emphasis that Weyiouanna had. He was, however, overseeing a new study that was, again—even as all that work was being done over at the Tin Creek site—considering alternatives. The new study would come up with three locations, including the option of keeping Shishmaref right where it was, only with more protection. There were three criteria for the site selection: economic sustainability, cultural sustainability, and cost-effectiveness.

When I'd seen Eningowuk in his office, he'd pulled from his shelf the June 2009 Government Accountability Office report "Alaska Native Villages: Limited Progress Has Been Made on Relocating Villages Threatened by Flooding and Erosion."[8] The GAO report noted that "federal disaster programs have provided limited assistance and no comprehensive relocation program exists" and that "without a lead federal entity to prioritize and coordinate assistance, individual agency efforts may not adequately address the growing threat." It went on to note a number of structural problems that prevent the federal government from being more responsive. For example, cost-effectiveness criteria are a problem when the value of infrastructure in need of protection is less than the cost of proposed erosion and flood control projects. And, while there's funding to respond to disasters, there's no program to help villages avoid disaster. This report identified thirty-one "imminently threatened" Alaska villages and twelve that were at least exploring relocation options. Shishmaref was one of four villages "likely to move all at once, as soon as possible" both because of its immediate peril and because its options for a gradual move were limited. Then there was this: Some "officials" feared that building new seawalls could slow the momentum toward relocating by creating a false sense of safety.

Eningowuk was clear himself about the need for Shishmaref to relocate. He showed me an aerial photograph of the island. "It looks like there's still a lot of room, but all this space"—he pointed to the green tundra on the south side of the island—"can't be developed because it's in the airport's clearance zone." And besides, when there were storm surges, the water came up on that side and flooded the area. Shishmaref was slated to get twenty-one new homes, but there was nowhere to put them. The newer houses in town—the ones on the old airstrip, which was abandoned when the island got too narrow—were set up to be plumbed, if they ever got water and sewer connections or were moved to a place that had them. Those houses had external septic tanks right now, so that "honey buckets" weren't necessary, but the tanks needed to be heated in winter, and people couldn't afford the cost.

Another major problem on the island was the lack of freshwater. Eningowuk had pointed to the map again—a rectangular "pond" on the east side of the island. It was just a hole in the ground with a visible white liner, and it collected rain and snowmelt. Aside from the rainwater that people collected from their roofs, that was the only source of freshwater on the island. In winter, the only water came from a tank filled before freeze-up, or from snow and ice melted by individuals. Running water and flush toilets weren't an option for the island, even if they were affordable, because there simply wasn't the water.

And then there were drainage issues. The snowmelt used to drain, but now the seawalls were higher than the land and dammed it.

My head had begun to hurt from this litany of what seemed insurmountable problems. I asked Eningowuk what he wanted to happen.

"Personally, I hope we relocate to the mainland, someplace close enough to the ocean, and within the next ten years. I'm supposed to be planning this all out, but I'm not the decision maker." He flashed his smile. "I hope we move a lot sooner than ten years."

And what would he want people outside of Shishmaref to know?

"People have the misconception we should do this on our own. We need help, just like the people of Louisiana."

I wasn't sure that, after Katrina, the people of Louisiana felt that they'd gotten very much, or the right kind, or cost-effective help. But I didn't say that.

Now, at the coalition meeting, the group of mostly middle-aged men discussed the need to update the website and put out a news-letter.[9] (The website, badly out of date, included a timeline that began with Otto von Kotzebue coming by in 1816 and ended with "2009—April 30 move to new site completed," an optimistic projec-tion from two years earlier.) The mayor said that, if they were going to relocate, they'd need more local people trained to operate heavy equipment and do other skilled work.

Behind me, the outside of the basement windows were covered halfway up by drifts of the fine-grained sand. Opposite, one big wall poster celebrated Jesus, and another, THE INUPIAQ WAY, listed Inu-piaq values—among them knowing the language, sharing, respect for nature, humor, and spirituality. The group was talking about an upcoming meeting, when representatives from the Alaska Depart-ment of Transportation would present an update on the road recon-naissance study. This was when they would learn about subsurface conditions for the road and site, get a look at aerial photos and pos-sible routes, and hear the cost estimates. They scheduled the meet-ing at the community hall, displacing bingo, and arranged for door prizes so that as many people as possible would come.

The final item of important business was a notice that a del-egation from the coast guard, including the admiral of the whole shebang, was coming to town, via helicopter, for a quick tour. The delegation wanted to see the sewage lagoon and the landfill, and to speak with elders. I knew from my stopover in Nome that the coast guard was visiting this whole coast, preparing to establish a base for patrolling Arctic waters. The coast guard expected Bering Strait to become a major traffic route now that climate change had made ship passage possible, and its role—in addition to patrolling the border with Russia, serving as a base for scientific research, keeping an eye on fishing fleets, and performing rescue missions—would include "marine traffic cop." There might also soon be increased oil development in the Arctic. In the Nome paper I'd read that the number of ships that docked in Nome had increased from 34 in 1990 to 234 in 2008.

I imagined that the coast guard wanted to look over Shishmaref—the closest American community to the north side of the strait—as a harbor and perhaps a transfer site for receiving supplies and offloading ship waste. And I'd heard that they wanted to reach out to the Native people and learn about the environment and weather from those who themselves relied on thousands of years of local knowledge. Hence, apparently, the request to speak with Shishmaref elders.

Stanley Tocktoo, the chair of the coalition, had an additional concern. He told the others, "The coast guard is looking at the opening of the Northwest Passage. They might use icebreakers, right through where we do our sea mammal hunting." The coast guard would need to understand that the ice, already fragile for hunting, was not an obstacle to the local people. "That's our grocery store out there."

After the meeting, I talked more with Tocktoo, a wiry man with a long history of leadership in Shishmaref. His fear for the community and its ability to maintain its deeply rooted way of life was apparent as his words tumbled over themselves. "To the rest of America," he said, "we're nowhere, but we have families. We're doing this for our kids, so they don't have to move to cities. We can't lose our subsistence and our culture." He talked about the catch-22 of not being able to fund the relocation while also not being able to secure funding for things like a new, badly needed health clinic—because how do you justify new infrastructure if you're going to move? The last time there'd been a virus in town, there'd been 146 cases in one month. He was not the first to mention to me fear about swine flu coming to the village. Back in 1918, when the global flu pandemic had wiped out neighboring villages, Shishmaref had survived by posting sentries and turning away anyone who tried to approach.

At the school, which would open its doors to students in another week, I avoided touching anything near the WET PAINT signs. Science teacher Ken Stenek, wearing shorts, met me in his classroom and showed me on his computer the plant and animal encyclopedia he and his students had begun.[10] The encyclopedia contains photos and science information along with community information that includes the Inupiaq name, local observations, and the role (often as food) in the culture. Stenek, who is married to a local woman and has small children, is one of the few non-Inupiat to live full-time in the village. For ten years, he'd watched the community grapple with change; he'd watched four seawalls be constructed and the first, made of sandbags, deconstruct. He'd seen permafrost thaw and sand crumble, and storms blow in over the open ocean. He'd seen ice thin and weaken. "This year was a good ice year," he told me, "but the two before that were very poor." Three years ago a young man fell through the ice and died, in a place that had never been a problem before.

There had not been a major storm since 2005, but Stenek was keeping an eye on a typhoon that had just killed dozens of people in Southeast Asia and required the evacuation of millions; its waves had been twenty-six feet high. The Chukchi Sea, he said, is known as "the graveyard of the typhoons," and the remnants of that storm could hit Shishmaref in another month.

Stenek taught his students, to the degree he could, about global warming and climate change. He was hampered by the school district standards, which were prescriptive about what students needed to learn. He worked it in, though. He taught about energy transfer and the albedo effect of ice, and he'd had the kids calculate the carbon footprint for the village.[11] (The electric generators burn one hundred thousand gallons of diesel per year, adding six hundred thousand pounds of carbon to the atmosphere.) In 2007 he'd contributed an article to the magazine *Connect*, for teachers of science and math, called "Global Climate Change: What to Teach and When."[12] In that, he wrote about the media people who descended on Shishmaref as the "poster child" of global warming and who asked young people about climate change as though they were experts on it. He'd given a lot of thought about how to teach what was not required but relevant to student lives, appropriate for each age group, and how to do that without either imposing a political agenda or creating panic. He believed in empowering our future citizens, wherever they may live, to help solve a global problem.

I asked, what did his students, now, think about the problem? Did they engage with it? Were they troubled?

"It's just something they live with," Stenek said. "If you ask a kid here, 'what's global warming?' he'll probably say, 'erosion.' I'm just trying to help them get the facts straight. A lot of it is correcting information they hear."

In Shishmaref, as elsewhere, most people had heard from the media about global warming causing higher tides. But that's not Shishmaref's immediate problem. The Arctic has small tidal ranges, and if there's a little more water—or water volume—out there to rise and fall, that doesn't make a huge difference. Stenek's effort goes into helping his students understand how storm surges not blocked by ice erode a coastline and how thawing permafrost loosens the sand.

I recalled a conversation I'd had with a University of Alaska atmospheric scientist, Dave Atkinson, who worked on storm tracks and the question of whether, or to what degree, storm frequency and intensity were increasing along Alaska's coasts. The models that existed were global—not a very useful scale for dealing with local problems. He'd traveled to villages, including Shishmaref, to install offshore buoys for recording wave dynamics, and to ask local people questions like "Which way does the wind come from when you get the big waves?" as a way of ground truthing.

"People are definitely looking for help and answers," Atkinson had told me. "Should they stay or go? It's ultimately a political decision." In his opinion, the government bore some responsibility. The government had settled nomadic people in one place, "sometimes over the objections of local people who knew the locations were unstable." The villages inherited problems caused by the bad decisions of others, who ignored available information they could have used.

Lots of similar research—collecting data on local conditions and trying to link to global models to provide information that might be useful for understanding what to expect and prepare for in particular places—was going on all over the north and beyond. The involvement with local people was a good thing, though it was less clear to me what individuals could reasonably do with information that merely reinforced what they already knew to be happening. Storm surges were eroding the coastline. Permafrost was thawing. Now what? Stenek had made a point of saying he didn't want to create panic. Or despair, I assumed.

Stenek told me where to find, near the new playground beyond the school, two PVC pipes stuck in the ground. In another example of university research, a permafrost expert had dug a borehole there and involved the school in helping track permafrost temperatures.[13] Stenek's students were doing that—checking the gauges, recording change, watching the "permanently" frozen earth beneath their feet warm.

There are, of course, other low-lying places in the world that have dealt with erosion and flooding, some more successfully than others.

There's New Orleans, for example, with its system of levees and pumps. We know how well that worked. And it's not at all clear—at least to me—what lessons have been learned from Hurricane Katrina.

I've been to the Netherlands, where more than a quarter of the country lies below sea level and the Dutch have engineered a truly remarkable system of water management and land reclamations going back centuries. One day we visited a museum with a huge old pumping system, where exhibits and a docent told the story of the country's polders, dikes, canals, and water management. Although our docent, a retired ship captain, said he didn't know if he entirely believed Al Gore—as though Al Gore had somehow independently, or politically, come up with the idea of global warming—the Netherlands was preparing a national plan for raising the height of sea walls and dikes to meet rising seas and increased rainfall.

With a large, three-dimensional map of the country stretching out before us, I at last understood that most of the western part of the country is river delta behind barrier islands, and what a polder is. (A polder is land that used to lie under the sea but has been dried out by building a dike around it and pumping the water out.) All along our bicycling route we'd heard the saying *God made the Earth, but the Dutch made Holland.* It's more than a little true.

Despite our docent's skepticism, the Dutch in general—the public as well as scientists and policy makers—take global warming and climate change very seriously. Signers of the Kyoto treaty, they've pledged to reduce their carbon emissions significantly, and wind energy is a major area of investment. Although the classic windmills that moved water are mostly relegated to tourist attractions now, lines of towering wind turbines rise everywhere over the landscape.

The Dutch, it's said, paid more attention to the New Orleans disaster than Americans did, and have applied its lessons to their own planning. They expect to spend $25 billion in the next decades on additional water management infrastructure. This seems like a lot of money until you consider they already have $2.5 trillion invested in that infrastructure and that they have both the technology and the wealth to build ever larger dikes, seawalls, and pumping stations.

Importantly, though, the Dutch have also adopted a policy of "making room for water" and are surrendering land to floodplains. The greater danger to them from climate change is not rising sea level, which can be addressed with higher dikes and seawalls, but a projected increase in precipitation and the flooding of rivers.

The Dutch are also experimenting with floating houses, even the idea of floating cities. Amphibious buildings rise and fall with the water level, much like the floats in our Homer harbor move up and down with the tides.

Behind all that Dutch infrastructure and in those floating buildings: population density, great productivity and know-how, national wealth. Behind the Shishmaref seawall: a subsistence culture rich in ways that don't include dollars and cents.

Of course, there are places much worse off than Shishmaref, places where seawalls or a government-funded relocation would not even be considered. In Bangladesh, 140 million impoverished people live on a floodplain. The Pacific island nation of Tuvalu, with eleven thousand inhabitants, will soon be underwater and has already lost the two things essential to the lives of its inhabitants—palm trees that have died from saltwater infusion and fish that have disappeared as the corals that shelter them have bleached and died.

In Alaska, while Shishmaref waits for studies and relocation help, other villages are already moving. Newtok, a Yup'ik village about four hundred miles down the coast, was facing issues similar to Shishmaref's—permafrost thaw, erosion, flooding. For twenty-five years it assessed the problem and worried over the solution, and in 2003 it made the decision to move. The Corps of Engineers estimated the cost of relocating the entire village of 350 residents to higher ground nine miles away at $80 to $130 million, but local and state officials called that cost excessive and inflated. A locally directed organization called the Newtok Planning Group went at the effort piecemeal, choosing a location, getting a few small grants, building a few new houses in the new location. (This is the gradual model the state's Mike Black had suggested to me.) Alaska came through with $3.3 million for a barge landing at the new site and the design for a road from there to a planned evacuation center.

The new Newtok evacuation center, when funded and built, will shelter residents who might need to flee their flooding town in a hurry, and can later, when the move is completed, serve as a community center. (The building has been designed with help from the Cold Climate Housing Research Center in Fairbanks to be energy efficient; one aspect, suggested by Newtok residents, is to save both fuel and water by using simple steam baths instead of showers.) In the summer of 2009 the army and marines arrived with a landing craft and a five-year commitment to helping with road construction and the move. That help comes through a government program called the Innovative Readiness Training Program, which provides community assistance while doubling as a military training opportunity. The argument goes, if America is to be prepared to build (or rebuild) towns in war zones, we can practice at home and create something of value for our own people.

Another village that has begun a gradual move is Unalakleet, on Norton Sound about halfway between Shishmaref and Newtok. As residents have made decisions about new houses, they've moved away from the low and eroding village, into foothills served by an existing road to an air force site. The problem, a friend from there told me, is that getting to the new site requires better transportation than most people—who generally rely on four-wheelers and snow machines—have.

I thought about another village I'd visited—Point Lay on the Arctic coast.[14] That village was once located on a barrier island but had moved to the mainland years before, and then moved again, all before there was much permanent infrastructure to worry about. At one time the village had just about disappeared, its people gone off to live in other villages, towns, and cities, even outside of Alaska. In the early 1970s, when Native land claims had been settled, many came back. The late Dorcas Neakok had told me that all six of her children had gone away to school. In an earlier book I quoted her, "I tell them one of them have to be electrician, one engineer for the light plant. I must have been dreaming. Sounds like I was lying but it come true." Her children and others returned to Point Lay with skills to build and maintain a village committed to its cultural values but functional in modern services.

But now, I heard, Point Lay was worried about the source of its freshwater, a lake threatened by erosion. Its citizens were also concerned about a proposed coal mine that would turn the country thirty-five miles to its south into a giant open pit, with the coal destined for mercury- and greenhouse gas–spewing Asian power plants.

In the end, the situation at Shishmaref might best be considered as one of human rights. Worldwide, so many of the people who will lose their homes and livelihoods as a result of global warming are among the populations that, at least historically, contributed the least to the problem. The International Panel on Climate Change has estimated that, by 2050, there will be 150 million climate refugees; other estimates range much higher.[15] (Almost a fourth of the seven billion people on earth reside today within one hundred kilometers of the coast and less than one hundred meters above sea level.) Already, the United Nations reports, more people are being displaced by environmental disasters than by wars. We are woefully unprepared for addressing the needs of these citizens—or even for agreeing on what terms to use.

The Inuit Circumpolar Council, an international non-govern-
mental organization that promotes the welfare of indigenous people in Canada, Greenland, Russia, and Alaska, has for years spoken
about climate change as a human rights issue. In its "call to action"
in advance of the Copenhagen climate summit, it called on world
leaders to work with Inuit (the general term for indigenous Arctic
people, not commonly used in Alaska) in their efforts to adapt to
the new Arctic with, among other things, an adaptation fund. (This
fund, to provide tens or hundreds of billions of dollars annually for
financial support and technical assistance, is the one Hillary Clinton
pledged U.S. support for in Copenhagen, although details of who
would pay and who would receive were left for future discussions.)
Members of the ICC argue that vulnerable communities within
developed nations as well as undeveloped nations should be eligible
for help; past governmental actions that reduced the adaptability
of Arctic people—that is, settling them down among permanent
infrastructure—requires assistance beyond the communities' own
resources.

In 2005 the former chair of the ICC, the Canadian Inuit activist
Sheila Watt-Cloutier, petitioned the Inter-American Commission
on Human Rights with a claim against the United States for failing
to curb greenhouse gas emissions.[16] The commission decided against
hearing the petition, but Watt-Cloutier has continued to be an outspoken campaigner on the issue. In 2007 she was a nominee for the
Nobel Peace Prize and in 2008 was one of *Time* magazine's "heroes
of the environment." She told *Time*, "Most people can't relate to the
science, to the economics, and to the technical aspects of climate
change. But they can certainly connect to the human aspect." As she
continues to speak in international forums, her goal is to "move the
issue from the head to the heart."

Deborah Williams, the impassioned former director of Alaska
Conservation Solutions and, before that, Alaska's representative
of the U.S. Department of the Interior, said to me not long ago,

about Shishmaref and the other eroding villages, "I believe we have a significant moral and human rights responsibility to ensure that global warming does not result in the elimination of tribal heritage or the cultural richness of Alaska Natives' subsistence activities. The tribes most affected now have lived together and survived as tribes for thousands of years, and they are federally recognized as unique cultural units. They live off the land that surrounds them." She spoke about the archaeological evidence that the people of Shishmaref have occupied their island for at least four thousand years. "The cultural heritage and traditional knowledge associated with occupying that site is invaluable. We have a political responsibility—since they're federally recognized tribes—to ensure that they can continue to exist as tribes in a location near their current location, so that their traditional knowledge can be applied."

"Obviously," Williams told me, "the United States engaged in tribal annihilation throughout much of our history. We're more enlightened now, kinder and more respectful. And we know what we lost both as a nation and as human beings by exterminating tribes and moving tribes. We'll be judged as human beings and a nation by how we respond to this crisis."

Robin Bronen, a human rights attorney who has directed the Alaska Immigration Justice Project in Anchorage for many years, also thinks a lot about what's happening to the coastal villages.[17] She dislikes the term *climate refugees* used by the IPCC and others because *refugee* has traditionally referred to a narrow category of people who have sought refuge, mostly outside their countries, from violence perpetuated against them. For the people who have to move as a direct result of climate change and who will not be able to return home, she's coined a new word—*climigrants*. (Others have adopted other terms, with perhaps the most accepted being *climate-change-induced displacees* or *climate-change-displaced persons* —CCDPs.) As part of her work on a doctorate related to governance and climate change, she told me in a phone conversation, she's been developing the framework of a governance structure that has as its guiding principles the involvement of climigrants in deciding where and how they should move and commitments to assisting whole communities—not just individuals or households—to relocate. "If not," she said, "people will be dispersed."

For several years Bronen participated as an observer with the Newtok Planning Group, which she credits with "creating the roadmap" for other Alaskan communities and beyond, globally. "People get focused on the funding piece," she told me, "but we don't know the true cost. Newtok has primarily been using existing funding streams," directing them to the new site. One thing was clear to Bronen: The sooner communities and government agencies recognize that relocation must occur, the sooner funding can go to relocation instead of to disaster relief.

Alaska, according to Bronen, is the logical place to develop climigration principles and guidelines that can then be transferred to the rest of the world. In her work she's identified what should be governmental responsibilities: allow affected communities to be key players in relocation processes, ensure that families and tribes can remain together, protect subsistence use and customary communal rights to resources, safeguard rights to basic needs like housing and potable water, and implement sustainable development opportunities as part of the relocation process. This last point deserves emphasis. If a variety of socioeconomic problems can be addressed in the relocation process, the benefits will be multiplied, for the health of the communities and—to the degree they use less fossil fuel and create less waste—for the world.

Get the relocation piece right in Alaska and perhaps the trauma and expense can be lessened elsewhere. As Bronen warned, "I really think what's happening in coastal Alaska is going to be the story in much of the rest of the coastal United States."

Newtok's organized effort at staging a relocation might be the model for one kind of response. The village of Kivalina, home to four hundred Inupiaq Eskimos on a narrow barrier island in the Chukchi Sea north of Shishmaref, has taken a different route. As another of the six Alaska villages most at risk from climate-induced thawing and flooding, it is within a decade or less of becoming uninhabitable. In 2006 a new $3 million seawall built of metal cages and sandbags was built, and the day after its dedication ceremony, a storm took out a critical section. The next year the entire community had to be evacuated from the low island, six hundred feet across at its widest point, when another fall storm threatened. This is a clear case where building and rebuilding erosion control structures and evacuating and then returning residents to the vulnerable place don't make sense. Permanent relocation is required, and the questions to be answered are when and how—and who will pay. The cost of moving the community to the mainland has been estimated at between $95 million and $400 million.

For Kivalina, compared to Newtok and Shishmaref, there's been less cohesion in the planning process, and the community has undertaken a unique strategy. The village sued the energy companies residents claim are responsible for greenhouse gas emissions and, especially, for the industry campaign to distort the truth about global warming.[18] The lawsuit for unspecified monetary damages was filed in federal court in early 2008 against twenty-four energy companies—ExxonMobil and eight other oil companies, one coal company, and fourteen electric utilities. The complaint says, "Each of the defendants knew or should have known of the impacts of their emissions on global warming and on particularly vulnerable communities such as coastal Alaskan villages." The complaint also alleges a conspiracy by some of the companies, especially Exxon-Mobil, to "suppress the awareness of the link" between emissions and climate change "through front groups, fake citizens organizations, and bogus scientific bodies." (This strategy is similar to that used successfully against the tobacco companies in the 1990s, when it was established that cigarette manufacturers had lied about the consequences of smoking.) The law firms spearheading the suit are human rights ones—the San Francisco–based Center on Race, Poverty, and the Environment and the Native American Rights Fund.

As reported in *The New York Times*, the American Justice Partnership, a business-oriented group, has argued that the conspiracy accusations make the Kivalina case "the most dangerous litigation in America."[19]

In a 2009 ruling, a U.S. District Court judge dismissed the lawsuit on the grounds that it dealt with a political question properly reserved for the legislative, not judicial, branch of government. Kivalina has since appealed. The field of legal responsibility for global warming is a developing one, sure to reach the U.S. Supreme Court before we're done. No one seemed to think there'd be a definitive answer anytime soon, certainly not in time to save Kivalina.

One alternative the people of Shishmaref had turned down unambiguously was "colocation"—that is, moving the community to another, established one. The likely places analyzed by the Corps of Engineers were Nome and Kotzebue, both regional centers near Shishmaref, both with much larger and mixed populations. "That's not something we want to do," Brice Eningowuk had told me, emphatically. "Everyone here is family."

Shishmaref residents are certainly aware of the example of the King Islanders. King Island, a steep volcanic island in the Bering Sea, about eighty-five miles northwest of Nome, was inhabited by Inupiaq Eskimos for at least a thousand years.[20] As a winter home built along cliffs, it was surrounded by the biological richness of the Bering Sea—seals, walrus, fish, crabs, seabirds. In summer, the people typically migrated by boat to the mainland for different hunting, fishing, and gathering opportunities, and to trade. In 1959 the Bureau of Indian Affairs closed down the school, and the people were forced to move to Nome full-time. There, they lived on the south end of town in substandard housing and suffered economic and social ills along with outright discrimination. Some reversed the old migration pattern—for years, when school was out, spending some of the summer on the island.

Non-Native friends in Nome have told me that when they were growing up there the worst thing a person could be called was "a K-I-er" and that young people today still used the expression in derogatory name-calling. The community, described by outsiders as "clannish," struggles to maintain an identity that lives, in its heritage and heart, elsewhere.

We would not, in America in this day and age, either mandate moves or leave migrants and refugees entirely to their own devices, but the King Island experience lingers in people's memories and adds to their fears.

What do I think will happen to Shishmaref? Many people I spoke with, including some in Shishmaref, told me that, despite all the best intentions and all the desire and effort, they don't expect that the community will actually move. The cost is too great, the impediments too many. The most likely scenario, I believe, is that planning and studies will continue, but that the residents of Shishmaref will get tired of waiting, the anxiety that comes with every storm, and doing without water and sewer and an adequate clinic—infrastructure they would have if they knew they were staying, or if they were building in a new place. I expect that they'll gradually move away— the young people who might make a start elsewhere, and family by family—scattering to other villages, to Nome and Kotzebue, to Anchorage, as they already have begun to do, until only the most determined remain. Some—the most committed to a traditional life—might well move to the mainland and "live out," as some people always have, and others might still return seasonally, as the King Islanders did to their island for years after their move to Nome. But the village itself will eventually be gone, dropped into the sea, and the community bonds and culture that flourished in its unique fashion for so very long will be gone with it.

When I was first beginning to think about the consequences of global warming and climate change for Alaska's villages, a friend said to me, "For these communities that are already stressed, climate change will either be the glue that will help hold them together, or it will be the straw that finally breaks them."

The same thing could be said for the rest of us, all of us who will, individually and collectively, either find new ways of living that sustain ourselves and the earth as we know it, or who will not.

Shishmaref is just the beginning.

In Shishmaref, so many people I'd met had looked me directly in the eyes and asked, "How do you like it here?" or "What do you think of Shishmaref?" or "What do you think of us?" I had thought at the time it was a way of trying to assess me, but also an expression of pride in who they were, and also, perhaps, a small show of insecurity. Do we matter? Are we important enough to save? Is anyone going to help?

PART FIVE

THE OCEANIC REALM: BERING SEA

In a conference room in Bethel, Alaska, twenty-some Yup'ik elders from surrounding Bering Sea villages bent their heads over three tables spread with maps. In Yup'ik and the occasional English translation, they talked about the colored sections and shared their own personal knowledge of the parts of the Bering Sea near and sometimes not so near their villages, where they fish and hunt for walrus, seals, ducks, and beluga whales. Except for two women, they were all men, mostly in their seventies and eighties, mostly peering from behind eyeglasses. They wore knitted vests and fleece, or jackets with tribal names on their backs. David Bill, the chairman, wore a bright blue shirt and equally blue ball cap. Arthur Lake, the group's executive director, sported a diamond in one ear.

The maps were the result of earlier interviews with these elders and many others, about their subsistence uses and the habitats important to the fish and animals on which their families and cultures relied. The elders, members of the Bering Sea Elders Advisory Group, were checking the maps to see if they agreed with the lines that were drawn, and they were marking more detailed information about the times animals were in particular places, the conditions in which they hunted in different places, and the numbers of animals they had seen in different years.[1]

The elders were from small-dot places like Kwigillingok, Quin-
hagak, Mekoryuk, Toksook Bay, and Kipnuk, and they talked
together about changes they had seen. Most had long histories of
hunting and fishing in the Bering Sea, going back to the time of
kayaks and harpoons and knowing how to navigate by reading the
ocean currents. They had been told how things were by their own
elders.

At the table with the seal map, the men talked about ice thick-
ness and the danger of hunting on ice that's too thin. In an area they
marked for a lot of bearded seals, they noted that the ice is usually
thick enough by the end of November. "We stay home when it's not
safe," a white-haired man said. Someone else said, "We used to tell
the weather by the ice. Now we can't."

The table's scribe asked, "How do you tell the weather now?"

"TV," someone said, and they all laughed.

At another table, David Bill tapped his finger on a portion of
the fish map. The elders there were talking about their subsistence
catches of salmon and whitefish, anadromous species that live in the
Bering Sea and travel up the Yukon and Kuskokwim Rivers.

A couple of important lines were drawn on all the maps. One cutting through the Bering Sea was the international date line, dividing U.S. waters from those of Russia. The other, extending from
the south end of Kuskokwim Bay in jagged steps around Nunivak
Island and then west around St. Matthew Island before straighten-
ing north to intercept the date line, the elders referred to as "the
northern boundary." Above the line, put into effect in 2007 as a precautionary, interim measure, bottom trawlers shall not go. Even as
the Bering Sea warms and fish and ice coverage both move northward, the trawlers—those boats that drag big nets weighted with
chains and tires across the ocean floor—may not, for now, follow
them.

The line up to which trawling was allowed was already as close as
fourteen miles to some of the communities from which the elders in

the room had come, and places they'd marked for their fishing and hunting were in some of those same waters.

The ice is different now, the men with the walrus map were saying. Sometimes the winds blow it farther south, but then it goes out faster in the spring. It's thinner. The ice edge—that's where it all happens—is different; it's hard to know where it will be and how it will move. They have to travel farther to get to the walrus. That takes more fuel, and they don't know the area as well. It's more dangerous. Here—they pointed to a spot in Kuskokwim Bay. Here's a heart-shaped rock that only the best hunters go out to.

In 2011 the North Pacific Fisheries Management Council, responsible for most fisheries in Alaska's federal waters, will reconsider the northern boundary, and bottom trawlers may be allowed to follow the fish northward, into waters they haven't previously fished. Those same waters are home to ice-dependent sea mammals like walrus and seals, crabs, threatened species like the spectacled eider, and the Yup'ik, Inupiaq, and Siberian Yupik people who depend in profound ways on the health and bounty of the northern Bering Sea.

First, though, a large area above the line—called the Northern Bering Sea Research Area—is supposed to have a "research plan." The plan is primarily meant for research into the potential impacts of trawling on bottom habitat, but it is also meant to provide some protection for vulnerable species along with the subsistence needs of the people.

Over at the first table, the woman acting as a facilitator rolled up the maps the elders were finished with and laid out another one. "This is a *science* map," Dorothy Childers explained, making clear the difference between the maps generated from local and traditional knowledge and this new one, which had come from scientific data. "The science maps show where the animals are when you're not hunting them." The particular map was of Alaska's four species of eiders, sea ducks that nest on land but winter at sea. The men studied the map with interest, locating uninhabited St. Matthew Island far to the northwest and placing their hands on the circular shape marking the winter habitat of spectacled eiders. That part of the ocean was far from anywhere they knew and in winter well beyond the travels of any Native people.

Who would have thought that frozen place would also be home to such life? It wasn't until 1995 that researchers tracked a transmitter implanted in a spectacled eider to discover the wintering ground of that species. A fly-over and subsequent research confirmed that the entire world's population—some 360,000 spectacled eiders—winter in open-water leads in the otherwise frozen Bering Sea and in those leads dive to the bottom to feed on clams. Childers set a photo of one of these polynya (Russian for "little field") areas beside the map; the thousands of birds squeezed into it looked like grains of brown sand filling a crack in an otherwise vast expanse of white.

The elders looked to the areas they knew along the Yukon-Kuskokwim Delta and discussed the places marked there as eider breeding grounds. One man remembered that in 1983 there had been a lot of king eiders. Not anymore. "We don't hunt them like we used to," another said. When they were sea mammal hunting, they sometimes saw eiders migrating past.

Their eyes went back to the polynya area in the Bering Sea. "This needs to be protected," they told Childers. "Let the fish and the rest grow out there."

Childers wrote that down.

"We rely on the sea for subsistence," someone said. "All the sea. We need to take care of it."

The Bering Sea might best be known to most Americans as the setting for a ridiculously popular television show, the Discovery Channel's *Deadliest Catch*. I say "ridiculously" because most of this reality-type series involves watching giant crab pots being hauled over boat rails, with various numbers of king or opilio crabs in them, some worthy of the crews yelling "Yeah, baby!" and others not so much. Let me admit right here that I personally love this show. Regardless, the truth is that the words *Bering Sea*, if they mean anything to most people, bring to mind images of thirty-foot waves, broken ice, and exhausted men swearing at one other.

It is true that the Bering Sea, that semienclosed part of the Pacific Ocean that extends from Alaska to Russia and the Aleutian Islands to the strait also named for explorer Vitus Bering, can be a ferocious place in winter, when the crab fisheries take place, and that boats go down and men die on a regular basis there. It is also true that the Bering Sea, because of physical properties including its broad continental shelf and general shallowness, the movements of currents and ice, and upwellings, is a prodigiously rich biological basin, one of the most productive environments in the world.[2] Its biodiversity is profound: more than 450 species of fish, crustaceans, and mollusks; fifty species of birds including twenty million individual seabirds; and twenty-five species of marine mammals including the world's rarest whale, the North Pacific right whale.

The Bering Sea's great bounty has supported people who've lived on and around it for a very long time—"from time immemorial," as the Natives say. On the American side lie sixty-five communities, home to 27,500 people. Although this human population is small, the villages that line the coast—on the Russian side as well as the American—today remain intricately connected to all aspects of Bering Sea weather, seasons, and nourishment in all its forms. This part of Alaska was late to be influenced by the trappers, traders, and outside interests of all kinds, and it maintains more cultural intactness—including language and traditional foods—than much of the rest of Alaska, where cultural change came earlier and hard.

For the elders in the Bethel conference room, the Bering Sea is home, the center of their universes, their gardens and breadbaskets, the place of their ancestors back to the beginning. One said to me, "It's not the Bering Sea. That's the name from a newcomer. It's

Imarpik." *Imarpik* translates literally to "big container," identifying the sea as a big bowl, full of resources. Less literally it refers to the one ocean that means everything. The elders spoke of their own elders, and what their elders instructed. "My grandmother told me, you will protect the Bering Sea. When you talk about the Bering Sea, you're talking about me."

Today, though, the Bering Sea also feeds the world. The fish and shellfish catches on its American side make up almost half (by weight) of all fisheries production in U.S. waters. Dutch Harbor on its southern edge has ranked number one among U.S. fishing ports nearly every year since 1981. In the beginning, king crab was king. Now the largest catches belong to the trawl fleets—enormous schools of pollock caught in midwater (also known as pelagic) trawls out over the deep water and groundfish caught in bottom (nonpelagic) trawls on the continental shelf. In both cases huge cone-shaped nets sweep up everything in their paths, and in both cases there are environmental consequences. The midwater trawls catch tons of "nontarget" species, including salmon intended for subsistence and commercial fisheries elsewhere. The bottom trawls tear up the sea bottom—toppling corals, overturning rocks, busting apart crabs, scraping up the sediments that are home to the clams and worms that other creatures eat.

In the regional center of Bethel, forty miles up the Kuskokwim River from the Bering Sea, the elders who gathered to document their resource use knew about trawling, and they didn't like it. Many had been involved in efforts to "cap" the pollock fleet's bycatch— to make them stop fishing when they've caught too many salmon. They don't want the bottom trawlers to go any farther north; in fact, they would like to see them confined to a smaller area than they already fish. They want them to leave the bottom of the Bering Sea alone, in the wholeness that provides the habitat and food for so much else.

When the elders spoke, the throaty sound of strange consonants and catches, of Yup'ik words flowing and colliding, was simply beautiful. The skillful interpreter, Fred Phillip, sometimes translated passages to English, sometimes summarized, and sometimes—if the conversation was "internal"—just let it go. The Yup'ik was frequently peppered with enough English that I could at least figure out the general topic. Yup'ik speakers generally use English for numbers and dates—their own number system is a more complicated base-twenty—and, although they're good at creating new words, they've borrowed a certain amount of English. I heard in English "disaster declaration," "Magnuson-Stevens Act," "Norton Sound," "tribal consultation," "memorandum of understanding," "$1,000," and "2011."

These men might have lived subsistence lives, more familiar with hunting gear and judging ice and weather than with the teachings of Western education, but they were no slouches when it came to organizing and participating in modern governance systems. They knew the laws that affect how they live, and they knew the strength they bring, through tribal rights and their own citizenship, to influencing regulations and the decisions of government agencies. In addition to chairing the elders' group, David Bill, who lives in the village of Toksook Bay, served on a subsistence halibut board created by the National Marine Fisheries Service, the board of the nonprofit Bering Sea Fishermen's Association, and his local school board. Interpreter Fred Phillip was a leader in his own right; the natural resources director for the Native village of Kwigillingok, he has also served on many organizational boards and traveled dozens of times to Washington DC to represent the interests of his people before Congress.

Outside, the temperature was at zero, and the November sun skidded low across a pale blue sky. Snow machines zipped along the frozen Kuskokwim River, and taxis ($5 to anywhere in town) plied the icy roads. A thin snow cover was just enough to brighten the landscape: no trees but the wooden buildings squatting on pilings. Smoke drifted sideways from a few stovepipes, evidence of shifts away from expensive heating oil to the burning of wood pallets and cardboard. (There was talk of importing firewood from the forests of southeast Alaska.)

The elders all well understood why they had come to Bethel, and each of the three days, they were seated at the tables, ready to work, well in advance of starting times. They stayed in those seats for hours, more attentive than any meeting-goers I've seen in my life. Now and then a cell phone rang and one reached into a pocket to hold a brief and muffled conversation.

The elders knew that they had until 2011 to influence where the bottom trawlers go and to make their case for protecting the subsistence use that lies at the heart of their lives and culture. They knew that they couldn't just say, "We want to protect as much as possible of the sea that provides for us," and expect the rightness of that principle to prevail over the tremendous economic value of all those fish that might be caught if bottom trawling was allowed to follow the climate shift north. They would need to identify, in a way that resource managers and policy makers could understand and quantify, exactly what areas they and the animals depended on for their lives. They would have to present a concrete proposal—data—that said, this is the value here and here and here, and this is the reason this area—this exact piece of Imarpik—should be protected. What was once a wholeness already had lines drawn across it; they had to participate in the system that would further divide up the big container. The scientists knew science, but only they—the elders—held the wealth of generational knowledge about the animals and what they ate, the seasonal cycles, the way water and ice moved, and how things changed over time, all those interwoven aspects scientists called an ecosystem. And only they were looking out for the needs of their people and the future generations.

The elders, revered in their communities for their knowledge and
connections to the wisdom of the past, know about change. They've   *Ethos*
seen more than most, in every aspect of their lives. For years they'd
been speaking out about the changes they've seen in and around
the Bering Sea. They'd watched sea ice form later and retreat earlier and faster. They'd witnessed surprising storm patterns, different
movements of fish and marine mammals, new species showing up,
sudden die-offs of seabirds, unusual plankton blooms, and other
environmental oddities beyond their usual experience or what they
had learned from their elders to expect as "normal." They're well
aware that, as rich as the Bering Sea is, its productivity is less than
it used to be. They've seen steep declines in species of marine mammals, birds, and fish. They've caught smaller salmon and mammals
with thinner fat layers.

In my own travels through the Bering Sea, in the four years I
worked on adventure cruise ships and stopped in villages all the way
to Russia, I heard repeated concerns about the difficulty in predict-
ing weather or anticipating storms, about decreasing numbers of
fur seals at the Pribilof Islands and evidence that the young animals
were starving on the rookeries, about kittiwakes failing to lay eggs.
On a Russian island I looked down from a cliff top at thousands
of walrus hauled out on a single rocky beach. From our Zodiacs, I
pointed out schools of jellyfish and the fins of salmon sharks, and
very few of the endangered Steller sea lions. I explored the remains
of an ancient whaling culture in Russia, studied through fog the
more recently abandoned King Island village near Nome, and heard
from the people of Little Diomede about their reliance on winter ice for airplane access—and that shortening season. I watched
gray whales stirring up the bottom along the beach at St. Matthew
Island, was shown the hide of a brown bear that had ridden the ice
from Russia to St. Lawrence Island, and heard about hunters having to go farther after prey. I heard about the hunting party—with
children—that drowned when their boat overturned in a storm.

Scientists now were documenting the same changes local people had been reporting for years.[3] They spoke of ecosystem stress and nutritional stress, of "regime change." They studied ice and the relationship of ice to productivity. Regular surveys had shown that forty-five fish species had shifted their ranges northward. Predator species were altering their diets and sometimes traveling greater distance to find food. "Grabs" of the sea floor from research vessels were finding fewer clams and other benthic species.

Due to its remoteness, size, and often fierce weather, it has always been a challenge to conduct scientific research in the Bering Sea. If the science had lagged what local people observed, mounting data supported the need for a new approach to fisheries management. The old method had centered on single species; survey the "biomass" (how much of the species was out there) and then allow for a percentage take each year, based on what was guessed to be a "maximum sustainable yield." (In other words, fish those commercial species as hard as possible without depleting them.) Conservation organizations had begun hammering on the need to consider the entire ecosystem and be precautionary. They argued that fishery managers should look beyond the population numbers of commercial species and calculations of sustainable catches. In this new world, managers need to be able to predict population trends in a rapidly changing environment and factor in a new degree of environmental variability. In light of so much uncertainty, they need to manage conservatively, carefully track trends, and identify and protect ecologically important areas under stress from climate change. They need to do all this against the pressure of a high-stakes fishing industry that wants to catch as much "product" as can be justified.

And thus it was that tribes from the Bering Sea region, with a number of conservation organizations, in 2007 won that rare victory at the industry-dominated North Pacific Fisheries Management Council. The council unanimously agreed that as-yet-unexploited portions of the northern Bering Sea should be at least temporarily protected from an expansion of industrial fishing. The managers noted specifically that rising temperatures could result in a redistribution of fishery resources into and within northern waters and that they bore a responsibility for making sure that, before fisheries were allowed to expand, adequate protections would be in place for marine mammals, crabs, animals listed under the Endangered Species Act, and subsistence resources depended on by local people.

Dorothy Childers, representing the Alaska Marine Conservation Council, said at the time, "The Bering Sea faces diminishing sea ice and other uncertain changes caused by global warming. Now more than ever, it is important to prevent the introduction of new sources of impact like bottom trawling in the sensitive northern region."

During most of the elders' group gathering, Childers, a slight woman in a Shetland sweater and jeans, was nearly invisible. She sat off to one side, headphones for the translations around her neck, dark hair loose around her face, pen and notepad in hand. Only when scribes were needed for the mapping did she come to the tables and assist with questions for the elders.

This was not her meeting, and yet she was essential to it.

Since 1995, Childers had worked for the Alaska Marine Conservation Council as either its executive director or program director and had established a solid reputation for working with coastal communities. She'd earned this reputation because she genuinely cared—not just for the seals and the fish and unpolluted seas but for the people who depend on marine resources for their lives and livelihoods. She sees absolutely no contradiction between conserving the marine environment and supporting the people who use that environment. That ethic, in fact, is at the heart of all AMCC's work; the grassroots organization exists to protect habitat, prevent overfishing and waste, and promote "clean," community-based fishing opportunities. (In full disclosure, I was one of the organization's founding members in 1992.)

Childers, in her support role, looks like a shy person, nonthreatening. In fact, she's a brainy strategist, and a warrior, a force to be reckoned with. In addition to directing AMCC, she has sat on various marine-related panels and committees and is currently a member of the North Pacific Research Board (a Ted Stevens creation, with $1.6 billion to fund research that will "enable effective management and sustainable use of Alaska's marine resources"). Childers is also one of five international recipients of a 2007 highly competitive and prestigious Pew Fellowship in Marine Conservation.[4]

Childers's original idea for her Pew Fellowship was to address challenges of fisheries management in the Bering Sea in the face of climate change. In particular, she wanted to encourage Natives, fishermen, and field scientists to fully share their perspectives and help develop new approaches to managing fisheries in a way that would foster resilience to the warming ocean. She had in mind the development of a zoning plan to limit adverse fishery effects as fish move northward—and that local people would help drive policy changes regarding both fisheries management and climate change.

"So how do you think it's gone?" I asked her one evening in Bethel, while she and AMCC program assistant Julia Beaty taped together maps in a hotel room.

"Better than I imagined," she said, with a look that suggested she was still surprised by how it had turned out. "I'd envisioned using existing information to identify important areas that needed protection, but I didn't imagine this sort of engagement. The villages were fired up from the beginning." She'd sent information about the boundary issue out to villages, and David Bill, who understood the federal process, had stepped forward as a leader. Elders from eight tribes formed the advisory group as an organized way to provide traditional guidance; soon twenty tribes were involved, then more, until the membership reached thirty-seven and stretched all the way to Little Diomede in the Bering Strait. (A second elders meeting, like the one in Bethel, would soon be held in Nome, to gather the members from the northern region.) Childers and AMCC helped with fundraising and logistics. AMCC's western Alaska coordinator, a high-powered Inupiaq woman named Muriel Morse, supported the elders project by traveling to villages to work with tribal leaders and to interview elders selected by the tribes. Beaty, the assistant who had started out as an AMCC intern, learned to make GIS maps.

The Bering Sea Elders Advisory Group took on its own life, and Childers would claim little credit for any of it. She denied to me having anything to do with empowering others. "They're already empowered. It was totally the tribes that decided to speak out. All they need is access to information so they can influence decision makers." The information she could help with was how to put together what they knew, how to package it in a way that was not just acceptable in the Western, science-based, political world, but that would be convincing as well. She padded in sock feet across the hotel room. "What I do is just technical assistance. They know they have to make the case for what they want. They're the only ones who can do that. We're just helping."

The mission adopted by the elders' group doesn't speak to climate change directly but is driven by it implicitly. The goal is "to enable Alaska Native tribes to fully participate in the federal fishery management process regarding upcoming decisions affecting the Bering Sea." Their "deliverable," as we say in the world I come from, is to be a unified proposal justifying the protection of the areas most valued for both ecological significance and subsistence use. In other words, they hope to weave their traditional knowledge into the data and understandings of Western science, to help fishery managers decide how best to protect the Bering Sea—or at least key areas of it. The final product, Childers imagined, would be a proposal for protected areas, in the form of a booklet that would include maps, justifications, and the specific statements of individual elders. It would come from the tribes, with their endorsements.

On its web page, the group's executive director, Arthur Lake, is quoted: "Our people have survived since time immemorial due to a complete understanding and respect for the land and waters that provide food, clothing, and spiritual sustenance. We are now facing challenges before unseen by our people. This project engages our villages and will help our children to stay connected to their roots and the wisdom of the Elders."

In the Bering Sea, it's all about the ice. That puts it too simply, of course, but Native people and scientists know that ice plays an essential role in the life of the Bering Sea, just as it does in the Arctic. Sea ice is, of course, the habitat of species like seals and walrus. Algae grow on it, in turn feeding species that live under the ice and at the ice edge. The formation, movement, and melting of ice affect not just the sea's biological productivity but ocean currents and the exchange of heat between ocean and atmosphere, in an enormously complex system.

Scientists who speak of a "reorganizing of the Bering Sea biogeography" are just now teasing out some of the effects of climate and ice changes there. They're challenged by many factors—not just the difficulty of working in such an extreme environment, but by a lack of historical data, the complex interactions among processes, and the inherent uncertainties in how events will play out.

Always, the weather and climate in the Bering Sea have been both harsh and variable. Caught between the cold, dry Arctic air mass to the north and the moist, relatively warm air mass to the south, the climate and weather systems of the Bering Sea are influenced by natural cycles including the Pacific Decadal Oscillation (PDO), the Arctic Oscillation (AO), and El Niño/La Niña—as well as by global warming. We were, in late 2009, in both a cold phase of the PDO and an El Niño warming trend.

From temperature-related research, we now know this: Since 1950, the ice cover in the Bering Sea has decreased. (There is considerable variability here including, in 2008, winter ice extending southward past the historic mean, but the overall trend line for this period has been down. And aside from spatial coverage, the ice has gotten thinner.) We also know that, since 1980, water temperatures in the Bering Sea have increased by about 1.8 degrees Fahrenheit. (Again, lots of variability. Based on temperatures recorded at moorings, from 2001 to 2005 the southern shelf of the Bering Sea warmed; then in 2007–2008 it cooled.) A poster I studied in the basement of the Alaska Fisheries Science Center in Kodiak showed the relationship between ice cover and the catch of opilio crab (*Chionoecetes opilio*); the more ice, the more crab. It also showed the southern Bering Sea "cold pool"—an area of cold bottom water on the continental shelf, formed under ice—contracting and moving northward by 143 miles since 1982. The text read "As cold bottom water moves north, Arctic species (like opilio crab) are lost from the southern Bering Sea." When I visited the lab, they were preparing to chill water to replicate Bering Sea conditions and to test the effects on the metabolisms of various Arctic species.

The evidence—experiential and scientific—of a rich Bering Sea becoming less rich is backed by some decades-long data. One study of chum salmon weights since the 1960s showed a steady decline in size, indicating they were getting less to eat. In 2000 an analysis of carbon isotopes in historic samples of whale baleen suggested a 30 to 40 percent decline in average seasonal primary production since 1970. "Primary production" is, essentially, phytoplankton (those microscopic, free-floating, photosynthesizing organisms) at the base of the food chain, which feed everything above it.

This is what we know about phytoplankton production: It is generally controlled by sunlight and available nutrients, but in the Bering Sea it has also depended on seasonal sea ice. When the ice melts in spring, the influx of water with lower salinity encourages a "bloom" of phytoplankton. And, the ice itself supports the bloom, with the sea algae that grow on it. Change the ice coverage and the timing of the melt and you change the size, timing, and the species makeup of the phytoplankton bloom.

The Bering Sea has changed, in my lifetime, from a primarily cold Arctic ecosystem dominated by sea ice to sub-Arctic conditions. There are winners and losers as the result of this change. When there was more sea ice and it melted in the spring, the resulting bloom occurred before there were many zooplankton (mostly microscopic animals) to feed on it, and it tended to fall to the sea bottom and feed species that live there. The lack of sea ice results in a later (and smaller) bloom, which gets eaten by the zooplankton and other species in the higher parts of the water column before it can fall to the bottom. Thus, to mention just two commercial fish species, the biomass of pollock has in recent years increased dramatically (despite heavy fishing) and the flatfish known as Greenland turbot, which lives close to the bottom and likes cold water, has declined in equally dramatic measure. The very rich benthic (bottom-dwelling) communities of worms, clams, and crustaceans—on which gray whales, walrus, diving birds, and other bottom feeders depend—are less rich than they so recently were.

Scientists also worry about the mismatch of prey availability and predator needs. A later phytoplankton bloom prolongs the winter hunger period of fish and shellfish; many won't survive their juvenile stages. Meanwhile, warmer ocean temperatures may cause some species to reproduce earlier, before foods they need are available. Studies of phenology (the interactions between the yearly life cycle of a species and the yearly climate cycle) have shown that most species, around the globe, are advancing their breeding, hatching, budding, and migrating times.[5] In a California study, the common murre (a diving bird that eats mostly small fish and zooplankton) was found to be breeding a remarkable two months earlier in 2000 than in 1975.

The loss of ice in the Bering Sea is likely to have additional effects. More open water in winter may add to the severity of rough seas and increase the mortality of birds at sea. Warmer water requires cold-blooded fish to increase their metabolism, which requires more food; this is a particular problem for young fish, which rely on fat reserves to get through their first winter.

Even the Discovery Channel is doing its part to help educate its viewing public about the environment in which the *Deadliest Catch* crabs live.[6] A Q&A on its website discusses ice, the warming climate, and ecosystem research, and ends with a quote from oceanographer Phyllis Stabeno: "The one thing you can say is, it's going to change. And if you like what you've got, change may or may not be good."

On the first day at the Bering Sea elders' gathering, the elders listened (via their translator) to a presentation by Tom Van Pelt, the program manager for the North Pacific Research Board, about the science that organization funds. One of the NPRB's primary programs is specific to the Bering Sea—an integrated ecosystem research program to look at, among other things, changing ice and currents, food availability, and how those changes cascade through the whole system. The idea, Van Pelt said, is for the one hundred scientists working on specific projects to think beyond their particular projects and disciplines and try to gain a larger understanding of how all things relate and interact. After three years of field seasons, two years (2011–12) would be given to synthesizing the results.

I thought I detected in the room a certain amount of puzzlement. Were the scientists only coming to realize, at this late date, that all things were connected?

One of Van Pelt's slides, among those that showed scientists taking sediment and ice cores, collecting plankton, and darting walrus with satellite transmitters for tracking their movements, was a cartoon from *The New Yorker*. In it, several ladies in dresses were socializing around a silver tea service, and one was saying, "I know I should care about the bottom of the ocean, but I just don't."

Nobody laughed.

There were questions following the science presentation, and they were all about the effects of bottom trawling on the ocean floor and the bycatch caught in trawlers' nets. These were not parts of the NPRB's program, and Van Pelt could only say that he wasn't the right person to ask about those specifics. The science currently being conducted is more basic to the workings of the Bering Sea, though I knew the scientists would agree that maximum sharing of information—science, traditional knowledge, the effects of fishing and other activities—would be a good thing, something to work toward for the holistic understanding they sought.

The elders' immediate concern about trawling was whether areas for bottom trawling would be expanded in the Bering Sea, but they also expressed alarm about the amount of pollock fishing taking place in deeper waters—and the bycatch from that fishery.

The most valuable fish (considering volume) in Alaska and the world's most abundant food fish is one that most Americans wouldn't recognize and may never have even heard of. Alaska pollock or walleye pollock (*Theragra chalcogramma*), a North Pacific member of the cod family, is a modest-looking, one- or two-pound, speckled fish with a lot of fin area, top and bottom. Landings of pollock from the Bering Sea are the largest of any single fish species in the United States, some 2.5 billion pounds a year, valued at hundreds of millions of dollars. On an individual basis, pollock is a low-value fish; with its white flesh and mild taste, it ends up not in fish markets or fancy restaurants but made into fish sticks, fast-food fish fillets, and artificial crabmeat. Since the late 1970s, as a result of changes in the Bering Sea, pollock have done very well; only recently have their numbers begun to drop and catches been reduced.

What both fishermen and scientists have found is that pollock are indeed moving northward. Generally, pollock spawn each winter in the southern Bering Sea, near the Aleutian Islands, then follow their food (plankton and small fish) north as waters warm in the spring. The bulk of them, following the outer contour of the continental shelf, now migrate to and beyond the international border with Russia. In effect, Alaska's pollock are becoming Russian pollock.

Andrew Rosenberg, a former deputy director of the National Marine Fisheries Service, was quoted in the *Los Angeles Times* in 2008: "It [the northward pollock movement] will be a food security issue and has an enormous potential for political upheaval."[7] He expected that pollock would be a test case in a growing pattern of fish driven by climate change across jurisdictional borders.

Once in Russian waters, the pollock are caught by Russian fishermen in a poorly managed, probably overexploited fishery that's known to be plagued by lax enforcement and poaching. Catches there have been increasing as the Alaskan catches have been throttled back to stay at sustainable levels.

Pollock is just one of the species moving north in the Bering Sea, but because of its enormous economic value, it has gotten serious attention. Twenty-five years of scientific surveys have shown that dozens of other fish species are also shifting to the north.[8] The range shift—thirty miles for pollock, thirty-four for halibut, fifty-five for opilio crab—is occurring two or three times faster than that of terrestrial species. According to the scientists, these species appear to be shifting in response to the extent of seasonal ice, itself moving northward and correlated to climate change.

As vital as the Bering Sea is for the men and women meeting in Bethel, the climate change–induced threats we see there extend far beyond Alaska's shores. It's not just the Bering Sea's rich ecosystem that's at stake, it's also the life support systems that the Bering Sea influences and the entire world needs.

If we know little about the effects of global warming on the Bering

Sea, we know barely more about those effects on any of the oceans—which cover three-quarters of our earth and house 90 percent of the planet's biomass. Compared to land, oceans have been inadequately studied; everywhere, ocean research is difficult, resource intensive, and expensive. The Intergovernmental Panel on Climate Change, for example, gave little attention to the marine system.[9]

Consider: Ocean temperatures may be a better indicator of global warming than air temperatures, because the ocean stores more heat (90 percent of the heat in the earth's climate system) and responds more slowly to change. Recent studies suggest the ocean is warming 50 percent faster than the IPCC reported in 2007 (and that thermal expansion rates and sea level rise were thus also underestimated by a similar amount). The next IPCC report is expected to give greater attention to ocean science, including the uncertainties in understanding and modeling climate change because of deficiencies in the knowledge base.

What we do know at this point is "big picture"— global warming affects ocean temperatures, the supply of nutrients that enter the ocean from the land, ocean chemistry, marine food webs, wind systems, ocean currents, the volume of ocean water, and extreme events such as hurricanes. The ecological responses to these are already playing out in processes ranging from primary production (where all the eating begins) to biogeography (where organisms live) to evolution.

Considerable attention has been given to the effect of warming on thermohaline (*thermo* as in temperature and *haline* as in salt content) circulation (also known as the ocean conveyor belt), which is what moves both energy and material around the world and thus has a huge influence on climate. Most of that attention has gone to the possibility of the slowing, or even shutdown, of the North Atlantic "conveyor." In the North Atlantic, pools of cold, dense water sink, pulling warm surface waters north from the tropics. With warming and the addition of freshwater from the melt of glaciers and the Greenland ice cap, the sinking of cold water has lessened in recent years. A map of the path of the thermohaline circulation looks somewhat like a picture of the human body's blood circulation; blue lines mark the deepwater currents, red the surface currents, and they all tie in and keep moving.[10] The oldest waters, with a transit time of some sixteen hundred years, end up in the North Pacific, finally in the Bering Sea. Clearly, if that first deepwater formation in the North Atlantic quits on us, the entire ocean circulation will be altered—kind of like your heart stopping.

There are many other implications of climate change for our oceans, poorly understood at present. A warmer ocean will hold less oxygen, for one thing. A warmer ocean will increase stratification, potentially locking nutrients away from those who need them. A warmer ocean with less ice appears to be freeing up mercury and other pollutants, raising contaminant levels throughout the food web and accumulating at the top, in marine mammals and those who eat them.[11] A warmer ocean already appears, in the Arctic, to be releasing methane clathrate (hydrate) compounds—large frozen methane deposits that lie mostly under sediments on the ocean floor, though some also underlie permafrost on land. Methane, remem-*Dct* ber, is roughly twenty times more potent as a greenhouse gas than carbon dioxide. The carbon in these frozen deposits is thought to exceed that in all other fossil fuels on earth combined. Not to be too alarmist here, but there is strong evidence that runaway methane clathrate release may have caused major alterations of the ocean *Pathos* environment and earth's atmosphere on a number of occasions in the past, most notably in connection with the Permian-Triassic extinction event (the Great Dying) 251 million years ago. At that time, 96 percent of marine species and 70 percent of terrestrial vertebrate species went extinct.

Of the nine "tipping elements" scientists have identified where global warming could push the world past tipping points to force abrupt, potentially irreversible changes and large, long-term consequences for the earth's climate, seven relate to the ocean and its dynamics.[12]

While warming itself alters the chemistry of the ocean, so does the absorption of carbon dioxide from the atmosphere.

When I first talked to Dorothy Childers about her work with the Bering Sea elders, I'd asked if the elders involved in the project were also considering ocean acidification. Her face had taken on a pained look. "No," she said. "It just hasn't come up because we've been so focused on documenting culturally important areas we want considered in fisheries management. The combination of a warming Bering Sea and ocean acidification is a lot to swallow all at once."

At the Bethel meeting, I never heard the words *ocean acidification*. In a context of the need for his elders to add their knowledge to the scientific system, one younger man who participated spoke of fish becoming smaller as a result of the ocean's "carbon dioxide absorption." And perhaps it had been suggested in the presentation about research, when Tom Van Pelt showed slides of water sampling—how samples were taken at different depths to see what lived there, and to check temperature and chemistry.

I can track my own education about ocean acidification by looking in a file folder in my office. The first clippings are from 2006, when a report by two dozen concerned scientists was mentioned in *The Washington Post* with a headline "Growing Acidity of Oceans May Kill Corals." Later that year Elizabeth Kolbert's article "The Darkening Sea: What Carbon Emissions Are Doing to the Ocean" appeared in *The New Yorker*. In 2007 the headlines proliferated and grew more urgent: rising acid levels threaten shellfish, oceans' growing acidity alarming, oceans are being choked to death. Dorothy Childers's organization, the Alaska Marine Conservation Council, took an early lead in bringing "OA" to the attention of its membership, made up largely of coastal residents and commercial fishermen. AMCC spearheaded the development of a "coastal community climate change compact," adopted by a number of municipal governments in support of policies, actions, and initiatives aimed at mitigating both climate change and ocean acidification.

"Climate change's evil twin," Richard Feely had called acidification, on an AMCC-sponsored visit to Alaska early in 2008. At that time, Feely, a chemical oceanographer at the National Oceanic and Atmospheric Association's (NOAA) Pacific Marine Environmental Lab in Seattle, was still largely introducing ocean acidification to people hearing about it for the first time. Even at that late date there was no direct government funding for research on acidification, something he lamented to me when we met for lunch. A mild-looking man, with graying hair and studious glasses, Feely told me that in the course of studying the ocean carbon cycle, he'd found himself on the front lines of discoveries that were truly alarming, and the lack of direct research coupled with the ticking of the clock compelled him to speak out. In 2007 he'd testified to Congress that ocean acidification was an emerging scientific issue in need of a coordinated research program; he called it "one of the most significant and far-reaching consequences of the buildup of anthropogenic carbon dioxide in the atmosphere."

Simply put, ocean acidification (a term coined in 2003 by Ken Caldeira and Michael Wickett of Stanford University) is "the other CO_2 problem."[13] All that carbon dioxide we've been putting into the atmosphere hasn't stayed in the air. About 30 percent of all human-caused CO_2 emissions—which include those resulting from land clearing, cement production, and other activities, as well as burning fossil fuels—end up in the oceans. Today the oceans hold about 140 billion metric tons of human-contributed carbon.[14] Scientists used to think this "buffering" of global warming was a good thing and even tried to think of ways to direct more CO_2 into the oceans. The oceans are so enormous, after all. Who ever imagined that humans could significantly change their chemistry? But that is, in fact, what has happened.

As we might recall from high school chemistry, pH measures the acidity of water, with 7.0 being neutral. Surface ocean waters are slightly alkaline, ranging from 7.8 to 8.5, and polar waters are less alkaline than the global average. In the last two hundred years, the global average pH has dropped by about 0.1. That doesn't sound like much, except the pH scale is, like the Richter scale for earthquakes, logarithmic; that is, a 0.1 decline represents a 30 percent increase in acidity.

Maybe even that doesn't sound so frightening, until you consider that by the end of this century, seawater pH is expected to drop by as much as 0.3 to 0.4, a 150 to 200 percent increase in acidity. The last time it was that acidic was more than twenty million years ago. Since the atmosphere and ocean normally work to establish an equilibrium, balancing out their gases, the ocean will be absorbing atmospheric CO_2 for a long time to come, even if we were to stop burning fossil fuels today.

To be clear, it's not that ocean waters are turning to acid. As the CO_2 is absorbed from the atmosphere by the ocean, it mixes with water to create corrosive carbonic acid. The water becomes less alkaline, thus more acidic. The danger of this acidification is that marine organisms have evolved to thrive within certain pH ranges, and the abrupt change in chemistry will stress them in ways only now suggesting themselves. For one (big) thing, the dissolved CO_2 (by creating carbonic acid and depleting carbonate ions) reduces the calcium carbonate available to shell builders including corals, crabs, mussels, clams, snails, oysters, sea stars, and many planktonic calcifiers at the base of the food chain. The chemistry problem is referred to in scientific terms as "undersaturation with respect to aragonite," with aragonite being a principal form of calcium carbonate.

Some scientists have likened the effects of acidification to osteoporosis, the disease that in humans causes the thinning of bone tissue and loss of bone density over time. If you don't have the material with which to build structures, the structures will be compromised.

Carbon dioxide is more soluble in cold water than in warmer water, and areas closest to the poles are expected to be the first affected by acidification.[15] And it's not just the amount of anthropogenic CO_2 that's a factor in cold waters. Other processes work in combination to increase acidification and lower the concentrations of forms of calcite used in shell building.[16] There's the freshening of water as ice melts, increased biological activity after ice melts (which produces more CO_2 when organic matter decays in subsurface waters), and upwellings of low-pH waters—all contributors to the problem.

Feely and colleagues had been involved in water sampling all along the West Coast, from Mexico to Canada; he was the lead author of an article published a few months after his Alaska visit in the journal *Science*, detailing the analysis that showed surprisingly acidic waters.[17] The authors had not anticipated that deep ocean waters would, through the process of upwelling, already be topping the continental shelf and carrying corrosive waters to the biologically productive areas close to shore. Already, a large section of the North American continental shelf was affected by ocean acidification, and so likely were other shelf regions. Some pH levels were measured at 7.75. This was one hundred years earlier than the models had predicted.

How such acidification was affecting the complex ocean processes and interwoven ecosystems was not at all clear. There was almost no data about what was actually happening to marine life or systems. Feely emphasized to me, "The Bering Sea is where we really need to know what's happening."

Water sampling along Alaska's coast had shown that the most corrosive waters lay at the edge of the continental shelf and were rising at about a meter a year in the water column. The Bering Sea—where the water was not only cold but "old"—having risen from the deep after traveling the ocean's conveyor belt, picking up carbon all the way—was thus perhaps most at risk. Feely feared that acidification would harm Alaska's deepwater corals before those corals, first discovered just two decades ago, have even begun to be studied. While tropical coral reefs have gotten a lot of press due to acidification and "bleaching," it's Alaska's slow-growing corals, themselves essential habitat for so many northern species, that appear to be most vulnerable. When the acidic waters reach up over the shelf, "where the critters live," Feely expected dramatic effects.

What those effects might be are suggested by laboratory studies. Preliminary results had shown that increased CO_2 and acidification—even at levels already appearing in ocean waters—make it more difficult for organisms to form shells and tend to dissolve structures already formed. Observed results had included thinner and more porous shells, decreased fertilization rates, reduced growth, impaired oxygen transport, mortality, and greater susceptibility to disease. Juvenile stages are especially vulnerable.

Results, though, have not been uniform, and they depend in part on the type of calcium carbonate an animal makes and the ability of species to "pump out" hydrogen ions and give themselves more carbonate to work with. Recent studies have suggested that some crustaceans, like lobsters, are able to build *stronger* shells in response to more acidic water.[18] However, it's not clear what the cost in energy of such a response might be, or what happens to such animals at different life stages and if other species they depend on for food are compromised by the same acidification.

In Alaska, researchers at NOAA's Alaska Fisheries Science Center in Kodiak have experimented since 2006 with king crab larvae and altered pH levels. Preliminary results demonstrated that more acidic water, matching what modeling says will be the average ocean pH by the end of this century, reduced the survival, growth, and calcium uptake of the crab larvae as they grew to juvenile stages. The Kodiak studies were hampered by difficulties in controlling the pH levels, which were set by adding hydrochloric acid rather than CO_2, and when I visited in 2009, the lab was being fitted with a more complex system to deliver actual CO_2 and allow for the study of not just pH levels but the whole carbonate cycle.

Bob Foy, the affable director of the Kodiak lab, had been away at crab meetings when I was in Kodiak, but when I caught up with him later by phone, he told me that acidification research funding was just beginning to come through the system.[19] "Ocean acidification didn't hit the radar screen in the scientific community until two years ago. It takes that long to react. Now everybody's looking at it." In terms of research spending, Foy thought acidification would soon be equal with climate change.

None of the study would be easy, though. In normal circumstances, ocean chemistry changes all the time, with pH going up and down all day long depending on what's happening in a given piece of water—respiration, mixing, warming, and cooling. "It's hard to tease out what an animal's experiencing in everyday life," Foy emphasized. Physiological responses were complex, and there were differences between what an animal could tolerate in the short-term versus long-term effects of environmental change.

Although the focus at the Kodiak lab was on the commercially valuable crab species, Foy and his fellow researchers wanted— needed—to know what changes acidification might bring to the entire marine ecosystem, with all its intricate processes and relationships. "Our whole goal is to manage the stocks," Foy told me. "We manage based on what we know about them, but we have to factor in everything else that's happening." Coastal residents who depend on the crab and other fisheries need time to get ready for the changes ahead, in the water and in the management system. "We're trying to do two things. First, build robust models to help us with predictions. Then, build in a buffer that accounts for uncertainty. We need to leave a buffer for what we don't understand." He paused. "There's a lot we don't understand. We're just at the beginning of our knowledge about how this is going to impact animals."

On his Alaska trip, Richard Feely presented a slide show to a packed house at Homer's Pratt Museum. The audience, which included a large number of commercial fishermen, sat especially upright when Feely showed photos of pteropods—planktonic snails (or, in translation from the Latin, "flying feet") that are, Feely explained, "a prime food source for much of our salmon, herring, and pollock." Juvenile salmon, especially, depend on pteropods; one study of pink salmon showed that pteropods made up 60 percent of their diet. Predictions are that a 10 percent decrease in pteropods will lead to a 20 percent drop in mature pink salmon weight.

"We're moving evolution in reverse," Feely said, showing a picture of a mass of jellyfish. It's not that the marine ecosystem will die from acidification. It will shift, with huge repercussions for the entire food web including those "higher" species so commercially valuable. As calcifiers are compromised—as some decline and possibly even disappear from the ocean—noncalcifiers will take their places. Durable jellyfish, among the most ancient creatures in the sea, are able to tolerate CO_2-rich waters and, at least in warm latitudes, increase and spread as water temperatures warm. But relationships are never simple in the ocean, and the effects of increased acidification, again, won't be uniform even among jellyfish; a study of one jellyfish species—the red paper lantern jellyfish that lives off the coast of Japan—found that its juvenile stage roosts in pteropod shells.

During the 1990s the numbers of jellyfish in the Bering Sea ballooned to forty times what they were in 1982, and their ranges expanded. They were so numerous they interfered with commercial fishing operations. But then, their populations crashed and returned to more moderate numbers, leaving biologists to still puzzle over the relationship between jellyfish numbers and temperature, acidity, available food, and other factors.

Feely mentioned a *National Geographic* article, and that night I found it in my magazine pile.[20] Among a series of photographs of marine microfauna was one of a very beautiful pteropod, with its incredibly fragile shell and the "foot" that looked like a pair of gossamer wings. There was a separate series of photos of a pteropod shell exposed to seawater resembling that expected in the Antarctic Ocean, in terms of its CO_2 concentration, by the end of the century; in just two days of exposure the pteropod shell is pitted and turning opaque, and at day forty-five all the carbonate has dissolved, leaving what looks like snot.

In the same *National Geographic* article, a pair of maps shows the relative corrosiveness of oceans in 1995 and, based on computer modeling, in 2100. The first map has Arctic and Antarctic waters already leaning toward acidity, while most of the oceans, a deep blue on the map, are not at all corrosive. In the second map, based on assumptions that CO_2 emissions will continue to rise unchecked, the colors are startlingly different—red-hot north and south and green yellow—midrange on the corrosiveness scale—throughout the rest of the world's oceans; the blue is entirely gone. At that point, the text reads, scientists expect that polar waters would be hostile to any organism that requires a carbonate shell, and tropical corals would be beyond saving except in enclosed aquaria where the water chemistry can be controlled.

A year and a half after Feely's talk, another ocean scientist came to town.

First, we ate tanner crabs (*Chionoecetes bairdi*), pulled from a pot in Kachemak Bay just a couple hours earlier and cooked in a big kettle at Alan and Mindy Parks's Alaska Ridgetop Inn in Homer. Alan is, among other things including commercial fisherman, photographer, photography teacher, and innkeeper, a community organizer for the Alaska Marine Conservation Council. He had invited a number of locals involved in commercial fishing and oyster farming to come meet Jeremy Mathis, from the School of Fisheries and Ocean Sciences at the University of Alaska Fairbanks.

The fields of fireweed outside the windows were as brilliant as any we could remember—a result, perhaps, of the dry summer or the dustings of volcanic ash we'd gotten earlier in the year. Alan was quizzing his fourth-grader, Ella. "What's another name for tanners?"

"Snow crabs."

"And bairdi. That's the scientific name."

We dug into the crabs, tearing their shells with our hands and swabbing the tender leg meat in melted butter. I imagined we were all sharing a couple of simultaneous thoughts—how much we love to eat crab from our bay and that those crabs might not always be with us.

Mathis had been on statewide public radio a few days earlier, talking about his studies of ocean acidification.[21] Everyone in the room already knew about ocean acidification, but what we hadn't heard about until very recently were the details of Alaska-specific research.[22] The pH of seawater in Alaska's Chukchi and Bering Seas and the Gulf of Alaska, where Mathis had been sampling, was, he'd said on the radio, "already low enough to be corrosive to shell building." He'd also said, "This isn't a case of talking about an impact a hundred years from now. This is an impact that we're going to see over the next decade, that could potentially disrupt all the major fisheries in Alaska."

Mathis is not an alarmist kind of guy. Like Richard Feely, he's a chemical oceanographer—a youngish and slightly nerdy one, wearing a very short Vandyke-style beard and, that evening, an orange sweater and city shoes. His expertise is in the cycling and fate of carbon and nitrogen in marine environments. But he, like Feely, thinks that scientists ought to communicate with people other than other scientists, and that the threat of acidification needs to be part of public discourse. He had begun to talk about his work outside of professional conferences and classes, with whoever wanted to know.

When we'd filled up on crab and garden vegetables, Alan showed part of the documentary *A Sea Change*, about ocean acidification.[23] In the film, Sven Huseby, a retired educator, interviews various scientists, gets charmed by the swimming pteropods he likens to angels for their delicate beauty, and tries to explain what's happening to the ocean to his five-year-old grandson. "The power to effect change begins with knowledge," the cheery Sven tells us.

We watched as scientist Victoria Fabry told Sven how she accidentally discovered the effect of acidification on pteropods. She'd collected a number of them in a jar—too many, as it turned out. The pteropods respired, adding carbon dioxide to the jar's seawater, and their shells turned opaque and began to dissolve.[24]

I'd seen the film before and thought it did a great job of explaining the issue in human terms, though perhaps it tried too hard sometimes to spin the seriousness into something lighter and more entertaining, with kid-cuteness and silly music and an ending that suggests we can solve the problem by adopting renewable energies.

We all need hope, certainly.

Mathis had already told me about a presentation he'd made a couple months earlier at a North Pacific Fisheries Management Council meeting. It was an informal presentation, open to anyone, and about seventy people in the fisheries business had attended. He characterized the collective response as, "If we can't do anything about it, we may as well keep exploiting the resource just as we've been, as long as we can, until it's gone."

After the film, Mathis told us about his Alaska-specific studies that, like Fabry's work with pteropods, had an element of accidental discovery. Originally, he'd simply been looking at the carbon cycle in Arctic waters. He was certainly aware of the buildup of carbon dioxide in the deep oceans and the change that might make in ocean chemistry, but it had not occurred to him that he'd find actual acidification already happening. When he checked his samples from the Chukchi Sea, he discovered higher than expected levels of dissolved carbon dioxide and an aragonite undersaturation. It was not that shells were dissolving, but the undersaturation meant that the ability of organisms to build their shells was made more difficult, requiring more of their energy.

"That's energy they will not be spending on growth, foraging, and reproduction," he told a quiet room.

After his findings in the Arctic, Mathis did similar samplings in the Bering Sea and in the Gulf of Alaska—the waters near Homer. He found the same results of low pH and low aragonite saturation states, with the most troubling numbers coming from the Bering Sea.

In addition to what we already knew about the Bering Sea, with its old, cold water and broad shelves, Mathis theorized that its very productivity might be contributing to acidification. The spring plankton blooms and resulting biological fecundity all the way up the food chain use oxygen and emit carbon dioxide, from both respiration and decomposition. And as the waters warm, productivity should increase, exacerbating the problem.

"It's not a good time to be a crab in the Bering Sea," Mathis told us. "I don't think I'm overstating it. Alaska will be ground zero for ocean acidification, just as it is for climate change. Everywhere we look in Alaska we're finding areas that are already corrosive."

Could it be that Alaska's waters were just naturally corrosive, and its marine life already adapted to those conditions? A disturbing part of Mathis's work was that, when he subtracted from his data the amount of dissolved CO_2 that's come from human sources, the argonite undersaturation disappeared. That suggests that the undersaturation is anthropogenically induced—and that organisms living in that water are not adapted to the conditions in which they are now living.

We were left with a very sobering thought: The same things that have made Alaska's oceans so incredibly rich may make them the most vulnerable to ocean acidification.

There was also this: In the cold Bering Sea waters, marine invertebrates in particular have low metabolic rates and are consequently
slow to develop and grow. Compared to those elsewhere, they will
have fewer generations to adapt to change. Not only will polar
waters be the first to be affected by ocean acidification, their calci-
fying animals may be most vulnerable. Some of the calcifiers most
at risk, according to a paper coauthored by Mathis, are clam species
in the northern Bering Sea—the ones that live beneath the open-
water polynya just south of St. Lawrence Island and are fed on by
all those eider ducks in winter.[25] That was the area Bering Sea elders
had studied on the map, when they'd agreed, "Let the fish and the
rest grow out there."

After the evening with Mathis, I looked on the web at more photos of pteropods and the even smaller but equally beautiful (when
magnified) coccolithophores, single-celled algae that encase themselves in calcite plates and form such large algae blooms they turn
parts of the oceans a pale shade of blue. The coccolithophore's role
in the marine environment and carbon cycling, I discovered, is anything but simple.[26] On the one hand, the carbon in their plates
sequesters that carbon, largely in ocean sediments when the material sinks to the bottom. On the other hand, the chemical reaction
that creates the plates also releases CO_2 molecules, some of which
escape into the atmosphere.

If, as is projected, global warming in the short-term makes
the upper layers of the ocean more temperate, with less mixing,
such conditions would be ideal for coccolithophores. More coccolithophores, with all their biological activity, could contribute to
more global warming. *But* the blooms of more coccolithophores
could also increase the albedo effect (the lighter color reflecting the
sun's heat) and help mitigate global warming. *But* if it turns out that
acidification interferes with coccolithophores' ability to build their
structures, the oceans could lose an important food source along

with the present albedo contribution, and the rest of this tiny plant's complex role in the marine system and carbon cycling. And at least one species of coccolithophore seems to flourish in corrosive waters. It is exactly this *but-but-but* uncertainty that makes predictions so difficult, requires so much research, and creates confusion for the public.

In the late 1990s, surprisingly large blooms of coccolithophores covered vast areas of the Bering Sea. Such massive blooms had never been seen there before and seemed to displace the diatoms (larger, more nutritious single-celled plants) that normally dominate the Bering Sea's planktonic realm. Coccolithophores are associated with still, nutrient-poor waters of mild temperatures, and in 1997 a persistent high-pressure system in the Bering Sea meant that an unusual amount of sunlight heated surface water while a lack of wind suppressed mixing. Seabirds like the shearwaters, which feed on the zooplankton that feed on the type of plankton that were so greatly reduced, starved to death by the hundreds of thousands. A friend who was working on the Bering Sea coast in 1997 described to me the turquoise color of the water and the huge rafts of shearwaters resting lethargically on inshore waters, where they're not normally found. He wrote to me about the seabirds, "There were so many dead on the beaches that you could have walked miles stepping from one carcass to another."

At the elders' meeting in Bethel, the focus was on fisheries management. That, at least, was something the people present could actually do something about, if they put together a proposal supported by both traditional knowledge and science and capable of competing in the political realm. What could they possibly do about ocean acidification?

On my late-night flight home from Bethel, I stared from my window at blackness broken only by the flashing light at the end of the jet's wingtip. I fretted, as I always do these days, about the greenhouse gases my travel was spinning into the sky and about my large, American "carbon footprint." My tired mind turned from the elders to the young, and to a pair of teenagers I'd met two months earlier in Kodiak. Those students had participated in the "tsunami bowl," Alaska's version of the National Ocean Sciences Bowl for high schools.[27] In 2009 the issue to be researched and presented was hazards of ocean acidification to coastal communities. The Kodiak team's paper, "Projected Effects of Ocean Acidification on the Marine Ecosystem and Social Structure of Kodiak," emphasized Kodiak's dependence on fisheries and concluded that the community "will be affected profoundly by ocean acidification."

The two students I'd spoken to in Kodiak told me that neither they nor their parents had heard of ocean acidification before the assignment. They'd read up on the science and interviewed researchers at the Kodiak Fisheries Research Center, and they'd made a practice presentation before their local school board. They wrote in their paper, "As inhabitants of this planet, it is our duty to solve the problem of ocean acidification by decreasing our greenhouse gas emissions."

One of those students, Ray Garcia, said to me in Kodiak, "We're expecting big changes in the world. I decided to change small things in my life, to make a difference."

And then, shaking his head as though he still couldn't fathom it, he mentioned that when the Kodiak team traveled to the state meet in Seward, an aide to representative Don Young had been there—not to congratulate the young people who presented their work but to take the stage to tell them that Representative Young didn't believe in global warming and wouldn't act on it or ocean acidification "without hard evidence."

Both Ray and Adilene Castaneda—the other team member I met—expected to go to college and to become productive members of society. None of their immediate family members worked in commercial fisheries, but they knew that school, post office, and car rental jobs—positions held by their parents—all depended on the fisheries that built the base of Kodiak's economy. Their peers, they thought, were less likely to become fishermen than the previous generation; the future of the fisheries was too uncertain.

The oldest of the tsunami bowl team, Sam Horton, was already at college, where he was studying political science. He told me in an e-mail that he expected to make movies and eventually to run for public office. He wrote, "I am very determined to use what I have accumulated about global climate change and ocean acidification to bring about . . . awareness of our situation."

The jet hurtled through the sky, over unseen tundra, forest, frozen ground, and mountains. I was not hopeful, and yet I could not be without hope. The young people are inheriting the earth, such as it is and will be. I sent my wish out into the darkness, to those we've left the last chance: May you gather the wisdom of the elders, use the reason your large brains allow you, and adopt the resolve to do what must be done.

ACKNOWLEDGMENTS

This book could not have been written without the cooperation, assistance, and advice of many generous people. I thank all who appear in these pages, named and unnamed, and who otherwise provided my education in climate change and life in the north. It's not always comfortable or convenient to have your homeplace and ideas scrutinized by a writer, and I truly appreciate all who helped me along the way. I've tried to be respectful and accurate, and I hope my intrusions and any failures in understanding will be forgiven.

Books are our teachers, too, and I've relied on the work of scientists and other writers who have written so well about climate change and related subjects. Some of their books are included in my bibliography. The Internet has also been a tremendous source of up-to-date science, policy, and opinion.

I thank as well all of the following, who contributed in various ways to make this book possible:

A number of reviewers kindly and carefully read sections and in some cases the entirety of my manuscript and offered expert advice. These include Tom Kizzia, Ed Berg, Terry Johnson, Dave Aplin, Sue Mauger, Sue Libenson, Craig Gerlach, Elaine Velsko, Pete Velsko, Tony Weyiouanna, Ken Stenek, Susanne (Susi) Miller, Dorothy Childers, Fred Phillip, Jeremy Mathis, and Richard Feely. Any errors in fact or interpretation are of course my own.

My agent, Elizabeth Wales, offered incisive counsel from the beginning. Editors Jack Shoemaker, Laura Mazer, Roxanna Aliaga, and Elizabeth Mathews, with the rest of the team at Counterpoint Press, all supported this project and ably helped it along. Bill McKibben and Kathleen Dean Moore, among the wisest and most principled people I know, offered their encouragement.

Sue Libenson and the Boreal Songbird Initiative, Paul Rauber and *Sierra* magazine, Canadian River Expeditions & Nahanni River Adventures, and Northwest Territories Tourism combined to make my visit to the Mountain River and Fort Good Hope in Canada's Northwest Territories possible. My article "Lair of the North Wind" appeared in the March/April 2008 issue of *Sierra* magazine.

Early on, I was the grateful recipient of a fellowship to the Knight Center for Specialized Journalism for the seminar "Climate Change, Its Sweeping Impact." During the writing of this book I also benefited from residencies at Escape to Create, Ragdale Foundation, and the Artists' Enclave at I-Park. I thank all who made those opportunities possible and who shared with me their friendship, expertise, and art.

Toward the end, I found new inspiration in Linnea Rain Lentfer of Gustavus, Alaska. Linnea, who is six years old and rides her bike to school, told me, "We need to take care of the earth, the water, and the air, because they take care of us."

Finally, as always, I thank my partner, Ken Castner, for his continuing support and place in my life.

ENDNOTES

Introduction

1. See map images, by season, at http://data.giss.nasa.gov/gistemp/2005/.
2. An excellent plain-language summary of climate change specific to Alaska can be found at http://downloads.globalchange.gov/usimpacts/pdfs/alaska.pdf. This is one chapter of "Global Climate Change Impacts in the United States," which looks at changes by region. The report, issued in June 2009, was prepared under the Bush administration and its draft withheld from the public until environmental groups successfully sued to have it released. See the entire 196-page publication at www.globalchange.gov/publications/reports/scientific-assessments/us-impacts.
3. For explanations of this, see page 15 in the summary of the Arctic Climate Impact Assessment (ACIA) at www.amap.no/acia/highlights.pdf; a commentary by Cecilia Bitz, professor of Atmospheric Sciences at the University of Washington, at www.realclimate.org/index.php/archives/2006/01/polar-amplification/; and a temperature trend analysis by NASA's James Hansen at http://data.giss.nasa.gov/gistemp/2007/.
4. Homer, Alaska's plan can be found at www.ci.homer.ak.us/CLPL.pdf. Homer, a member of ICLEI (Local Governments for Sustainability, an international association), has, among its actions, conducted a detailed energy use study of city buildings and established an energy monitoring program, developed a policy guidebook for city employees, purchased energy-efficient vehicles, adopted an ordinance regulating residential wind turbines, revised procurement policies to advance "green" purchasing, and replaced and adjusted lighting and boilers. It was an early signatory to the Alaska Coastal Communities Global Climate Change Compact (www.akmarine.org/pressroom/alaska-coastal-communities-global-climate-change-compact/) and actively pursues funding to implement more energy efficiency and renewable energy strategies identified in its plan. First-year energy (electrical) savings at city hall were 13 percent.
5. Up-to-date climate science, prepared in advance of the 2009 Copenhagen summit, can be found at www.copenhagendiagnosis.org/default.html.

6. The IPCC's 2007 summary for policy makers is a good place to grasp the basics: www.ipcc.ch/pdf/assessment-report/ar4/wg1/ar4-wg1-spm.pdf.
7. The radio show quote is from National Public Radio, February 12, 2008, www .npr.org/templates/transcript/transcript.php?storyId=18913804. On another occasion, Young suggested that artificial ice floes, made of plastic, could be floated in the ocean to help the bears. He also likes to say, regarding global warming, "My opinion is as good as anyone's."
8. See the fact sheet from the International Union for Conservation of Nature, http://cmsdata.iucn.org/downloads/species_extinction_05_2007.pdf.
9. See IPCC FAQ 6.2 at http://co2now.org/index.php?option=com_content&task= view&id=75&Itemid=87.
10. See www.ecoadapt.org/.
11. See www.iser.uaa.alaska.edu/Publications/Juneclimatefinal.pdf.

Part One
My Salmon Home: Kenai Peninsula

1. See Cook Inletkeeper's website for more information about the salmon stream project including Sue's presentation, "Changes in Alaska Salmon Stream Habitat Due to Climate Warming," made to the state panel: www.inletkeeper.org/salmon /reports.htm.
2. The referenced paper, an unpublished draft, is titled "Cumulative Impacts of Climate Change on Fraser River Sockeye: Potential for Mitigation."
3. The study is recounted in Richard Kocan's scientific paper "Effects of *Ichthyophonus* on Survival and Reproductive Success of Yukon River Chinook Salmon" (2003), Final Project Report No. FIS 01-200 for the U.S. Fish and Wildlife Service. See also "Ichthyophoniasis: An Emerging Disease of Chinook Salmon in the Yukon River" (2004), in *Journal of Aquatic Animal Health* 16. A good article about Kocan's work, "Alaska salmon may bear scars of global warming," by Kenneth R. Weiss, can be found at www.latimes.com/news/science/environment/la-na-ichfish15 -2008jun15,0,6335392,full.story.
4. A high school science paper, "The Effects of Sedimentation on Skilak Lake Due to Glacial Melting," can be found at http://seagrant.uaf.edu/nosb/papers/2005 /soldotna-worms.html. It cites a number of scientific papers and includes a discussion of some possible engineering solutions—silt fences and still ponds—as well as the need to deal with CO_2 emissions on a national and global scale.
5. Ed Berg, whom we will meet later, is the lead author of "Spruce beetle outbreaks on the Kenai Peninsula, Alaska, and Kluane National Park and Reserve, Yukon Territory: Relationship to summer temperatures and regional differences in disturbance regimes," published in *Forest Ecology and Management* 227 in 2006 (pp. 219–232).
6. For some examples, see "Spruce Bark Beetles and Climate Change," by Charles Wohlforth in *Alaska Magazine*, www.wohlforth.net/SpruceBarkBeetles.htm; *The New York Times*, www.nytimes.com/2002/06/25/science/on-hot-trail-of-tiny -killer-in-alaska.html?pagewanted=2; and *The Christian Science Monitor*, http://

features.csmonitor.com/environment/2008/08/28/alaska-climate-change
-frontier/. The "take no prisoners" quote is from *Reuters*, "Warming Climate Threatens Alaska's Vast Forests," August 19, 2008, www.alertnet.org/thenews/newsdesk/N19282797.htm. Berg also contributes to a regular notebook series from the Kenai National Wildlife Refuge, http://kenai.fws.gov/current.htm.

7. Berg wrote up his work in a Refuge Notebook article April 24, 2009: http://kenai.fws.gov/overview/notebook/2009/april/24april2009.htm.

8. Berg is the lead author of a paper about the recent woody invasion of refuge wetlands, published in the *Canadian Journal of Forestry Research*, vol. 39, no. 11, November 2009. The full text is here: http://pubs.nrc-cnrc.gc.ca/rp-ps/inDetail.jsp?jcode=cjfr&vol=39&is=11&lang=eng.

Part Two
Boreal Forest: At the Arctic Circle

1. *Popular Mechanics* featured ice roads and the challenges to them from global warming at www.popularmechanics.com/outdoors/adventures/4212314.html.

2. See www.nwtpas.ca/.

3. This thousand-page scientific report of very dense material is an international product of the Arctic Council and the International Arctic Science Committee and was released in 2004. The entire report is available online at http://amap.no/acia/. Chapter 14 discusses forests specifically.

4. See http://carbon.cfs.nrcan.gc.ca/CBM-CFS3_e.html.

5. A good background paper about forest carbon is "Forest Carbon Sequestration and Avoided Emissions," from the Canadian Boreal Initiative/Ivey Foundation, October 2007, www.forestsandclimate.org.

6. This is discussed in chapter 14 of Arctic Climate Assessment Impact (ACIA), pages 820–821.

7. Descriptions of studies and their results were carried in the press and were based on articles published in *Nature* (January 2, 2008) and *Science* (January 23, 2009).

8. This is discussed in ACIA and elsewhere.

9. Glenn Juday and Terry Chapin from the University of Alaska Fairbanks discussed likely landscape changes in an article in the *Fairbanks Daily News-Miner*, July 29, 2008, reported by Stefan Milkowski.

10. There have been many studies regarding permafrost carbon. For one, see "Vulnerability of Permafrost Carbon to Climate Change: Implications for Global Carbon Cycle" in *BioScience* vol. 58, no. 8 (September 2008), pp. 701–714. Another, "The effect of permafrost thaw on old carbon release and net carbon exchange from tundra" was published in *Nature*, May 28, 2009, see www.nature.com/nature/journal/v459/n7246/abs/nature08031.html. See also a *Scientific American* article about the study at www.scientificamerican.com/article.cfm?id=permafrost-melt down-bogs-global-warming.

11. See http://cgc.rncan.gc.ca/permafrost/climate_e.php.

12. A very good interview with Romanovsky, with additional links, can be found at www.arcticwarming.net/node/70.

13. See "Bubbles of warming, beneath the ice" for a portrait of Anthony and her work: www.latimes.com/news/science/environment/la-na-global-warming22 -2009 feb22,0,646220.story. Video clips of Anthony lighting methane bubbles are also popular on the Internet. Her website, www.alaska.edu/uaf/cem/ine/walter/, has additional information about her work. An article in *New Scientist* from March 25, 2009 (www.newscientist.com/article/mg20127011.500-arctic-meltdown-is-a -threat-to-humanity.html), also mentions the work of Anthony and the problem of thawing permafrost and methane release, as well as other aspects of how a warmer Arctic will change the entire planet, and has many links to researchers and their scientific papers.

14. See www.climatecommunication.org/PDFs/GEO2008.pdf for the report "Methane from the Arctic: Global warming wildcard." This report, part of the United Nations Environmental Programme's Year Book 2008, discusses the issue of the release of methane from thawing permafrost soils and from deposits of methane hydrates. It includes photos and graphics as well as scientific citations.

15. See www.borealbirds.org/. The website has links to many news items and reports related to the importance of the boreal to birds and wildlife and for storing carbon.

16. Root, a lead author of the International Panel on Climate Change report on impacts of climate change on wildlife, also coauthored the 2002 book *Wildlife Responses to Climate Change: North American Case Studies* (Island Press).

17. "Birds and Climate Change: Ecological Disruption in Motion, A Briefing for Policymakers and Concerned Citizens on Audubon's Analyses of North American Bird Movements in the Face of Global Warming," February 2009, www.audubon .org/bird/bacc. An Alaska-specific article about the study, "Snow Birds," was published in the *Anchorage Daily News*, February 13, 2009.

18. This was *The Sahtu Atlas: Maps and Stories from the Sahtu Settlement Area in Canada's Northwest Territories*, edited by James Auld and Robert Kershaw for the Sahtu GIS Project, 2005.

19. The quote comes from Eric Hebert-Daly, national executive director of the Canadian Parks and Wilderness Society, CPAWS. See www.ens-newswire.com/ens /jun2009/2009-06-09-02.asp.

20. Representative Don Young's visit was reported in the *Homer News* of August 6, 2008. See www.homernews.com/stories/080608/news_1a_003.shtml.

21. Glenn Juday, from the University of Alaska Fairbanks, is a frequent speaker at science conferences and the lead author of the forest chapter (ch. 14) of the Arctic Climate Impact Assessment.

22. See www.uaf.edu/accap/research/interior_land_use.htm for the full description of this project housed at the Alaska Center for Climate Assessment and Policy.

23. For more information about the restoration project, see www.wc.adfg.state.ak.us /index.cfm?adfg=game.restoration.

24. Senator Ted Stevens was convicted of all counts just a week before the 2008 election, in which he lost to Democrat Mark Begich. The convictions were later vacated by U.S. attorney general Eric Holder, who cited prosecutorial misconduct during the trial. Son Ben left the public scene to crew on a boat supporting

Arctic oil drilling and has never been indicted on corruption charges. See http://
alaskacorruption.blogspot.com/2010/03/why-havent-ben-stevens-and-don-
young.html for an update on the corruption scandal.

25. "Yukon Flats villages opposed to drilling," by Tom Kizzia. *Anchorage Daily News*,
July 21, 2008.

Part Three
Sea Ice and Ice Bears: Barter Island

1. There is often confusion between the words *Inupiaq* and *Inupiat*. Per the University of Alaska Fairbanks Editorial Style Guide, *Inupiaq* is used to refer to the
language of the Alaska Inuits (the people from the North Slope and Northwest
Alaska) or to one person of that culture, and as an adjective. *Inupiak* is the word
for two people. *Inupiat* refers to three or more people, the people collectively, and
the culture.

2. Much history of Barter Island and Kaktovik is recounted in "Kaktovik Area Cultural Resource Survey" by David Libbey, a paper funded by the North Slope Borough and the National Park Service in 1983. The reference to "the sea where there
is always ice" is cited on page 7 of that report. Even at the time of the report, in
1983, the ice pack at Kaktovik was described (on page 2) as "never far out from the
land and a changing wind can bring it back in at any time."

3. The U.S. Geological Survey has conducted a number of recent studies regarding
erosion along the Arctic coast. See www.usgs.gov/newsroom/article.asp?ID=2141
as well as a report in the *Anchorage Daily News* from February 18, 2009, "Beaufort
Sea rapidly erodes Arctic shoreline."

4. Find extensive sea ice information, including maps, graphics, and videos, at http://
nsidc.org/arcticseaicenews/.

5. I first saw it stated this way in Daniel Glick's essay "Fever Pitch: Understanding
the Planet's Warming Symptoms" in *The Last Polar Bear* (Braided River, 2008).

6. See www.nsidc.org/arcticseaicenews/faq.html. According to the National Snow
and Ice Data Center, today's global average temperatures are approaching those
of the Eemian age, the last major interglacial period, but carbon dioxide levels are
already higher, indicating more warming is to come.

7. See www.tundradaisy.org.

8. See www.climatescience.gov/Library/sap/sap3-4/final-report/default.htm. This
report, titled "Abrupt Climate Change," was done for the U.S. Climate Change
Science Program. In addition to addressing sea level rise, it also addresses the
hydrologic cycle (drought and flooding), Atlantic Ocean circulation, and the
release of methane to the atmosphere.

9. See www.polarartproductions.com/ and www.icebearsofthebeaufort.com/Home
.html. The film, which has now won a number of awards, makes the case for creating a polar bear sanctuary, protected from oil and gas development, in the eastern
Beaufort Sea.

10. See links to a number of relevant studies at www.usgs.gov/newsroom/special
/polar_bears/. These studies were conducted for the USGS by a team of scientists

to inform the decision about whether to list the polar bear under the Endangered Species Act.

11. "Effects of sea ice extent and food availability on spatial and temporal distribution of polar bears during the fall open-water period in the Southern Beaufort Sea," by S. Schliebe et al., 2008.

12. See www.worldwildlife.org/species/finder/polarbear/polar-bear-research /introduction.html for a diary of the spring capture effort by WWF's polar bear expert, Geoff York. The recapture and related studies are also reported in an *Anchorage Daily News* article, "Scientists go to extremes for Arctic research," on December 21, 2009. See www.adn.com/626/story/1063313.html.

13. This was reported in the *Anchorage Daily News*, in an AP story ("State will sue over polar bear listing, Palin says") by Dan Joling, on May 22, 2008.

14. A good discussion of the pizzly bear and what its occurrence means can be found on pages 10–14 in Anthony Barnosky's *Heatstroke: Nature in an Age of Global Warming* (Island Press, 2009). A good article, with photos, can be found at www .dailymail.co.uk/news/article-1130064/Plight-pizzly-bear-A-leading-filmmaker -tells-story-discovery-cruel-fate-grizzly-8211-polar-bear.html.

15. See a video that shows the patrol at work, using sticks and stones to keep bears away from a village, at http://belyemedvedi.ru/video/videoup2008.html. Learn more about the polar bear patrol and other WWF polar bear projects at www .worldwildlife.org/species/finder/polarbear/projects.html.

16. *The Last Polar Bear*, by photographer Steven Kazlowski, includes many photographs shot on and around Barter Island, with text of his own and separate essays by others.

17. The students were responding to her article "Drill Here. Drill Now." *National Review* online, July 21, 2008.

Part Four
When a Village Has to Move: Shishmaref

1. A partial list of media reports appears in anthropologist Elizabeth Marino's "Imminent threats, impossible moves, and unlikely prestige: Understanding the struggle for local control as a means toward sustainability," which also lays out a history of the Shishmaref relocation effort, its publicity strategies, and the tensions between local control and government planning. See www.ehs.unu.edu/file /get/3615.

2. GAO Report GAO-04-142, "Flooding and Erosion in Alaska Native Villages," 2003.

3. The $179 million estimate for relocating Shishmaref to the mainland breaks down like this: $20 million for moving 150 homes; $26 million for moving or rebuilding a school, city hall, and clinic; $25 million for an airport; $23 million for roads; and $25 million for a water and sewer system.

4. The carbon offsets from the Banner Wind Project are sold through the Bonneville Environmental Foundation, an Oregon-based nonprofit organization. For a primer on carbon offsets, see http://science.howstuffworks.com/carbon-offset

.htm. Those who, like me, occasionally buy offsets to assuage our guilt for the "carbon footprint" we produce by activities like airplane travel, may be supporting Nome's new turbines.

5. An interactive map created at the University of Arizona allows views of anywhere in the world with sea level rises from one to six meters. See http://www .geo.arizona.edu/dgesl/research/other/climate_change_and_sea_level/sea _level_rise/sea_level_rise_old.htm#images. For an animation of North America see http://www.geo.arizona.edu/dgesl/research/other/climate_change_and_sea _level/sea_level_rise/north_america/slr_north_america_a.htm.

6. For Alaska's Climate Change Strategy detail, see www.climatechange.alaska.gov/, which has links to the legislative commission report, the subcabinet working group reports, and much more. The final report of the immediate action workgroup is at www.climatechange.alaska.gov/docs/iaw_finalrpt_12mar09.pdf.

7. An eloquent discussion of coastal dynamics can be found in *The Corps and the Shore* (Island Press, 1998), by Orrin Pilkey and Katharine Dixon Wheeler. The authors, critical of the Corps of Engineers, argue for using coastal science, not engineering, to improve coastal management.

8. The report, GAO-09-551, can be found at www.gao.gov/new.items/d09551.pdf.

9. See the website at www.shishmarefrelocation.com. The public information and media efforts had largely come to a halt when Tony Weyiouanna left his position with the coalition. Weyiouanna had told me that, for a while, the "help us" link on the website was bringing in about $25,000 a year in donations.

10. http://wiki.bssd.org/index.php/Category:Plants_and_Animals_of_the_Bering _Strait. For the McKay's bunting, a bird that breeds only on a couple of Bering Sea islands in the summer, the community text reads, "The McKay's Buntings come to Shishmaref each October. During the 2007-08 winter, there were approximately 100 birds of this species as well as many Snow Buntings. Locally they are not distinguished between Snow Buntings and both are called Snow Birds or God's Birds. Their local [Inupiaq] name literally translated means Winter Bird, which is very fitting. Local resident Albert 'Yabo' Olanna feeds them each winter on the roof of his shed behind his home. These birds are very intelligent and recognize those that fed them."

11. There's often confusion in such calculations between carbon and carbon dioxide. Carbon dioxide is what is actually emitted, but scientists generally refer to carbon when speaking of what ends up in the atmosphere, and governments refer to carbon when discussing things like "carbon caps." A good explanation of the difference can be found at www.grist.org/article/the-biggest-source-of-mistakes -carbon-vs-carbon-dioxide/.

12. See www.synergylearning.org/cf/displayarticle.cfm?selectedarticle=672.

13. Kenji Yoshikawa, a University of Alaska Fairbanks scientist in the Water and Environmental Research Center, toured northwestern Alaska on a snow machine in the winter of 2008 to dig boreholes in the frozen tundra and to engage local schools in a monitoring program. Watch a video of Borehole Expedition 2008 at www.arcticclimatemodeling.org/scientists_yoshikawa.html.

14. I wrote about Point Lay and its annual beluga whale hunt in my book *Beluga*

Days, Counterpoint Press, 2004, and Mountaineers Books (paperback edition), 2007.

15. For an excellent 2007 analysis of the climate refugee issue, see "Preparing for a Warmer World: Towards a Global Governance System to Protect Climate Refugees," www.sarpn.org.za/documents/d0002952/Climate_refugees_global _governance_Nov2007.pdf.

16. The *Time* magazine article in which she is quoted "Heroes of the Environment 2008," September 24, 2008, is found at www.time.com/time/specials/packages /article/0,28804,1841778_1841779_1841797,00.html.

17. Bronen has published several papers, including "Forced Migration of Alaskan Indigenous Communities Due to Climate Change: Creating a Human Rights Response." See page 70 at www.ehs.unu.edu/file.php?id=600.

18. The filing is Native Village of Kivalina v. ExxonMobile Corp., 08-CV-1138 (ND Cal. Feb. 2008). The case document can be found at www.climatelaw.org/cases /country/us/kivalina/Kivalina%20Complaint.pdf. The court document dismissing the suit can be found at http://theusconstitution.org/blog.warming/wp-content /uploads/2009/10/kivalina-decision.pdf. A good analysis of the Kivalina ruling and related ones can be found at www.nytimes.com/gwire/2009/10/19/19greenwire -courts-follow-landmark-2nd-circuit-ruling-with-62336.html?pagewanted=all.

19. "Courts as Battlefield in Climate Fights," January 27, 2010.

20. Photos taken of King Island and its residents taken by teachers Rie and Juan Muñoz in 1951, can be found at www.riemunoz.com/kingIsland.htm.

Part Five
The Oceanic Realm: Bering Sea

1. See www.beringseaelders.org.

2. A good overview of the Bering Sea, only somewhat dated, is *The Bering Sea and Aleutian Islands: Region of Wonders*, by Terry Johnson, 2003. This Alaska Sea Grant publication, with lots of illustrations, describes in common language the Bering Sea's global context, physical environment, life, cultures, and challenges. It includes a CD of well-produced science radio reports.

3. Just in recent years a flood of research funding has been available through the North Pacific Research Board. See www.nprb.org/index.html for information about its projects and research papers.

4. See www.pewmarinefellows.org/.

5. A good discussion of these studies is found in *Heatstroke*, pp. 38–40. Barnosky's notes section cites numerous specific studies. See also *Wildlife Responses to Climate Change: North American Case Studies*, by Stephen Henry Schneider and Terry L. Root (Island Press, 2002).

6. See http://dsc.discovery.com/fansites/deadliestcatch/crab-fishing/bering-sea -science.html.

7. The *L.A. Times* article ("U.S. fishing fleet pursues pollock in troubled waters") by Kenneth R. Weiss, appeared in that paper October 19, 2008, and was reprinted in the *Anchorage Daily News* November 3, 2008.

8. This research is related in "Sea Ice Retreat Alters the Biogeography of the Bering

Sea Continental Shelf" by Franz J. Mueter and Michael A. Litzow, *Ecological Applications* 2008, www.faralloninstitute.org/Publications/Mueter%20and%20Litzow%202008.pdf.

9. An International Union for Conservation of Nature 2009 report, "The Ocean and Climate Change," may provide the best summary of what is currently known, along with recommended actions, such as reducing "human stressors" including fishery impacts and pollution. It's available as a pdf at www.iucn.org/about /work/programmes/marine/marine_our_work/climate_change/publications .cfm. Another useful report is "In Dead Water: Merging of climate change with pollution, over-harvest and infestations in the world's fishing grounds," United Nations Environmental Programme, February 2008, www.unep.org/pdf/InDead Water_LR.pdf.

10. See http://en.wikipedia.org/wiki/Thermohaline_circulation.

11. See "Poison Ice" by Elizabeth Grossman at www.salon.com/news/feature /2008/04/30/arctic_pollutants/.

12. See www.pik-potsdam.de/news/press-releases/archive/2008/tipping-elements -in-the-earths-climate-system/.

13. There now exist several excellent primers on ocean acidification. These include a 2009 IUCN introductory guide for policy advisers (http://cmsdata.iucn.org /downloads/ocean_acidification_guide.pdf), which includes a bibliography of additional references; a layperson's guide (http://na.oceana.org/sites/default/files /reports/Acidification_Report1.pdf) with extensive citations, from the marine conservation organization Oceana; and "Covering Ocean Acidification: Chemistry and Considerations," www.yaleclimatemediaforum.org/2008/06/covering -ocean-acidification-chemistry-and-considerations/, by Marah Hardt and Carl Safina. An additional source of up-to-date scientific info about OA is the Ocean Acidification Network, www.ocean-acidification.net/. Read there the Monaco Declaration, signed by 150 prominent marine scientists from twenty-six countries, imploring policy makers to reduce CO_2 emissions sharply or risk widespread and severe damage from OA. The website includes a link to a blog on which researchers share their work.

14. See S. Khatiwala, F. Primeau, and T. Hall, "Reconstruction of the history of anthropogenic CO_2 concentrations in the ocean." *Nature* 462: 346–349, 2009. A principal finding of this research is that the oceans are reaching some limits of CO_2 absorption; since 2000 the amount taken up by the oceans has declined by as much as 10 percent—meaning more greenhouse gas has remained in the atmosphere, adding to global warming. As the ocean warms and acidifies, it becomes less able to absorb CO_2.

15. "Ocean Acidification at High Latitudes: The Bellwether," an article in *Oceanography*, vol. 22, no. 4, December 2009 (p. 160–171), makes this point explicitly. The authors argue that the Arctic and Antarctic Oceans should be considered ecosystem laboratories for studying OA; what happens there first is a bellwether for what will later happen in the mid and low latitudes. Moreover, the authors make the case that immediate and intense OA monitoring and research is essential, while a baseline against which to compare future change still exists.

16. See http://oceanseanet.ning.com/profiles/blogs/sea-ice-melt-has-implications

for an article detailing scientific papers that address ocean acidification in the Arctic and the role of sea ice melt. (Access to the SEANET site, on which an informal network of people communicate about research in Alaska's seas, requires a free subscription.)

17. This paper was first published in *Science Express* on May 22, 2008, and in *Science* June 13, 2008. Its findings were reported in the *Seattle Post-Intelligencer*, "Corrosive ocean water moving inland; increased acidity wasn't expected for 100 years," on May 22, 2008. See http://seattlepi.nwsource.com/local/364242_acid23.html.

18. See http://sciencenow.sciencemag.org/cgi/content/full/2009/1201/1.

19. See an interview with Foy at *ClimateWire*, www.eenews.net/tv/transcript/890.

20. "Acid Threat," November 2007. The photos are by David Liittschwager, text by Jennifer S. Holland.

21. The press release on which the radio account (and other news reports) was based is at www.sfos.uaf.edu/oa/.

22. A scientific paper coauthored by Mathis, about saturation states in Arctic waters, can be found at www.agu.org/pubs/crossref/2009/2008JC004862.shtml. He is also a coauthor of "Ocean Acidification at High Latitudes: The Bellwether," in *Oceanography*, vol. 22, no. 4, December 2009 (pp. 160–171).

23. For more about *A Sea Change*, see www.aseachange.net.

24. Fabry's discovery, back in 1985, is also recounted in Elizabeth Kolbert's *New Yorker* article "The Darkening Sea: What carbon emissions are doing to the ocean," November 20, 2009 (pp. 66–75).

25. "Ocean Acidification at High Latitudes: The Bellwether," in *Oceanography*, vol. 22, no. 4, December 2009 (pp. 160–171).

26. See photos and read about the relationship between coccolithophores and global warming at http://earthobservatory.nasa.gov/Features/Coccolithophores/coccolith_3.php.

27. The research papers by the Alaskan school teams are archived at http://seagrant.uaf.edu/nosb/papers/2009/index.php.

Selected Bibliography

After the Ice: Life, Death, and Geopolitics in the New Arctic. Alun Anderson. Smithsonian, 2009. By the former editor of *New Scientist* magazine, this book takes a circum–polar look at the effects of sea ice loss.

An Inconvenient Truth: The Planetary Emergency of Global Warming and What We Can Do About It. Al Gore. Rodale Books, 2006.

Arctic Climate Impact Assessment. This 1,042-page report from 2004 is entirely avail-able online at www.acia.uaf.edu/pages/scientific.html. A 139-page book version, titled *Impacts of a Warming Arctic*, is written in plain language and packed with very helpful graphics; this is available from Cambridge University Press (2004). The assessment, conducted by the Arctic Council, involved an international effort by hundreds of scientists and is comprehensively researched, fully referenced, and independently reviewed.

Climate Change 2007: The Physical Science Basis, the Fourth Assessment Report by the Intergovernmental Panel on Climate Change. See the IPCC website, www.ipcc. ch. The website includes a newsletter and many other reports and publications. The Fifth Assessment is under way and due to be completed in 2013–14.

Climate Change: Picturing the Science. Gavin Schmidt and Joshua Wolfe. W. W. Norton, 2009. Essays and photos that explain how scientists measure and have come to understand the risks of climate change.

Climate Code Red: The Case for Emergency Action. David Spratt and Philip Sutton. Scribe Publications, 2008. The writers and publisher are Australian, and the book has had far too little attention in the United States. See www.climatecodered.net/ for excerpts, updates, and what Spratt has to say about "the Arctic challenge."

Climate Cover-Up: The Crusade to Deny Global Warming. James Hoggan. Greystone Books, 2009. Well-sourced research by a Canadian.

The Climate Crisis: An Introductory Guide to Climate Change. David Archer and Ste-fan Rahmstorf. Cambridge University Press, 2010. An unofficial guidebook to the IPCC Fourth Assessment Report.

The Copenhagen Diagnosis: Updating the World on the Latest Climate Science, online at www.copenhagendiagnosis.org/default.html. Authored by twenty-six climate scientists from eight countries, this report is based on more than two hundred cited and peer-reviewed science papers that have appeared since the last IPCC report.

The Discovery of Global Warming: Revised and Expanded Edition. Spencer Weart. Harvard University Press, 2008. This book teaches that there's a long history to the issue built on a robust science of climate.

Down to the Wire: Confronting Climate Collapse. David W. Orr. Oxford University Press, 2009. A synthesis of science, politics, and public policy, with attention to human dignity and social change.

Eaarth: Making a Life on a Tough New Planet. Bill McKibben. Times Books, 2010. McKibben, founder of 350.org, starts with the premise that we now and in the future will live on a different and less hospitable planet; he then proposes creative ways of surviving and living more sustainably in functioning communities.

The Earth Is Faster Now: Indigenous Observations of Arctic Environmental Change. Igor Krupnik and Dyanna Jolly, editors. Published by Arctic Research Consortium of the United States in cooperation with the Arctic Studies Center, Smithsonian Institution, 2002. In their introduction, the editors state this volume's "main messages": Arctic residents are witnessing far-reaching changes in their environment, and they have much to contribute as collaborators in observing and understanding those changes.

Earth Under Fire: How Global Warming Is Changing the World. Gary Braasch. University of California Press, 2007. Photojournalist Braasch traveled the world to document climate change, in both photos and words. The book also includes essays by experts and excellent documentation for further reading.

Ecological Impacts of Climate Change, by the Committee on Ecological Impacts of Climate Change, National Research Council, available online at www.nap.edu /catalog.php?record_id=12491. The National Academies Press, 2008.

The End of Nature. Bill McKibben. Random House, 1989. This is now a classic, the first text to alert the general public to the dangers of greenhouse gas emissions and the consequences of altering the earth's atmosphere.

Field Notes from a Catastrophe: Man, Nature, and Climate Change. Elizabeth Kolbert. Bloomsbury USA, 2006, and paperback updated with a new afterword, 2007. This well-researched and very readable book may well still be the best primer on the issue of climate change.

Heatstroke: Nature in an Age of Global Warming. Anthony D. Barnosky. Shearwater, 2009. A paleoecologist takes a long, biological view at the ways in which global warming is fundamentally changing the natural world.

High Tide: The Truth About Our Climate Crisis. Mark Lynas. Picador, 2004. In this experiential account, the author travels to Alaska, China, Peru, England, Florida, and the South Pacific to portray communities experiencing the effects of climate change.

In Dead Water: Merging of climate change with pollution, over-harvest, and infestations in the world's fishing grounds. United Nations Environmental Programme, February 2008. See www.unep.org/pdf/InDeadWater_LR.pdf.

The Last Polar Bear: Facing the Truth of a Warming World. A Photographic Journey by Steven Kazlowski. Braided River, 2008. Kazlowski spent years photographing in the Arctic, with an emphasis on polar bears and their habitat. The text, which includes some of his journal entries, also brings together important essays by others.

The Long Thaw: How Humans Are Changing the Next 100,000 Years of Earth's Climate. David Archer. Princeton University Press, 2009. A leading climatologist looks well into the future, with a focus on the long-term carbon cycle.

Our Choice: A Plan to Solve the Climate Crisis. Al Gore. Rodale Books, 2009. Solutions-based and loaded with great photos and useful charts.

Science as a Contact Sport: Inside the Battle to Save Earth's Climate. Stephen H. Schneider. National Geographic, 2009. Details how scientific theory evolves and how the disinformation campaign by global warming deniers has interfered with science and science education.

Storms of My Grandchildren: The Truth About the Coming Climate Catastrophe and Our Last Chance to Save Humanity. James Hansen. Bloomsbury USA, 2009. The director of NASA's Goddard Institute for Space Studies covers the geopolitics of climate change as well as up-to-date science.

The Weather Makers: How Man Is Changing the Climate and What It Means for Life on Earth. Tim Flannery. Atlantic Monthly Press, 2005. This Australian scientist is especially good at presenting climate change from a historical perspective.

The Whale and the Supercomputer: On the Northern Front of Climate Change. Charles Wohlforth. North Point Press, 2004. An Alaskan journalist documents climate change in Alaska as experienced by Inupiaq whale hunters and observed by scientists.

The Winds of Change: Climate, Weather, and the Destruction of Civilizations. Eugene Linden. Simon & Schuster, 2006. An environmental journalist weaves together science, history, personal narrative, and political analysis in a very readable account.